T5-CVQ-549

Corporate First Amendment Rights and the SEC

Corporate First Amendment Rights and the SEC

Nicholas Wolfson

Q

Quorum Books
New York • Westport, Connecticut • London

Library of Congress Cataloging-in-Publication Data

Wolfson, Nicholas.
    Corporate first amendment rights and the SEC / Nicholas Wolfson.
        p. cm.
    Includes bibliographical references (p.
    ISBN 0–89930–450–8 (lib. bdg. : alk. paper)
    1. Advertising laws—United States.   2. Corporation law—United
States.   3. Freedom of speech—United States.   I. Title.
KF1614.W65   1990
342.73'0853—dc20
[347.302853]   90–8412

British Library Cataloguing in Publication Data is available.

Library of Congress Catalog Card Number: 90–8412
ISBN: 0–89930–450–8

First published in 1990

Quorum Books, 88 Post Road West, Westport, CT   06881
An imprint of Greenwood Publishing Group, Inc.

Printed in the United States of America

The paper used in this book complies with the
Permanent Paper Standard issued by the National
Information Standards Organization (Z39.48–1984).

10 9 8 7 6 5 4 3 2 1

Contents

Introduction

In this book we examine the impact of the First Amendment on speech regulated by the Securities and Exchange Commission (SEC). At first blush it appears rather strange to consider for even a moment the possibility that corporate financial and business disclosure rises to the dignity of speech protected by the First Amendment. Nevertheless, since at least 1976, with the rise of the so-called commercial speech doctrine of the Supreme Court, it is clear that SEC speech receives some level of protection under the Constitution.

In 1976 the Court, for the first time, explicitly held that the advertisement of a prescription drug in the form "I will sell you the X prescription drug at the Y price" was speech protected by the free-speech clause of the Constitution.[1] The Court, in a series of cases, argued that advertisements conveyed information and belief to the consumer. That dissemination was undoubtedly of real interest to the public, frequently more so than campaign speeches and the like. The Court held that undue governmental interference with the conveyance of information and belief, however economically motivated, is subject to the protection of the First Amendment.[2]

The Court did not grant the advertisements the full measure of protection afforded to political and artistic speech. It argued that commercial speech is hardier than political or artistic speech, hence less effectively chilled by regulation and censorship. The Court also maintained that the government can more readily distinguish the true from the false in commercial speech than in political speech. Therefore, the government can pre-screen advertisements for accuracy, criminally prosecute false advertisements, and even ban truthful commercial speech under certain circumstances.

The definition of commercial speech is hardly free of fateful ambiguity. The Court agrees that the advertisement of a product or a service for a business purpose is commercial speech. Therefore, the advertisements of shampoo and of legal services fall within the term. Any extension of the concept beyond that creates enormous difficulty. Assume that a group of trial attorneys organize a campaign to defeat no-fault insurance. Their self-interest is clear. If they are successful they will, no doubt, maintain or increase the demand for their services. Assume that a group of farmers put together a series of publications and speeches designed to maintain government price support of specified farm products. If they succeed, they will maximize their income. Any small exercise of memory and imagination demonstrates to all of us that much, if not most, of political speech is moved by economic self-interest. Arguably, much of artistic speech too. Any effort to place economically driven speech within the category of commercial speech threatens, however, to move a vast array of speech and publication within the dread word, commercial speech.

SEC-regulated speech is not, on its face, the advertisement of a product or a service for a profitable purpose. When a shampoo corporation advertises shampoo, that is commercial speech. Even that receives some measure of constitutional protection. When a publicly held shampoo corporation is involved in a proxy battle for control, and rival management groups appeal to shareholders for their vote, the SEC regulates the campaign literature. It is, at best, a dubious proposition that the proxy speech is, in effect, an ad for a product. It is obviously a dispute about the governance of an organization that is in the form of a stock corporation. When an investment advisor recommends a stock, again, it is scarcely clear that the advice is the same as an ad for a product or a service of the investment advisor. It is opinion (similar to that appearing every day in the *New York Times*) about the financial and business health of a corporation. We can multiply these examples of SEC speech.

In order to adequately analyze the constitutional status of SEC-regulated speech, we must consider the purposes of the constitutional protection, the meaning of commercial speech as contrasted to political speech, and the nature of SEC-regulated speech. We must also evaluate the basis for the Court's refusal to grant full constitutional protection to commercial speech. In this book we attempt to accomplish those aims.

Perhaps the most famous exposition of the liberal statement on the freedom of the individual to express his or her individuality, in word or deed, is John Stuart Mill's essay "On Liberty."[3] The scholar Gertrude Himmelfarb went so far as to say, "Like all successful textbooks, ["On Liberty"] no longer has to be read to make itself felt. We imbibe its 'truth' by osmosis, so to speak, from the culture at large."[4]

In his opening discussion, Mill states that his object is to assert one very simple principle, as entitled to govern absolutely the dealings of society with the individual in the way of compulsion and control, whether the means used be physical force in the form of legal penalties or the moral coercion of public opinion. That principle is that the sole end for which mankind are warranted, individually or collectively, in interfering with the liberty of action of any of their number is self-protection.[5]

Mill admits that "the mischief which a person does to himself may seriously affect, both through their sympathies and their interests, those nearly connected with him and, in a minor degree, society at large."[6] However, Mill sharply defines the third-party effect as follows: "When, by conduct of this sort, a person is led to violate a distinct and assignable obligation to any other person or persons, the case is taken out of the self-regarding class and becomes amenable to moral disapprobation in the proper sense of the term."[7]

In Chapter 2 of his work Mill defends the right of free speech and discussion as part of the well-being of individuality. He does so on the, by now, familiar grounds that (a) the opinion silenced may be true; (b) the silenced opinion, although in error, may contain "a portion of the truth";[8] (c) even if the "received opinion" be the whole truth, it will be held as a little understood prejudice, unless suffered to be vigorously contested[9]; and (d) the meaning of the doctrine itself will be "lost or enfeebled" unless contested.[10]

Mill had a touching nineteenth-century faith in the power of rational debate to produce the truth in political and social affairs. Frank Knight, a great American economist, has warned us that

genuine, purely intellectual discussion is rare in modern society, even in intellectual and academic circles, and is approximated only in very small and essentially casual groups. On the larger scale, what passes for discussion is mostly argumentation or debate. The intellectual interest is largely subordinate to entertainment, *i.e.,* entertaining and being entertained, or the immediate interest of the active parties centers chiefly in dominance, victory, instructing others, or persuading rather than convincing, and not in the impartial quest of truth.[11]

The modern age's assault on reason, as Francis Canavan, in his recent essay on the First Amendment, points out, affected Professor Zechariah Chafee, Jr., one of the great American exponents of the First Amendment.[12] Chafee confesses that on reading Knight he "can no longer think of open discussion as operating like an electric mixer, which is the impression left by Milton and Jefferson—run it a little while and truth will rise to the top with the dregs of error going down to the bottom."[13] Still, Chafee asserts that reason "remains the best guide we have."[14]

In chapter 3 Mill argues that men and women should be free also to "act upon their opinions" so long as "it is at their own risk and peril."[15] Although he concedes that "[n]o one pretends that actions should be as free as opinions," he brigades action and opinion only at some relatively extreme level.[16] Thus some six decades before Justice Holmes' expression about "falsely shouting fire in a theatre,"[17] he asserts that "[a]n opinion that corn dealers are starvers of the poor, or that private property is robbery, ought to be unmolested when simply circulated through the press, but may justly incur punishment when delivered orally to an excited mob assembled before the house of a corn dealer."[18]

He eloquently asserts that "[i]t is desirable, in short, that in things which do not primarily concern others individuality should assert itself."[19] It is in this plea for individuality that Mill would probably ground the freedom to speak, as well as the somewhat more circumscribed freedom to live one's own life.

This vision of freedom was called forth some seventy years later by Justice Brandeis' eloquent concurrence in *Whitney v. California* : "Those who won our independence believed that the final end of the State was to make men free to develop their faculties. . . . They valued liberty both as an end and as a means. They believed liberty to be the secret of happiness and courage to be the secret of liberty."[20]

Mill also contends that the principle of liberty entailed the "liberty . . . of combination among individuals; freedom to unite for any purpose not involving harm to others."[21] More than a century later the Supreme Court emphasized that "[a]n individual's freedom to speak, worship, and to petition the Government for the redress of grievances could not be vigorously protected from interference by the State unless a correlative freedom to engage in group efforts toward those ends were not also guaranteed."[22]

Finally, he recognizes the political liberty aspect of individuality in the context of democratic governments. He emphasizes that majoritarian power through the vote and voice of the people created the risk of "the tyranny of the majority."[23] In a prescient mood, reminiscent of Orwell's *1984* he emphasizes that a democracy (including people's democracy?) untrammeled by individual rights can exercise "a social tyranny more formidable than many kinds of political oppression, since . . . it leaves fewer means of escape, penetrating much more deeply into the details of life, and enslaving the soul itself."[24] Therefore, protection for human individuality, even for personal eccentricity, in thought and action to the maximum extent possible, consistent with Mill's principle stated above, is necessary.[25]

Mill thus recognizes the role of free speech in countering the oppression of government, even a democratic republic. But he does not rest the value of free speech on a narrow definition of the political. Hence he escapes the danger of limiting protection of free speech to discussion of issues of civics, excluding art and science and economics and commercial information.

Writers beyond count in addition to Mill have expressed themselves on this subject. We shall consider and evaluate the modern arguments for and against the applicability of the great principles of the First Amendment to commercial speech and, more specifically, the speech regulated by the SEC.

It is not too great an oversimplification to assert that Mill has, in some sense, encapsulated the three principal arguments for the First Amendment: as a process for truth-seeking; as a surety for the expression of one's individuality, whether as speaker or as listener; and finally, as an assurance against government-overreaching, or bureaucratic orthodoxy.

It is also not too great an oversimplification to point out that the Court and some commentators have argued that First Amendment protection of commercial speech satisfies some or all of the above purposes or goals. The consumer gains information from the advertisement, retains the option of expressing his or her individuality through the use of ads to choose services and products, from medical and legal advice to beauty aids, and, with the assistance of expert advisors, winnows out the true from the false. As the Court noted in the leading commercial speech case, the First Amendment approach is "to assume that . . . information is not in itself harmful, that people will perceive their own best interests, if only they are well enough informed, and that the best means to that end is to open the channels of communication rather than to close them."[26] The Court rejected a paternalistic attitude to commercial information: The choice "among these alternative approaches is not [the Court's] to make or the Virginia General Assembly's. It is precisely this kind of choice, between the dangers of suppressing information, and the dangers of its misuse if it is freely available, that the First Amendment makes for us."[27] The Court also pointed out that "[s]o long as we preserve a predominantly free enterprise economy, the allocation of our resources in large measure will be made through numerous private economic decisions. It is a matter of public interest that these decisions, in the aggregate, be intelligent and well informed. To this end, the free flow of commercial information is indispensible."[28] We shall argue in this book that the Court is correct.

Commercial speech, as we have noted, receives less protection from the Court than political or artistic speech. The distinction between the two kinds of speech is less than clear. Whatever the treatment of commercial speech, we shall maintain that SEC-regulated speech is not "mere" commercial speech, but speech that deserves the full protection of the First Amendment.

NOTES

1. *Virginia State Board of Pharmacy v. Virginia Citizens Consumer Council, Inc.,* 425 U.S. 748, 761 (1976).

2. *See* J. Nowak, R. Rotunda, and J. Young Constitutional Law 909–24 (3d ed. 1986).

3. J. S. Mill, "On Liberty" (Currin V. Shields ed. 1956) (1st ed. London 1859) [herinafter "On Liberty"].

4. G. Himmelfarb, *On Liberty and Liberalism: The Case Of John Stuart Mill* xxi (1974).

5. "On Liberty" at 13.

6. *Id.* at 98–99.

7. *Id.* at 99.

8. *Id.* at 64.

    9. *Id.*
   10. *Id.*
   11. Knight, *The Planful Act*, in *Freedom and Reform* 349 (1947).
   12. F. Canavan, *Freedom of Expression, Purpose as Limit* 133 (1984).
   13. Z. Chafee, *The Blessings of Liberty*, 107 (1957).
   14. *Id.* at 110.
   15. "On Liberty" at 67.
   16. *Id.*
   17. *Schenk v. United States*, 249 U.S. 47, 52 (1919).
   18. "On Liberty" at 67–68.
   19. *Id.* at 68.
   20. *Whitney v. California*, 274 U.S. 357, 375 (1927) (Brandeis, J., joined by Holmes,
J., concurring).
   21. "On Liberty" at 16.
   22. *Roberts v. United States Jaycees*, 468 U.S. 609, 623 (1984).
   23. "On Liberty" at 7.
   24. *Id.*
   25. *Id.*
   26. *Virginia State Board of Pharmacy*, 425 U.S. at 770.
   27. *Id.*
   28. *Id.* at 765.

1

Commercial Speech Doctrine

In 1942 a unanimous Supreme Court, in a brief opinion, upheld the conviction of an entrepreneur who violated a sanitary code provision banning the distribution of a handbill. The advertisement promoted the tour of a submarine for a fee. On the reverse side of the handbill was a protest against New York City's denial of wharfage facilities for the exhibition.

The Court dismissed the political protest message as a mere appendage designed to evade the ordinance. With reference to the advertisement for the submarine exhibit the Court said:

> This court has unequivocally held that the streets are proper places for the exercise of the freedom of communicating information and disseminating opinion and that, though the states and municipalities may appropriately regulate the privilege in the public interest, they may not unduly burden or proscribe its employment in these public thoroughfares. We are equally clear that the Constitution imposes no such restraint on government as respects purely commercial advertising.[1]

A distinguished scholar, in an influential piece on commercial advertising, stated that the Court, "without citing precedent, historical evidence, or policy considerations, . . . effectively read commercial speech out of the first amendment."[2]

Additional evidence for a commercial speech exception to the First Amendment was developed in *Breard v. Alexandria,*[3] in which the Court affirmed a conviction for violation of an ordinance forbidding door-to-door soliciting of magazine subscriptions without prior consent of the homeowner. The

Court asserted: "The selling...brings into the transaction a commercial feature"[4]; it distinguished *Martin v. Struthers*,[5] a case in which the Court overturned a conviction for door-to-door distribution of religious tracts. In the *Martin* case, "no element of the commercial entered into this free solicitation."[6]

Subsequent cases determined that not all advertisements are commercial speech. In *New York Times Co. v. Sullivan*[7] a city employee of Montgomery, Alabama, commenced a libel suit against clergymen and the *New York Times*. The clergymen had run an advertisement in the *Times* attacking police behavior with respect to workers in the civil rights movement. The Court held the advertisement fully protected by the First Amendment. The Court said: "That the *Times* was paid for publishing the advertisement is as immaterial in this connection as is the fact that newspapers and books are sold."[8]

The Court, in a later opinion, *Pittsburgh Press Co. v. Pittsburgh Commission on Human Relations*,[9] explained: "If a newspaper's profit motive were determinative, all aspects of its operations—from the selection of news stories to the choice of editorial position—would be subject to regulation if it could be established that they were conducted with a view toward increased sales. Such a basis for regulation clearly would be incompatible with the First Amendment."[10]

In the *Pittsburgh Press Co.* case, Justice Powell, in often-cited language, went on to conclude that "the critical feature of the advertisement in *Valentine v. Chrestensen* was that, in the Court's view, it did no more than propose a commercial transaction, the sale of admission to a submarine."[11]

The justice emphasized that the advertisement in the *New York Times v. Sullivan* case expressed opinions, criticized alleged abuses, and communicated information on matters of great public interest.[12] The *Valentine* case involved merely an advertisement for services, in this case a submarine exhibit.

In the *Pittsburgh Press Co.* case, petitioner was charged with violation of a city ordinance forbidding newspapers to carry job advertisements in sex-designated columns. The Court stated that the job ads fell within the *Chrestensen*, not the *Sullivan*, category.[13] Each advertisement amounted to a "proposal of possible employment,"[14] not an article on "social policy."[15]

The newspaper contended that if the employment ads were indeed commercial speech (which it did not concede), then commercial speech should be accorded some degree of First Amendment protection. The newspaper argued that "the exchange of information is as important in the commercial realm as in any other."[16]

The Court did not have to reach this issue. It concluded, in a 5–4 decision, that the sex-designated ads proposed illegal discriminatory commercial activity. Hence, since the activity was illegal, speech advertising such illegal activity was without First Amendment protection. As the Court put it: "Any

First Amendment interest which might be served by advertising an ordinary commercial proposal and which might arguably outweigh the governmental interest supporting the regulation is altogether absent when commercial activity itself is illegal and the restriction on advertising is incidental to a valid limitation on economic activity."[17]

Notice that the Court arguably left open the possibility that commercial advertising might enjoy some degree of First Amendment protection when the activity itself was not illegal.

Justice Stewart dissented. Justice Douglas joined in his dissent. Stewart argued that nothing in the *Valentine* case supported the Court's decision. He observed that Douglas had stated that "[t]he [*Chrestensen*] ruling was casual, almost offhand. And it has not survived reflection."[18]

Stewart argued that the *Pittsburgh Press Co.* case was the first that permitted a government agency to dictate the layout and makeup of the newspaper's pages. This was not a purely commercial transaction, as in *Chrestensen*, but involved the editorial judgment of the newspaper. The paper makes a judgment whether or not to run the ad as the advertiser requests.[19] (This issue is involved in a recent insider-trading case that is discussed in Chapter 5) Douglas, in his separate dissent, added a few words to the effect that commercial speech should have First Amendment protection. Further, he felt that the advertisements were protected even though an employer might be lawfully punished if he in fact discriminated in hiring. This was not a case, in his opinion, in which "speech and action are so closely brigaded that they are really one."[20] Chief Justice Burger also dissented, believing that it was a "disturbing enlargement of the 'commercial speech' doctrine."[21]

The next significant case in the commercial speech development was *Bigelow v. Virginia.*[22] The Court, in a 7–2 decision, reversed the conviction of the managing editor of a weekly Virginia newspaper that published a New York City organization's advertisement of abortion placements for women in New York clinics and hospitals at "low cost."[23]

Justice Blackmun, speaking for the Court, pointed out that the *Pittsburgh Press Co.* opinion "indicated that the advertisements [in question there] would have received some degree of First Amendment protection if the commercial proposal had been legal."[24] Blackmun also stated that the abortion advertisement conveyed more than commercial information; it transmitted social or political information about a constitutionally protected activity in New York State.[25] Virginia possessed no power under the guise of implementing internal police powers to chill dissemination of information about abortions that were legal in another state.[26] Then, in language that the Court developed in later cases, Justice Blackmun asserted that advertising "may be subject to reasonable regulation that serves a legitimate public interest."[27] This regulation had not been demonstrated to do that.

The Court also emphasized that the advertisement was not deceptive or fraudulent. It did not infringe any protected rights or invade the privacy of others.[28] The Court concluded that the Virginia statute, as applied to the advertisement, violated the First Amendment.

Justice Rehnquist wrote a dissenting opinion, in which Justice White joined. Rehnquist argued that the advertisement was predominantly commercial in nature. To argue otherwise would permit any merchant to evade a regulation by adding a moral or political message to his ad.[29] Even if the advertisement is conceded to be more than purely commercial, Rehnquist argued that Virginia has a legitimate interest in banning commercial advertising in the health area to protect its citizens from shady practices in other states.[30]

In the next term the Court met the commercial speech exception directly and repudiated it. Consumers brought suit against the Virginia State Board of Pharmacy and its members, attacking a Virginia statute that provided that a pharmacist is guilty of unprofessional conduct if he or she advertises the prices of prescription drugs.[31]

Justice Blackmun pointed out that, unlike *Bigelow*, the advertisements in question did not, in any sense, editorialize on the cultural, political, or philosophical. The pharmacist wished to communicate simply the proposed sale of X prescription drug at Y price.[32]

Blackmun began the analysis by emphasizing that speech does not lose the shield of the First Amendment because it is in the form of a paid advertisement,[33] or is in a form that is sold for money.[34] Any contrary approach would chill speech in all its modern forms. Speech today is transmitted not by isolated individual printers, but by great publishing and communications corporations run for profit.

Clearly, then, the justice argued, the species of commercial speech that arguably lacks all First Amendment shield must be distinguished by the content of the ad, not the profit motive of the communicator.[35] But the prohibited content cannot simply be economic or commercial. Certainly pharmacists may speak and debate in public and private on the pros and cons of regulating pharmaceutical prices.[36] Further, they may claim protection for nonopinionated statements, whether in the form of advertisement or not, that simply state facts of public interest.[37]

The speech at issue is that which does "no more than propose a commercial transaction."[38] The question is, does such speech stray so far from the purposes of the First Amendment as to lose its protection? The Court answered in the negative.

The Court had already decided that selfish motive was no bar to protection. Justice Blackmun also pointed out that the particular consumer may have a greater interest in commercial speech than the most stimulating political debate.[39]

This was a factor in the Court's conclusion; but as we will see in later sections of this book, some commentators in later years argued that indifference to political issues perhaps calls for less regulation so as to stimulate more speech, whereas keen demand for the commercial product and the ad would permit the state to regulate the speech without chilling its supply.[40]

The Court next argued that advertising benefited the poor, the sick, and the aged. They spend much on drugs, yet can least price shop by traveling from drugstore to drugstore.[41] But the Court then made a more general argument that is crucial in this area, even if the particular point about the sick and others is not. Advertising of price and product or service plays an important role in our free enterprise society. Free flow of such information facilitates the allocation of resources in an efficient manner. As the Court put it[42]:

So long as we preserve a predominantly free enterprise economy, the allocation of our resources in large measure will be made through numerous private economic decisions. It is a matter of public interest that these decisions, in the aggregate, be intelligent and well informed. . . . And if it is indispensible to the proper allocation of resources in a free enterprise system, it is also indispensible to the formation of intelligent opinions as to how that system ought to be regulated.

The defendants argued that price advertising will destroy the professionalism of pharmacists. Low-cost competitors will advertise their cheap prices; other pharmacists will have to follow suit, and will no longer have the comfortable profits necessary to maintain their former professional services of handling and compounding medications and advising customers in a safe and quality manner.[43]

Further, defendants alternatively argued that advertising might not result in cheaper prices for the poor and the aged. Indeed, prices might rise because of the expense of competitive advertising. Also, defendants argued that advertising will lead to price shopping and the decline of stable customer-drugstore relations. Finally, advertising would ruin the professional nature and image of pharmacists.[44]

Defendants' contentions were not without merit, the Court observed. They would, the Court stated, sustain an attack on due process and equal protection grounds.[45] But the challenge in this case was on First Amendment grounds. In a powerful opinion by Justice Blackmun the Court argued that the approach of the state was based on the paternalistic benefits of keeping consumers in ignorance. It is this very choice that the First Amendment prevents. The free market in ideas, often cited in core political cases, should operate in economic and commercial matters. It is preferable that the public seek out their preferred interests based on the free flow of commercial information.[46]

Yet the Court, in dicta (but extremely important dicta), reserved the right of government to regulate, in certain cases, commercial speech to a greater degree than political speech. Justice Blackmun asserted that there are "commonsense differences between speech that does 'no more than propose a commercial transaction,' *Pittsburgh Press Co. v. Human Relations Comm'n,*

413 U.S., at 385, and other varieties."[47] First, the truth of commercial speech is more verifiable by the advertiser than the truth of political speech. The advertiser, the Court argued, knows more about his or her product than anyone else.[48]

This is clearly an empirical observation that is plausible but not necessarily accurate. We return to this crucial argument in later sections of this book.

Second, the Court asserted that commercial speech may be hardier than political speech. Businessmen will, the Court assumed, not be chilled by advertising regulation, since they need commercial speech so desperately for their profits.[49] This, too, is an empirical claim that may be wildly inaccurate. This argument is also discussed in later sections of the book.

The Court used these two arguments to justify its dicta that government may be able to lawfully regulate commercial speech to a much greater extent than political speech. In this regard, the Court states that the government may be able to ban or regulate commercial speech that is false or misleading. Regulation may include a form of mandatory disclosure of additional information, cautions, and caveats. The government also may be able to impose prior restraints.[50]

These two arguments were the only reasons given by the Court for distinguishing, in any manner, commercial speech from political speech. We shall see in later cases and sections of this book to what extent the Court or scholars offer other differentiations.

Next, the Court asserted that the ads in the instant case did not propose an illegal transaction. Hence the case was distinguished from *Pittsburgh Press Co. v. Human Relations Commission*.[51] The Court concluded in another note that pharmacists, unlike attorneys and physicians, dispense standardized products; the latter two professions offer more complex services that involve greater possibility of deception and confusion.[52] Soon, as we will see, however, the Court would consider attorney advertising and grant it limited First Amendment protection.

In conclusion, the Court held that the state may not completely suppress the truthful ads in question about legal activity merely because of fear about the information's impact on the pharmacist disseminators and the customers. The complete extent of permissible regulation, as distinguished from absolute ban in this case, was left for another day.[53] Furthermore, even a total ban of truthful advertisements might be permitted if the state could make a much stronger case for detrimental impact than it made in this case.[54] The extent and nature of what a stronger justification must be were not described.

Justice Stewart, concurring, addressed the major policy issue created by the elimination of the commercial speech exception. He recognized that this decision threatened to nullify regulation of false or deceptive advertising.[55] He wrote to answer this danger.

To begin with, he observed that the Court had limited protection for false statements in libel cases.[56] Thus, even in core political speech, libel actions exist for defamation. He quoted the Court in *Gertz v. Robert Welch, Inc.* that "there is no constitutional value in false statements of fact."[57] However, imposition of legal sanction for error could chill political debate.[58] Thus even suits for libel must face considerable limits.[59]

The justice then argued that the rationale underlying libel actions indicated that the states could regulate even more vigorously false commercial speech.[60] He asserted that in defamation cases, the press, under deadline pressure, cannot easily verify the data. The commercial advertiser, he maintained, knows his or her product or service. Hence, government regulation of commercial advertising will not chill truthful expression.[61]

The justice pointed out that in labor relations, employers' speech may be limited by the condition that it be based on fact. The Court has relied on the alleged "employer's intimate knowledge of the employer-employee relationship" to adhere to the truth.[62]

The contention that the speaker in commercial cases can easily verify the truth is similar to the argument advanced by the majority opinion, and is subject to empirical proof or disproof. We address this argument and its offspring in later sections of the book. Certainly it is apparent that plausible arguments also could be made that disseminators of political and general economic views are frequently able to verify the truth of the factual component of their assertions. The holes in First Amendment protection such analysis would create are obvious.

Justice Stewart next advanced the notion that fully protected speech (i.e., "[i]deological expression, be it oral, literary, pictorial or theatrical"[63]) is something more than the conveyance of factual information.[64] It is something grander; it is "thought that may shape our concepts of the whole universe of man."[65] Hence such grand thought, even if factually in error, is fully protected.[66] In fact, falsity may legitimately be used to advance the idea.[67] "Indeed, disregard of the 'truth' may be employed to give force to the underlying idea expressed by the speaker."[68]

Commercial speech, he maintained, relates primarily to presentation of facts about goods or services, not ideas, and therefore, as mentioned above, may be verified and corrected by government regulation.[69] Indeed, because the only reason commercial speech receives First Amendment protection is its assistance to the exchange of information about goods and services, false information must be regulatable.[70]

In later sections of the book this argument and others used to distinguish commercial speech from fully protected speech are analyzed. On its face it contains possible problems. Certainly Stewart must face the argument that ideas that depend on the truth of certain facts must be treated identically to commercial speech. We cannot prove or disprove the existence of a supreme being, but the fact, for example, of the Jewish Holocaust can be proved; shall we then censor and regulate false speech about that historical tragedy? Also, so-called commercial speech that advances an idea (defined in this case as an opinion), for example, that ABC shampoo will beautify your hair and maximize your romantic attachments, must then be treated as fully protected speech. Further, if only "grand" ideas deserve full protection, we must distinguish the puerile from the grand in politics and art, as well as in commerce.

Stewart's argument implicitly assumes that core political speech advances causes other than the simple conveyance of information. As discussed in subsequent sections of the book, First Amendment protection for political speech has been justified on such bases as the facilitation of personal growth and autonomy, advancement of the democratic political process, and advancement of the truth through intellectual competition in the marketplace of ideas.[71] Other purposes have been advanced.[72] The last purpose, intellectual competition, is not much different from the conveyance-of-information concept. We will have to analyze in depth the relevance of commonly accepted purposes of core protection of speech and whether in fact commercial speech should be treated differently.

Rehnquist filed the sole dissent.[73] He argued that the advertisements in question contained no ideological content, hence they were not protected by the First Amendment.[74] The Court had asserted that protection of commercial speech was important in a capitalist society to facilitate knowledgable decisions as to allocation of resources. Rehnquist argued that there was nothing in the U.S. Constitution that required adherence to this Adam Smithian version of free-enterprise economics.[75] The Court uses this position to uphold state legislation regulating conduct against attack based on the alleged unwisdom of the legislation.[76] The Court, however, had viewed the ad as speech, and could find no constitutional justification for distinguishing the content of this speech from other speech, insofar as an absolute ban was concerned. Rehnquist felt that the government should be as free to regulate commercial speech as it is to regulate economic conduct.

Rehnquist emphasized that the consequences of the Court's decision would be revolutionary in scope. All advertising of products and services would now be protected to a significant extent. He predicted that the Court would find it difficult in the future to distinguish medical and legal advertising from that of pharmacists.

He also predicted that labor relations would be impacted by the decision. Current restrictions on the right of employers to threaten reprisal or make promises of benefit would soon fall under the First Amendment.[77]

He admitted that in the past, there was some difficulty in distinguishing between protected speech and commercial speech.[78] He viewed as worse, however, the decision to include all commercial speech within the protective umbrella. This meant, in his opinion, abandonment of the correct philosophy that only political, social, and other public-issue speech was protected. He quoted Justice Black that the First Amendment does not protect a " 'merchant' who goes from door to door 'selling pots.' "[79]

Because the Court will not protect false commercial speech, the Court, he asserted, must now face the task of distinguishing between truthful and mis-leading commercial speech. It is not so much the difficulty of making that distinction that is troublesome. More important, the government should be able to regulate with respect to factors more diverse than merely that of truth or falsity of commercial speech.

He believed that in the area of commercial speech, the legislature should be free to regulate and ban for reasons of health, safety, and all the other reasons legislatures make policy decisions. In that regard he warned of future difficulties with respect to governmental power to regulate the advertisement of liquor and tobacco, to name a few dangerous commodities.

The next Supreme Court case on commercial speech, *Linmark Associates, Inc. v. Township of Willingboro*, involved a town ordinance that banned the posting of real estate "For Sale" and "Sold" signs.[80] The goal was to chill the exit of white owners from a racially integrated area. The town believed that such signs were a major catalyst in precipitating panic-selling by whites.[81]

The Court, speaking through Justice Marshall, stated that in the *Virginia Pharmacy* case, it was not convinced that the Virginia law was "necessary" to achieve the goal of professionalism.[82] This point was apparently diluted by the additional statement that "in any event," the First Amendment bars a total restriction on the flow of accurate information.[83]

For similar reasons the Court struck down the housing ordinance. The Court found unpersuasive the evidence on panic-selling.[84] Further, Marshall repeated the *Virginia Pharmacy* point that the ordinance prevented residents from receiving information for fear that they would use it unwisely. The town's concern (similar to that of Virginia) was not with commercial aspects of the residential sales, but with the public policy implications of the infor-mation.[85] In Virginia the fear was that pharmacists would become less profes-sional; here the fear was that whites would flee. Presumably by commercial aspects the Court meant fraud, or potentiality for deceit, in the sale of drugs or houses.

The Court then quoted the earlier language in *Virginia Pharmacy* about the value of a free market in ideas and the value of more speech rather than less to cure error and fallacy.[86] The Court concluded with the caveat for the future that laws regulating false signs or requiring additional disclosure to prevent deception would raise a different constitutional question.[87]

Carey v. Population Services International was the third case after *Bigelow* to address the commercial speech doctrine.[88] The constitutionality of a New York statute making it a crime to advertise contraceptives was at issue.[89]

Justice Brennan, writing for the Court, cited *Virginia Pharmacy* as dispo-sitive precedent.[90] Further, as in *Bigelow v. Virginia*, the statute was directed at activity that in many respects the state could not ban. The contention that the speech would be "offensive to some" was rejected as a justification for suppression.[91]

Powell, in his concurrence, agreed that the state had not substantiated sufficient cause for a complete ban.[92] He did not, however, want to raise doubt about the state's power to impose less draconian regulation designed to prevent undue offensiveness or legitimation of youthful sexual promiscuity.[93] For example, he asserted that this or other state interests might justify regulation of the time, place, or manner of such commercial advertising.[94] Justices Stevens and White essentially agreed in their concurrences with this approach.[95]

The chief justice dissented without opinion.[96] Justice Rehnquist, in a dissenting opinion, made a kind of original-intent argument. He asserted with some rhetorical flourish that the men who drafted the First and Fourteenth Amendments did not intend to protect "the right of commercial vendors of contraceptives to peddle them to unmarried minors."[97] He offered no evidence for this opinion.

In *Bates v. State Bar of Arizona* the Court considered a state supreme court's disciplinary rule that forbade attorney advertising.[98] Two attorneys placed an ad that offered "legal services at very reasonable fees."[99] They listed their fees for certain services, such as uncontested divorces and changes of name.[100] The advertisement stated that information on other kinds of cases would be "furnished on request."[101] The firm in the ad was self-described as a "legal clinic."[102] The goal of the firm was to offer legal services at moderate fees to people of modest income who did not qualify for governmental aid.[103] One of the issues presented by the case was whether the application of the rule violates the First Amendment, made applicable to the states by the Fourteenth.[104]

Justice Blackmun delivered the opinion of the Court, in which Brennan, White, Marshall, and Stevens joined. Then Chief Justice Burger and Justices Powell, Stewart, and Rehnquist dissented on the First Amendment portion of the case.

Justice Blackmun summarized, as he saw it, the reasons given in the *Virginia Pharmacy* opinion for granting First Amendment protection to speech proposing a mundane commercial transaction:

1. The listener's desire to receive the message is often greater than his interest in political speech.
2. Frequently such speech will carry news on important societal interests.
3. Such speech informs the consumer, and hence facilitates the allocation of resources in a capitalist society.[105]

Blackmun stated that in the *Virginia Pharmacy* case, the state argued, inter alia, that the advertisement of prices would depreciate the professionalism of the pharmacist.[106] The *Virginia Pharmacy* Court reasoned that the speech ban was unnecessary, since the state maintained professionalism by close direct regulation, and that the ban on ads kept the public in ignorance, something the First Amendment was particularly designed to prevent.[107]

The *Bates* case involved attorneys, not pharmacists. Because attorneys, unlike druggists, dispense complex, nonstandardized advice, the Court in *Virginia Pharmacy* had specifically reserved judgment about attorneys.[108]

First, this case did not involve the advertisement of legal advice, such as "If you bought stock of ABC corporation on January of X year contact us; you may have a viable insider-trading case." Second, this case did not involve face-to-face, person-to-person solicitation. Third, the case did not involve a claim, false or otherwise, that the firm offered a distinctive quality of services.[109] The only issue presented was the legality of commercial dissemination of the prices at which various routine legal service will be performed.[110]

The Court then considered a number of arguments about the possible detrimental effects of legal advertising. None of these contentions would be seriously considered in a case dealing with political speech.

The first argument of the bar of Arizona was the adverse impact on professionalism of advertising. Huckstering will lead to excessive greed.

The Court responded with a number of reasonable rebuttals.[111] It pointed out that the public is fully aware that attorneys work for profit. It argued that advertising may inform the public of the availability of needed services. It pointed out that the ban on advertising began as a kind of snobbish rule of etiquette. Centuries ago upper-class British attorneys frowned on trade as undignified.[112]

A number of other arguments were made. The state bar maintained that advertising multiplies litigation.[113] The bar argued that advertising actually increases costs and fees.[114] Further, the bar claimed that advertising helps the larger, more established firms and hence chills the entry of young attorneys.[115] It claimed that advertising specific packages of services, as was done in the case, would cause attorneys to use the package whether it met the client's needs or not.[116]

Blackmun responded with an array of counterarguments. For example, he asserted that advertising will help to end the underutilization of legal services, rather than stir up unnecessary litigation.[117] Blackmun referred to studies indicating that advertising frequently lowered costs and prices.[118] He argued that attorneys who shade quality will continue to act in that manner no matter what the state rules on advertising.[119]

This kind of process underscores the difference between treatment of commercial speech and fully protected speech. The direct or indirect detrimental impact of political speech is, as a rule, irrelevant to its protection. Blackmun is deeply engaged in determining whether the speech in question harms the public interest. Assume that the speech at issue was political assertions on free trade versus protectionism. In a government-censorship case Blackmun would then, if he followed commercial speech doctrine, debate whether advocacy of free-trade had direct or indirect detrimental impact on society. He might argue that free trade speech causes great anxiety among textile workers in North Carolina and New York, harms their mental well-being, and, further, leads them to excessive labor strike agitation. He might research the economic literature and evaluate the bona fides of the particular free-trade arguments.

Because the Court is now granting some First Amendment protection to commercial speech, where is the edge, so to speak.? If the speech had no constitutional protection, would the analysis be different? For example, regulation of conduct must meet some diluted rationality test to avoid a constitutional due process attack.[120] Presumably, Blackmun is meeting a tougher test than that. The government must establish some significant measure of substantiality in its arguments before Blackmun will permit the ban. More exact measures perhaps will be set forth by later cases.

The state bar then made a different kind of argument. It maintained that legal advertising inherently is misleading.[121] Because earlier commercial speech cases had made it abundantly clear that deceptive commercial speech warranted no protection, this argument, if sustained, would carry the day. Remember that deceptive political speech, absent some exception such as libel, is presumably constitutionally protected.[122]

First, the bar argued that legal services are so unique that they cannot be advertised for a fixed price with any degree of honesty. The Court responded that attorneys would usually, as in this case, advertise only routine services for a fixed price.[123]

The second argument was that potential clients are unable to intelligently understand the advertisement. The Court simply had greater faith in the understanding of clients than did the bar.[124]

Third, the bar maintained that advertising might lead the public to select attorneys for the wrong reasons. For example, good ad layout might trump reputational advantage. Again, the Court had greater trust in the intelligence of the public than did the bar.[125]

Finally, the bar argued that a cumbersome regulatory apparatus would be needed to enforce truthfulness in advertising. The Court responded that, in its opinion, most attorneys would be honest.[126]

Justice Blackmun then considered the overbreadth analysis.[127] In the preceding arguments the Court had considered and accepted arguments that the bar regulation chilled speech in general. Hence appellants in a political speech case would prevail, regardless of their specific speech. Usually a challenge to a statute must prove that it applies unconstitutionally to the conduct of the party before the Court. In First Amendment cases the Court, because of the fragile nature of protected speech, will permit a showing that the statute chills, or might chill, speech not specifically before the Court in the particular case.[128] But Blackmun observed that this is not the case for commercial speech. Because commercial speech is hardier than political speech and more easily verifiable by the disseminator, it need not get the protection of the overbreadth doctrine.[129]

Blackmun then considered the particular advertisement before the Court.

He weighed and found wanting the bar's arguments that the advertisement was misleading in referring to a legal clinic, arguably a confusing term, claiming "reasonable" prices and failing to inform the public that it might obtain name changes without an attorney.[130] He reasoned that the public would understand that legal clinic referred to the provision of routine services. Blackmun examined fees in Arizona, and decided that appellants' fees were indeed reasonable. Finally, Blackmun noted that one of the appellants deposed that he would send some clients out to do the job without him in very simple cases.

Blackmun concluded, with the usual caveats, that the state could regulate misleading or false advertising. Finally, he warned that the state might be able to suppress claims as to the quality of legal services, something he said that might be unverifiable, or restrain, for a like reason, in-person contacts.[131]

Justices Burger, Powell, and Stewart basically agreed with the arguments of the Arizona Bar, and did not share Blackmun's faith in the counterarguments. Rehnquist continued his record of fundamental dissent, arguing, unlike the other dissenters, that the initial decision in the *Virginia Pharmacy* case to legitimate First Amendment limited protection of commercial speech was in error.[132]

In 1978 the Court, in *Ohralik v. Ohio State Bar Association*, considered a particularly egregious case of in-person attorney solicitation of business.[133] An Ohio attorney visited an automobile driver injured in an accident in her hospital room. He also approached the passenger at her home on the very day she was released from the hospital. Although both eighteen-year-old women dismissed him ultimately as their attorney, he was successful in receiving a piece of the driver's insurance proceeds in settlement of his litigation against one of them for alleged violation of their contract of employment. The bar grievance committee brought charges against him on the ground that he had violated the disciplinary rules prohibiting solicitation of business. The Ohio Supreme Court upheld the findings of the Board of Commissioners on Grievances and Discipline of the Ohio Supreme Court that he had violated the particular disciplinary rules. The Court increased the board's punishment of a public reprimand to indefinite suspension. The attorney argued that his speech was insulated by the First and Fourteenth Amendments.[134]

Justice Powell wrote the opinion of the Court. Concurrences were filed by Justices Marshall and Rehnquist, but no one dissented. Justice Brennan took no part in the case. Powell pointed out that commercial speech enjoys a limited protection "commensurate with its subordinate position in the scale of First Amendment values."[135] This is a different approach from language in some of the earlier commercial speech cases, which emphasized the danger of distinguishing speech by its content. They gave commercial speech lesser protection because of its hardiness and the ability of the disseminator to verify its truthfulness.

Justice Powell made another point that has been emphasized in subsequent cases. He argued that "[t]o require a parity of constitutional protection for commercial and noncommercial speech alike could invite dilution, simply by a leveling process, of the force of the amendment's guarantee with respect to the latter kind of speech."[136]

Next he emphasized that conduct may be made illegal even though accompanied or accomplished by speech. As examples he cited Securities and Exchange Commission (SEC) inside information doctrine, SEC proxy regulation, antitrust law, and labor law restriction of employers' threats against employees.[137] The justice characterized these cases as involving "commercial activity deemed harmful to the public."[138] The state could regulate it even though "speech is a component of that activity."[139] As we shall see in later sections of the book on SEC regulation, it is this kind of approach that the SEC and some courts will seize upon to justify the legality of SEC regulation of corporate speech in the securities industry setting.

Justice Powell asserted that in-person contact to seek legal employment is more conduct than speech.[140] Even so, he conceded that the speech component still gets some First Amendment protection, but less than that provided, for example, in the *Bates* case.[141]

The element of conduct was spelled out by the Court as follows:

1. In-person contact is very compelling. The layperson does not have a chance to reflect at leisure, as with a book or a newspaper advertisement.
2. Face-to-face communication gives less opportunity for the bar to rebut, control, or regulate evil counsel.
3. In-person solicitation discourages the potential client from comparing alternative services.[142]

The premise of the Court is that speech in a personal setting is transmuted into conduct because it may prove more persuasive than a book, pamphlet, or newspaper ad or letter. This is certainly a more questionable proposition than, let us say, the conclusion that an assault accompanied by speech is basically conduct.

As to persuasiveness, its relative degrees of compulsion are empirical questions. The Court's measure is plausible, but the counterproposition is also plausible. Books and newspaper articles have, and have had, enormous impact. It should be clear that if in-person solicitation (and advice) is fully or substantially protected by the First Amendment, a serious threat to professional licensing laws is at hand. Such laws act as forms of prior restraint, preventing professional speech without the prior possession of a state license.

Further, persuasiveness is not normally a First Amendment concern. The First Amendment does not permit government to chill more persuasive or more compelling writers in order to create some kind of intellectual-level playing field.[143]

The Court, however, returned to its relative rank of speech concept, and argued that attorney solicitation in this case had nothing to do with political speech, securing constitutional rights, or free associational rights involving union organization, for example. Hence the First Amendment protection was slight, and must be weighed against what the Court believed were "important" and "particularly strong" state concerns.[144] These interests were maintenance of ethical standards among attorneys, preservation of privacy of potential clients, temptation to sacrifice the interest of the client to the self-interest of the attorney, and prevention of unacceptible pressure by attorneys on clients.[145] Hence the Court, in light of the egregious facts of the case, concluded that the state could constitutionally bar in-person solicitation.[146]

Justice Marshall, in his concurrence, addressed in-person solicitation in settings that lacked the overreaching present in this case. He argued that such in-person solicitation should get the same kind of constitutional protection as the advertisement considered in the *Bates* decision. He referred to some scholarship that indicated that the antisolicitation rules were designed to protect establishment firms against lower-class immigrant lawyers.[147] Perhaps the state should be limited to a mandatory disclosure or fraud approach rather than a complete ban.[148]

The *Ohralik* case was decided on the same day as *In Re Primus*.[149] The latter case decided that solicitation by letter of free legal assistance from the American Civil Liberties Union in a governnment sterilization scandal was political speech and associational conduct fully protected by the First Amendment. The Court distinguished the solicitation from the *Ohralik* matter by its content and the attorney's motivation.[150] The Court pointed out that the use of a letter, rather than person-to-person solicitation, involved less pressure, less problem of policing, and no invasion of privacy.[151] The content was allegedly political, not commercial, and the motivation was to further ideas, not commerce. This was not, in the Court's view, a commercial speech case. Hence South Carolina, in disciplining the attorney, must meet the "exacting scrutiny" standard and must prove a "compelling" state interest.[152] It did not.

Justice Rehnquist dissented. He believed that it was improper to make such a distinction. He felt that First Amendment doctrine prevented content and motive distinction.[153] He believed that such distinctions were difficult to make. Most important, he argued that attorney solicitation, whatever the motive, and whether paid or gratis, involved dangers of overreaching and baseless litigation, such that the states should be free to ban it.[154]

The next Supreme Court commercial speech case involved the profession of optometry. A Texas statute prohibited the practice of optometry under any assumed name, corporate name, or trade name. The commercial (i.e., multioffice chain) practice of optometry continued to be legal, but the owner or franchisor of a chain of optometry offices could not disclose by way of a trade name that the organization was owned or franchised by him or was a single corporate entity. This seemed to make the practice of commercial optometry more difficult. In *Friedman v. Rogers* the Court upheld this statutory structure against First Amendment attack.[155]

Justice Powell, writing for the Court, reiterated the by now familiar litany that commmercial speech is different from fully protected speech because it is hardier and more easily verifiable.[156] This two-point rationale continued to be the principal Supreme Court distinction between commercial speech and political or artistic speech.

A trade name, after continued use, conveys information about the quality, kind, and price of services and also serves to identify the business. Powell maintained that the use of trade names is susceptible to deception. He gave examples of commercial optometrists who kept the same trade name while employees at particular shops changed. He gave examples of commercial optometrists who used different trade names to give the false appearance of competition. He also argued rather nonpersuasively that the ban on trade names did not forbid other kinds of effective advertisements of commercial optometry services.[157] The Court thus appeared to go out of its way to find significant potential for deception.

Justice Blackmun dissented on the First Amendment issue in the case.[158] He pointed out the value of the trade name operation. The owner of the trade name required a uniformity of standards from participating optometrists. They must purchase supplies from the operation, comply with standards on the examination of clients, and receive clients on a first-come, first-served basis.[159] The justice quoted a study that in part concluded that trade names facilitate customers to "locate the goods, services and prices they prefer on a continuing basis with substantially lower search costs than would otherwise be the case."[160] Blackmun also emphasized that the state ban in effect crippled the trade name operations of commercial optometrists.[161] Further, the justice argued that appropriate disclosure could rectify any confusion on the part of the public. The state could simply require disclosure of the professionals at work in an office along with the trade name.[162]

The next commercial speech case, the eighth since the *Bigelow* case, saw the first serious effort by the Court to articulate a fairly comprehensive test for the validity of regulation. *Central Hudson Gas & Electric Corporation v. Public Service Commission*[163] involved an order by the New York State Commission banning all advertising that promotes the use of electricity.[164] The regulation was premised on the determination that "the interconnected utility system in New York State does not have sufficient fuel stocks or sources of supply to continue furnishing all customer demands for the 1973–1974 winter."[165] Even after the emergency ended, the commission continued the ban on so-called promotional advertising in order to comply with the national policy of preserving energy.[166] Promotional was defined as advertising tending to increase the purchase of utility services.[167]

Justice Powell, writing for the Court, made two crucial points. He underscored that "[t]he First Amendment concern for commercial speech is based on the informational function of advertising."[168] This was reiteration of earlier points made in, for example, the *Virginia Pharmacy* case. Therefore, he concluded that "there can be no constitutional objection to the suppression of commercial messages that do not accurately inform the public about lawful activity." [169] He also reiterated the conclusion of *Pittsburgh Press Co.* that the state may also ban commercial speech on illegal activity.[170] Where neither condition exists, the state's power is more limited.

The Court, however, has also pointed out that there is no value in false and misleading political speech.[171] Yet the First Amendment bars state interference (with certain exceptions, such as libel actions) premised on the content of the speech. In support, then, of the Court's two-pronged conclusion above, Justice Powell repeated the arguments that one, commercial speech is more easily verifiable than political speech, and two, it is hardier.[172]

The Court then articulated the now-famous four-part test for regulation of commercial speech. This test, it asserted, arose necessarily from the prior opinions and decisions on commercial speech.

In commercial speech cases, then, a four-part analysis has developed. At the outset, we must determine whether the expression is protected by the First Amendment. For commercial speech to come within that provision, it at least must concern lawful activity and not be misleading. Next, we ask whether the asserted governmental interest is substantial. If both inquiries yield positive answers, we must determine whether the regulation directly advances the governmental interest asserted, and whether it is not more extensive than is necessary to serve that interest.[173]

Under this test the government may ban speech that is "more likely to deceive the public than to inform it."[174] It may also completely bar speech about illegal activity.[175] Where speech is neither of the above, the government must meet the remaining three tests in order to regulate.

The New York Commission did not assert that the speech in question was false or directed at illegal activity.[176] It did argue that because the utility held a monopoly, advertisements could not assist the choices of consumers. Justice Powell responded that oil and gas businesses compete with the electric utility, and that consumers needed information even in a monopoly market.[177]

Next, the Court considered whether the state interest in suppression was substantial. Justice Powell concluded that the state's interest in conserving energy was that.[178] Also, the state's interest in fair rates was substantial.[179] Because the utilities' rates were not based on marginal cost, the state alleged that promotional advertising would increase consumption, which would be charged at inefficient rates.

The Court must next find a direct link between the interest and the regulation. It found none where lack of equity in rates was alleged. The causal relation was remote and uncertain.[180] It found, however, a direct connection between commercial speech and the demand for electricity.[181]

The fourth element in the test is a requirement that suppression be necessary to advance the interest and that less restrictive regulatory approaches not be available. Justice Powell concluded that a flat ban was overkill. He argued that some of the advertising was directed at suggesting devices that would conserve energy, such as the heat pump.[182] He suggested that the commission might set up a pre-screening office that would ban purely promotional ads but permit advertising that was informative and that did not increase energy consumption.[183]

Because the complete suppression of advertising was unnecessary to accomplish the goals of the state, the Court struck down the ban as violative of the First and Fourteenth Amendments.

Justices Brennan and Blackmun, in their concurrence, made a crucial objection to the four-part test. Blackmun wrote, with Brennan's agreement, as follows: "I do not agree, however, that the Court's four-part test is the proper one to be applied when a state seeks to suppress information about a product in order to manipulate a private economic decision that the state cannot or has not regulated or outlawed directly."[184]

His reason for the statement is important and warrants quotation in full: "Even though 'commercial' speech is involved, such a regulatory measure strikes at the heart of the First Amendment. This is because it is a covert attempt by the State to manipulate the choices of its citizens, not by persuasion or direct regulation, but by depriving the public of the information needed to make a free choice."[185]

He read the *Virginia Pharmacy* case, not as an early example of the four-part test, but as a ban on Virginia's efforts to pursue its goals by keeping people ignorant.[186] Likewise, he read *Linmark* as a prohibition on white-flight prevention by means of chilling speech.[187] The Court, however, read those holdings as instances in which the regulation was not sufficiently related to the interests of the government.[188] Justice Blackmun emphasized that relaxed scrutiny of commercial speech applied only in the area of policing deceptive speech, not economic conduct that is otherwise permitted.[188]

One issue not adequately discussed at this point by either the Court or Justice Blackmun is the meaning of the first element of the test. Deceptive commercial speech gets no First Amendment protection. Truthful commercial speech gets it. To begin with, who first determines whether the speech is deceptive? For example, in the securities area (assuming for the moment that what the government regulates is commercial speech), should it be an executive department, or an independent agency such as the SEC, or the courts? Perhaps this issue is so delicate or important that the nonjudicial branches should have only a limited role. In that regard, should the process be subject to special safeguards, burdens of proof, and other procedural niceties, since determination of falsity acts to strip the speech of constitutional protection?

May the government pre-screen it to make sure that no speech shall in fact be deceptive now or in the future? Will such a process itself be subject to the second through fourth tests of the *Central Hudson* case? That is, must the structure be reasonably related to the goal of securing truth? That process is called mandatory disclosure in the SEC area, and involves proxy and pro-spectus regulation and pre-screening by the commission staff. The situation becomes complex in the SEC area, where vigorous and good faith disagree-ment can exist as to the truth or falsity of descriptions of financial transactions. Perhaps unusually strong burdens of proof should be met by the government before its determination of falsity should be upheld by a court. Later sections of the book will analyze these and the other considerations raised in the preceding paragraphs.

Justice Rehnquist dissented, and forcefully repeated his position as it had been set forth in previous dissents. He made, in addition, the powerful ar-gument that the Court's protection of commercial speech was in reality a repeat of the old, discarded notion, expressed in cases like *Lochner v. New York*,[190] that the Court could vitiate economic regulation based on the Court's notions of economic rights imbedded in the Constitution. Later sections of the book will address this argument.[191]

The next significant Supreme Court commercial speech case was *Metro-media, Inc. v. City of San Diego*.[192] This case involved a city ban on offsite commercial billboards. Onsite commercial displays were permitted. The or-dinance also prohibited onsite and offsite noncommercial billboards with specified content-based exceptions. A plurality of four justices struck down the ordinance on the ground that it violated the First Amendment by the ban on noncommercial displays.[193] With respect to the ban on offsite commercial billboards, the plurality asserted that the ordinance satisfied the four-part *Central Hudson* test.[194] The plurality rather casually adopted the city's asser-tions that the ban facilitated automobile driving safety and aesthetic goals.[195] The plurality, however, struck down the entire ordinance, subject to state court determination that the ordinance's severability clause might serve to uphold the commercial ban portion.[196]

Justice Brennan, joined by Justice Blackmun, agreed with the judgment but followed a different reasoning on the noncommercial displays. Insofar as commercial speech issues were concerned, the concurring justices empha-sized that *Central Hudson* "demands more than a rational basis for preferring one kind of commercial speech over another." [197] Further, they asserted that where controversies involve decisions as to whether certain speech is or is not commercial, such decisions cannot be made by nonjudicial government entities. Such a mode of regulation would grant too great a chill power in government to suppress speech. Courts may make such distinctions, but not cities.[198] This is especially true since "[t]he line between ideological and non-ideological speech is impossible to draw with accuracy."[199]

Justices Berger and Rehnquist dissented, and Justice Stevens dissented as to the final conclusion invalidating the ordinance but not as to the reasoning of the plurality on commercial speech.[200]

In the case of *In Re R.M.J.* the Court again considered attorney advertising.[201] The Missouri Supreme Court had laid down certain restrictions, one of which specified the permissible form of description of areas of practice. The attorney used the words "real estate" rather than "property."[202] Further, he used such descriptions as "contracts" and "securities," which were not on the official list.[203]

The Court, speaking through Justice Powell, in a unanimous opinion, applied the *Central Hudson* test. The Court perhaps liberalized the four-part test by stating that a total ban on "certain types of potentially misleading information, e.g., a listing of areas of practice,"[204] is not permissible if the "information also may be presented in a way that is not deceptive."[205]

Because the state could not articulate a substantial interest served by the regulation, and because the speech was not obviously misleading, the rule was held invalid.[206]

The Missouri Supreme Court also banned mailing announcement of office openings to a list broader than "lawyers, clients, former clients, personal friends and relatives."[207] The Court concluded that a less restrictive approach, such as pre-filing supervision of mailing announcements, would be an equally good solution.[208] Other regulations were similarly analyzed.[209]

It is apparent from the immediately preceding two cases that the four-part test can be applied liberally or conservatively by the Court. That is, a court may hold the state to a very onerous standard of proof with respect to the second through the fourth tests. Alternatively, a court may permit the government to engage successfully in fairly casual speculation about, let us say, the causal link between billboards and aesthetics. Likewise, the judiciary can demand greater or lesser standards with respect to proving the falsity of a statement.

A good example of the Court's ability, so to speak, to apply the test in a manner unfavorable to government is the next significant commercial speech Supreme Court case, *Bolger v. Youngs Drug Product Corp.*[210] This litigation tested the constitutionality of a federal statute prohibiting the mailing of unsolicited advertisements for contraceptives.[211]

Justice Marshall, writing for the Court, first concluded that the commercial speech was neither misleading nor applicable to unlawful activity.[212] Hence he proceeded to the second of the four tests, the alleged substantiality of the government's interest in the goals of the statute. The government argued that the statute "shields recipients of mail from materials that they are likely to find offensive."[213] The Court, citing *Carey v. Population Services International,*[214] emphasized that offensiveness was never, except in obscenity cases, a reason for denying speech First Amendment protection.[215] This is based on the fundamental idea that content should not be the basis for censoring speech.[216] In *Carey* the Court, quoting *Virginia Pharmacy*, had asserted that much advertising is, in any event, " ' tasteless and excessive,' and no doubt offends many."[217]

Justice Marshall specifically approved of the argument in *Carey* that the offensiveness argument is directed at ideas and mode of expression, something that is "the core of First Amendment values."[218] Presumably that which offends, transgresses someone's ideas, hence should be protected. Because much advertising is "excessive," presumably much advertising contains ideas, albeit offensive ones. Therefore, the Court would not apply the offensiveness argument to commercial speech, even though it is otherwise distinguished from political speech.[219]

Another way to put the argument is that if commercial speech is often tasteless (i.e., offensive), then it is often identical to core speech. This, in any event, seems to be the Marshall and *Carey* Court argument. Yet surely there can be a quality of commercial offensiveness that is not directed at ideas. We are now in murky water, however, on the verge of distinguishing ideas in their coldly rational sense from complex states that include sensations, feelings, beliefs, and sentiments. Yet if "idea" is broadly enough defined (e.g., to include in this case, involving condom ads, ultra-orthodox feelings of good taste and discretion, and I am not suggesting that one should not necessarily do so), I suppose one can concede the Marshall argument.

A second government interest, more substantial in the Court's opinion, was the promotion of parents' control over the education of their children on sexual matters.[220] Arguably, the unsolicited mailings would compete with and impair their power to guide.

The Court concluded that the third test was not met. That is, the causal connection between statute and goal was too remote.[221] The Court argued, among a variety of points, that parents can and do monitor access to the mailbox.[222] No data were mentioned by the Court to buttress this common-sensical conclusion. It was good anecdotal argument but perhaps false in fact.

Another significant aspect of the case involved a definition of commercial speech. The Court recognized that some of the materials analyzed the use of condoms without particular specification of the company's products.[223] The Court defined commercial speech as follows:

Most of appellee's mailings fall within the core notion of commercial speech—"speech which does no more than propose a commercial transaction...." Youngs' informational pamphlets, however, cannot be characterized merely as proposals to engage in commercial transactions. Their proper classification as commercial or noncommercial speech thus presents a closer question. The mere fact that these pamphlets are conceded to be advertisements clearly does not compel the conclusion that they are commercial speech.... Similarly, the reference to a specific product does not by itself render the pamphlets commercial speech.... Finally, the fact that Youngs had an economic motivation for mailing the pamphlets would clearly be insufficient by itself to turn the materials into commercial speech.

The combination of *all* these characteristics, however, provides strong support for the District Court's conclusion that the informational pamphlets are properly characterized as commercial speech.[224]

Justice Stevens, concurring, emphasized that the federal regulation was directed at noncommercial goals. That is, it was aimed at, for example, protecting parents' rights to counsel children, not the commercial failures of the product being touted. Therefore, the regulation chilled basic noncommercial First Amendment purposes.[225]

In *Zauderer v. Office of Disciplinary Counsel*[226] the Ohio court held that Ohio's disciplinary rules "forbade soliciting or accepting legal employment through advertisements containing information or advice regarding a specific legal problem."[227] The attorney's advertisement in question had asserted his readiness to represent women who had been injured by use of the Dalkon Shield intrauterine device.[228] The notice had cautioned women that their claims might not be time-barred.[229] The information in the advertisement concerning the device was neither false nor deceptive.[230]

One of the arguments made by the state was that despite appellant's truthfulness, "the State's prohibition ... is a prophylactic rule that is needed to ensure that attorneys ... do not use false or misleading advertising to stir up meritless litigation against innocent defendants."[231] The state went on to make a most provocative point: "Advertising by attorneys, the State claims, presents regulatory difficulties that are different in kind from those presented by other forms of advertising. Whereas statements about most consumer products are subject to verification, the indeterminacy of statements about law make it impractical if not impossible to weed out accurate statements from those that are false or misleading."[232]

The reader will recall that one of the central arguments made in the earlier cases for distinguishing between commercial speech and core speech is the allegedly relative ease of verifying the accuracy or falsity of the former.[233] The state turns this about and argues that commercial speech that is difficult to verify should be subject, therefore, to sweeping prophylactic ban. In response, Justice White, writing for the Court, argued that first, the ad in question was easily verifiable,[234] and second, verification of much nonlegal commercial speech "may require resolution of exceedingly complex and technical factual issues and the consideration of nice questions of semantics."[235] Because commercial information is valuable, the government must incur the burdens of winnowing out the false from the true, rather than opting for a flat ban.[236] The second argument is persuasive within its terms of reference, but at the cost of wiping out one of the major reasons given by the Court in earlier cases for the entire commercial speech-core speech dichotomy.

The advertisement also stated that cases would be handled on a contingent fee basis, and that if unsuccessful, the client would owe no legal fees. The authorities in Ohio asserted that this was misleading, since it omitted the possibility of paying litigation costs.[237]

Zauderer argued that this charge should be evaluated by the four-part *Central Hudson* test.[238] The Court disagreed. It asserted that there was a substantial difference between outright bans of speech and forms of mandatory disclosure of omitted information.[239] Because information was the key, a government call for more disclosure is valuable, and the speaker's constitutionally protected interest in withholding is de minimus.[240] Mandatory disclosure regulation will, therefore, not be subject to the *Central Hudson* "least restrictive means" leg of the four-part test.[241] The new test for required disclosure is to the effect that "advertiser's rights are adequately protected as long as disclosure requirements are reasonably related to the State's interest in preventing deception of customers."[242] Although a system of mandatory disclosure will no doubt fail to meet constitutional tests with respect to core speech, since it is a method of prescribing orthodoxy "in politics, nationalism, religion or other matters of opinion"[243] the state may "prescribe what shall be orthodox in commercial advertising"[244] because the value of commercial speech lies principally in the truthful information (as distinguished from opinion) it transmits to consumers. The state's conclusion that deception was involved in omission of legal costs disclosure, the Court held, met the diluted "reasonably related to the State's interest test."[245]

This distinction between ban and mandatory disclosure is extremely important. It serves as a basis for the mandatory disclosure system of the SEC. The structure of securities regulation relies heavily on required disclosure in the sale of securities, shareholder meetings, and takeover transactions.

If such disclosure must meet the four-part test, (not the diluted test, above) it may fail in the following sense: Another major mode of securities regulation is civil and criminal fraud prosecution after the fact by the government. This involves such well-known areas as insider-trading prosecution and takeover fraud litigation. In certain cases parties could argue, with some chance of success, that the "least restrictive means" analysis requires use of fraud enforcement rather than the more onerous mandatory disclosure plus fraud prosecution mode.

Justice Brennan (with whom Marshall joined) disagreed with the distinction, and would apply the *Central Hudson* four-part test to state disclosure requirements.[246] He put the issue as follows:

Much of the Court's reasoning appears to rest on the premise that, in the commercial-speech context, "the First Amendment interests implicated by disclosure requirements are substantially weaker than those at stake when speech is actually supressed." . . . I believe the Court greatly overstates the distinction between disclosure and suppression in these circumstances. We have noted in traditional First Amendment cases that an affirmative publication requirement "operates as a command in the same sense as a statute or regulation forbidding [someone] to publish specified matter," and that "a compulsion to publish that which 'reason' tells [one] should not be published" therefore raises substantial First Amendment concerns. *Miami Herald Publishing Co. v. Tornillo*, 418 U.S. 241, 256 (1974). Such compulsion in the advertising context will frequently be permissible, and I agree that the distinction between suppression and disclosure supports some differences in analysis. . . . Nevertheless, disclosure requirements must satisfy the basic tenets of [the four-part test].[247]

The difference in analysis essentially meant that Justice Brennan agreed that the state may require some manadatory disclosure, always subject to the four-part test, to assure the truthfulness of commercial advertising.[248]

As we shall soon see, the Supreme Court, on June 29, 1989, rejected the least restrictive means interpretation of the fourth prong of the *Central Hudson* test. The implication of that change will be explored when that case is discussed.[249]

In *Posadas de Puerto Rico Associates v. Tourism Co. of Puerto Rico*[250] the Court considered a Puerto Rican ban on advertising casino gambling to residents. The activity itself was not unlawful. Justice Rehnquist, writing for the Court, argued that the government could chill the speech, since it possessed the greater power to ban the activity.[251] As the justice argued, "it is precisely *because* the government could have enacted a wholesale prohibition of the underlying conduct that it is permissible for the government to take the less intrusive step of allowing the conduct, but reducing the demand through restrictions on advertising."[252] In this context he applied the *Central Hudson* four-part test and found the ban in conformity with the First Amendment. That is, he found that the commonwealth had a substantial interest in reducing demand for casino gambling, that the less intrusive step directly advanced that interest, and that the restriction was no less extensive than necessary to achieve the interest.[253] Because most economic activity can be regulated or even banned under relatively permissive Fourteenth Amendment rational state behavior tests, the Rehnquist argument presaged a retreat from the earlier *Virginia Pharmacy* protection of commercial speech doctrine. It also seemed to imply a relatively permissive interpretation of the *Central Hudson* test.

Justice Brennan, joined by Marshall and Blackmun, dissented, arguing, among other contentions, that the government could not, absent special circumstances, chill speech about lawful activity as a substitute for banning the activity. He argued that the prohibition would prevent citizens from gathering information about an activity that was lawful. Hence their ability to make decisions about that activity would be impaired. This impairment or manipulation by the government, he reasoned, went to the heart of the evil that the First Amendment was designed to prevent.[254] As he eloquently put it:

However, no differences between commercial and other kinds of speech justify protecting commercial speech less extensively where, as here, the government seeks to manipulate private behavior by depriving citizens of truthful information concerning lawful activities.... Accordingly, I believe that where the government seeks to suppress the dissemination of nonmisleading commercial speech relating to legal activities, for fear that recipients will act on the information provided, such regulation should be subjected to strict scrutiny.[255]

This debate may be significant in the area of SEC regulation. The government may contend that transactions in securities can be directly regulated. For example, the federal government could pass legislation imposing a kind of merit regulation pursuant to which bureaucrats could ban sale of excessively risky ventures or transactions at too high a price. The government could ban insider holdings in stocks of companies they manage. Instead, the government, regulates disclosure about the sales (and purchases) in order to protect the investor. The latter is a less pervasive regulation, hence, under the Rehnquist argument, is lawful as long as it otherwise meets the *Zauderer* reasonability test.

In *Shapero v. Kentucky Bar Association* Justice Brennan, writing for the Court, held that the state could not ban truthful attorneys' advertisements directed at people with known legal problems.[256] The particular case involved potential clients who had foreclosure suits filed against them.[257] The Court rejected the argument that this involved a form of overreaching and pressure similar to the face-to-face conduct regulated in the *Ohralik* case.[258]

Justice O'Connor, with whom Chief Justice Rehnquist and Justice Scalia joined, wrote an impassioned dissent.[259] Although she accepted the *Central Hudson* test, she emphasized the need to respect the justifications for state regulation of attorney advertising. The justice argued that the fundamental ethical responsibilities of attorneys warranted different treatment from other commercial speech cases:

One distinguishing feature of any profession, unlike other occupations that may be equally respectable, is that membership entails an ethical obligation to temper one's selfish pursuit of economic success. By adhering to standards of conduct that could not be enforced either by legal fiat or through the discipline of the market. . . . Precisely because lawyers must be provided with expertise that is both esoteric and extremely powerful, it would be unrealistic to demand that clients bargain for their services in the same arms-length manner that may be appropriate when buying an automobile or choosing a dry cleaner.[260]

Difficult and complex arguments and assumptions are present in the dissent. It is hardly clear that the legal profession operates other than any other trade or occupation. But assuming that it does, her argument raises new problems. Much of her argument turns on the power of the attorney to do harm. Hence there is a need for a permissive attitude toward state regulation. But surely politicians can do even more harm, yet their speech is certainly protected by the full breadth of the First Amendment. She also argues that attorneys are more than businesspersons hawking wares, hence their speech should be more regulated. Yet if their speech is more political, and less commercial, than that of used car salesmen, it should be more protected, not less. Conversely, if their speech is different from commercial speech because emanating from noneconomic agents, surely that, too, is an argument for applying the same rigorous requirements to politicians that she would apply to the speech of attorneys.[261]

The *Posadas* case, as I have mentioned, seemed to signal a partial victory for the Rehnquist skepticism about the *Virginia Pharmacy* commercial speech doctrine. In the 1988–1989 term the new conservative majority on the Court (Chief Justice Rehnquist and Associate Justices White, O'Connor, Scalia, and Kennedy) handed down a series of opinions that signaled a shift in Court opinion on affirmative action cases and abortion.[262] In *Board of Trustees of the State University of New York v. Todd Fox* Justice Scalia delivered the opinion of the Court, joined by Justices Rehnquist, White, Stevens, O'Connor, and Kennedy, which significantly diluted the fourth prong of the *Central Hudson* case.[263]

The State University of New York (SUNY) had promulgated a resolution that read as follows: "No authorization will be given to private commercial enterprises to operate on State University campuses or in facilities furnished by the University other than to provide for food, legal beverages, campus bookstore, vending, linen supply, laundry, dry cleaning, banking, barber and beautician services and cultural events."[264]

American Future Systems, Inc. (AFS) merchandised housewares, such as china and silverware, to students at the university. As the Court put it, the company "markets its products exclusively by the technique popularly called (after the company that pioneered it) 'Tupperware parties.' This consists of demonstrating and offering products for sale to groups of ten or more prospective buyers at gatherings assembled and hosted by one of those prospective buyers (for which the host or hostess stands to receive some bonus or reward)."[265]

Again, as the Court described the facts, campus police requested that an AFS representative, who was demonstrating company products in a student's dormitory room, leave. She refused, and they arrested her and charged her with trespass, soliciting without a permit, and loitering. Students and the company employee sued for declaratory judgment that the university resolution violated the First Amendment. First, the district court granted a preliminary injunction[266]; later, after trial, the court held for the university "on the grounds that the SUNY dormitories did not constitute a public forum for purposes of commercial activity and that the restrictions on speech were reasonable in light of the dormitories' purpose."[267] In a 2–1 vote of a panel of the Court of Appeals for the Second Circuit the Court reversed the judgment and remanded to the district court to determine whether, one, the regulation directly advanced the substantial state interests, and two, was the regulation the least restrictive means to accomplish the interests.[268] On the day the Court granted certiorari the district court struck down the regulation because it failed to reach the state's goals by the least restrictive means available.[269] The district court stayed its mandate by stipulation of the parties awaiting the Court's decision.[270]

The Court, after concluding that commercial speech, not fully protected speech, was involved, considered the four-prong *Central Hudson* test. Justice Scalia, for the Court, agreed with the court of appeals that the speech proposed a lawful transaction and was not misleading. That is part one of the test. The Court also agreed with the court of appeals that the government interests asserted—promoting an educational atmosphere, promoting safety and security, preventing commercial exploitation of students, and preserving residential tranquillity—are substantial. That is test number two.[271]

The court of appeals did not decide whether the regulation "directly advances those interests"[272] and "whether the regulation...is more extensive than is necessary for that purpose."[273] Those issues were remanded to the district court, and "it is the terms of the remand...that are the major issue here—specifically, those pertaining to the last element of the *Central Hudson* analysis."[274] The court of appeals equated the *Central Hudson* fourth prong—whether it is "not more extensive than is necessary"—with the phrase "least restrictive measure" that could adequately sustain the State's concerns.[275] This demanding test was the focus of the Court's opinion.

The Court recognized that what it termed dicta in some of its prior opinions, supported a tough least restrictive means test. The Court referred to the language of *Central Hudson* itself, where it was stated that "if the governmental interest could be served as well by a more limited restriction on commercial speech, the excessive restrictions cannot survive."[276] The Court also referred to *Zauderer*, in which the least restrictive means test was assumed in the context of distinguishing outright bans from mandatory disclosure regulation.[277] *Zauderer* retained the narrow construction for bans, but adopted a more permissive test for governmental regulation by way of mandatory disclosure.

The Court, however, relied on *In Re R.M.J.*, where Justice Scalia cites to the statement that restrictions against deceptive advertisements must be "narrowly drawn" and "no more extensive than reasonably necessary to further substantial interests."[278] The justice also draws upon *Shapero v. Kentucky Bar Association* for a similar formulation.[279] The Court also referred to *San Francisco Arts & Athletics, Inc. v. United States Olympic Committee*, where the Court upheld the trademark "Olympics" against attack by a gay sports event using the term. Justice Scalia asserted that the latter opinion equated the *Central Hudson* test to the application of the test for validity of time, place, and manner restrictions, a test that does not require least restrictive means.[280]

Justice Scalia then stated that the Court is in the instant case focusing "upon this specific issue for the first time," as distinguished from its dicta of the past.[281] The justice made the following arguments for rejecting the narrow test.

First, he emphasized that commercial speech enjoys only a subordinate position in the hierarchy of First Amendment values.[282] Therefore, a least restrictive means test would unduly raise commercial speech to a higher position of protection than it deserves.[283]

Next, the justice argued by analogy, a popular form of legal reasoning, to be sure. He pointed out that a least restrictive means test has not been used for the time, place, and mannner restrictions of core political speech.[284] The Court has upheld such regulations, provided they are "narrowly tailored" to achieve a significant governmental interest.[285] Justice Scalia pointed out that the Court has followed a similar approach with respect to state regulation of "expressive conduct, including conduct expressive of political views."[286] Further, the Court has been "loath to second-guess the Government's judgment to that effect."[287]

Third, Justice Scalia maintained that "[n]one of our cases invalidating the regulation of commercial speech involved a provision that went only marginally beyond what would have served the governmental interest."[288] The restrictions disallowed have been "substantially excessive."[289]

Fourth, Scalia asserted that the Court decisions upholding the regulations "cannot be reconciled with a requirement of least restrictive means."[290] The justice referred to the *Posadas* case, and stated that "we did not first satisfy ourselves that the the governmental goal of deterring casino gambling could not adequately have been served (as the appellant contended) 'not by suppressing commercial speech that might *encourage* such gambling, but by promulgating additional speech designed to *discourage* it.' "[291] Scalia emphasized that the Posadas Court said it " 'was up to the legislature to decide' that point, so long as its judgment was reasonable."[292]

Justice Scalia made the same point with respect to *Metromedia, Inc. v. City of San Diego*, plurality opinion, "where we upheld San Diego's complete ban of off-site billboard advertising, we did not inquire whether any less restrictive measure (for example, controlling the size and appearance of the signs) would suffice to meet the City's concerns for traffic safety and aesthetics."[293] The justice finally refers to *San Francisco Arts & Athletics, Inc. v. United States Olympic Committee*, where "it was enough to uphold the restrictions placed on commercial speech by a federal trademark statute that they were 'not broader than Congress reasonably could have determined to be necessary.' "[294]

Justice Scalia provided the following restatement of the fourth prong of the *Central Hudson* test. It is a reformulation that appears to construe the third prong as well.

In sum, while we have insisted that the " 'free flow of commercial information is valuable enough to justify imposing on would-be regulators the costs of distinguishing ... the harmless from the harmful,' " Shapero, 486 U.S. at—, ... quoting *Zauderer*, 471 U.S. at 646, ... we have not gone so far as to impose upon them the burden of demonstrating that the distinguishment is 100% complete, or that the manner of restriction is absolutely the least severe that will achieve the desired end. What our decisions require is a 'fit' between the legislature's ends and the means chosen to accomplish these ends," *Posadas*, 478 U.S., at 341 . . . a fit that is not necessarily perfect, but reasonable; that represents not necessarily the single best disposition, but one whose scope is "in proportion to the interest served," *In re R.M.J.*, *supra*, 455 U.S. at 203 . . . ; that employs not necessarily the least restrictive means, but as we have put it in other contexts discussed above, a means narrowly tailored to achieve the desired objective. Within those bounds we leave it to governmental decisionmakers to judge what manner of regulation may best be employed."[295]

The justice went on:

We reject the contention that the test we have described is overly permissive. It is far different, of course, from the "rational basis" test used for Fourteenth Amendment equal protection analysis. . . . There it suffices if the law could be thought to further a legitimate governmental goal, without reference to whether it does so at inordinate cost. Here we require the government goal to be substantial, and the cost to be carefully calculated. Moreover, since the State bears the burden of justifying its restrictions . . . it must affirmatively establish the reasonable fit we require. . . . Far from eroding the essential protections of the First Amendment, we think this disposition strengthens them. "To require a parity of constitutional protection for commercial and noncommercial speech alike would invite dilution, simply by a leveling process, of the force of the Amendment's guarantee with respect to the latter kind of speech."[296]

The Court, in this case, is clearly signaling a turn in commercial speech doctrine. Although the new "means narrowly tailored" test could be interpreted by some judges to strike down many a government regulation, the Court's rejection of the least restrictive means test signifies a stronger affirmation of the lower value the new majority places on commercial speech.

Justice Blackmun wrote the dissenting opinion, joined by Justices Brennan and Marshall. They emphasized that the Court was rejecting "repeated assertions" in the past in support of the least restrictive analysis.[297]

The *Zauderer* opinion distinguished between outright bans and mandatory disclosure regulation. It applied a "reasonably" related to the goals test to evaluate the latter, rather than use the then applicable least restrictive means test. The new Court test, replacing the older versions of the four-prong test, might apply equally to bans as well as mandatory disclosure. The Court may in the future, however, continue to apply an even more permissive test for governmental regulation of mandatory disclosure because of the argument that it creates more information, rather than less. Indeed, in *Riley v. National Federation of the Blind of North Carolina, Inc.*, in 1988, the Court, in dicta, distinguished the charitable solicitation at issue from the securities field, which it considered commercial speech, approvingly mentioned the *Zauderer* opinion, and stated that "[p]urely commercial speech is more susceptible to compelled disclosure requirements."[298]

The reason for this distinction is hardly compelling. It appears to turn, as

mentioned above, in the discussion of *Zauderer*, on the argument that commercial speech is protected because of its mundane informational value, not
its opinion or idea value. However, as discussed at length in Chapter 5, the
power to create a governmentally imposed orthodoxy in "information" creates grave dangers not dissimilar from a governmental orthodoxy in political
speech. The government may be biased, the government may err, and the
government may seek power, not truth. In the *Riley* case the Court asserted
that "compelled statements of opinion" in fully protected speech cannot be
distinguished from "compelled statements of 'fact'."[299] The Court stated that
it would not "immunize a law . . . requiring a speaker favoring an incumbent
candidate to state during every solicitation that candidate's recent travel
budget."[300] The Court, quoting *Wooley v. Maynard*, argued that "[t]he right
to speak and the right to refrain from speaking are complementary components of the broader concept of 'individual freedom of mind.' "[301]

Respondent students also made an overbreadth claim. That doctrine permits people who are themselves not affected by a statute to attack it facially
on the basis that it may be applied unconstitutionally against others.[302] The
Court refused to make that determination at this point. Justice Scalia stated
that "[w]e remand this case for determination, pursuant to the standards
described above, of the validity of this law's application to the commercial
and noncommercial speech that is the subject of the complaint; and, if its
application to speech in either such category is found to be valid, for determination whether its substantial overbreadth nonetheless makes it unen-
forceable."[303]

The overbreadth doctrine does not apply to purely commercial speech
because it is allegedly hardy (i.e., "less likely to be 'chilled' ").[304] Justice Scalia
concluded that the university regulation at issue did apply to noncommercial
speech as well as to commercial speech. He emphasized that it applied to
tutoring, legal advice, job counseling, and medical consultation (all for a fee).
"While these examples consist of speech for a profit, they do not consist of
speech that *proposes* a commercial transaction, which is what defines commercial speech."[305]

His brief analysis of the distinction between commercial speech and fully
protected speech inadvertently illustrates the fuzziness of the distinction. The
justice, for example, categorized legal advice as noncommercial speech. Yet
a non-licensed attorney cannot give personalized legal advice without violating criminal or civil law in virtually all of the fifty states. The same is true
for medical advice. That same non-licensed attorney can write a book on
legal matters, and the book will be protected fully by the First Amendment.
The same is true for law student notes and articles published in law reviews.[306]
Presumably, the justice meant that the student had a First Amendment right
to receive legal advice from a licensed attorney or doctor. But presumably
that same student did not have the same unfettered right to be solicited for
said legal service by the attorney, since that involved the proposal of a com-

mercial transaction. That commercial transaction, however, is the hiring of the attorney so as to receive the advice that is protected by the First Amendment. This utter confusion, at least as I see it, demonstrates the difficulty of distinguishing, in any coherent manner, between economically motivated speech and economically motivated speech that proposes a "commercial transaction." All economically motivated speech is designed to accomplish down the road a commercial transaction. But because so much of political and artistic speech is economically motivated, the broader definition of commercial speech as economically motivated speech would include too much. Hence the Court must usually limit the definition to the direct advertisement of a product or a service for a profit. But where the service is itself speech, the narrower definition begins to break down. If the product involves symbolic speech, something that may depend on the elusive motives of the buyer (or seller), the narrower definition also begins to break down.

NOTES

1. *Valentine v. Chrestensen*, 316 U.S. 52, 54 (1942).
2. Redish, *The Frist Amendment in the Market Place: Commercial Speech and the Values of Free Expression*, 39 Geo. Wash. L. Rev. 429, 450 (1971).
3. 341 U.S. 622 (1951).
4. *Id.* at 642.
5. 319 U.S. 141 (1943).
6. 341 U.S. at 643.
7. 376 U.S. 254 (1964).
8. *Id.* at 266.
9. 413 U.S. 376 (1973). Justice Powell's opinion for the majority was joined by Justices Brennan, White, Marshall, and Rehnquist. Chief Justice Burger and Justices Douglas, Stewart, and Blackmun each filed dissenting opinions.
10. *Id.* at 385.
11. *Id.* at 385.
12. *Id.*
13. *Id.*
14. *Id.*
15. *Id.*
16. *Id.* at 388.
17. *Id.* at 389.
18. *Id.* at 401, n. 6. The Justice was citing Justice Douglas in his concurring opinion in *Cammarano v. United States*, 358 U.S. 498, 574 (1959).
19. *Id.* at 402 and n. 7.
20. *Id.* at 398.
21. *Id.* at 393.
22. 421 U.S. 809 (1975).
23. *Id.* at 812.
24. *Id.* at 821.
25. *Id.* at 822.

26. *Id.* at 824.

27. *Id.* at 826.

28. *Id.* at 828.

29. *Id.* at 832.

30. *Id.*

31. *Virginia State Board of Pharmacy v. Virginia Citizens Consumer Council*, 425 U.S. 748 (1976). Blackmun, J., delivered the opinion of the Court, in which Burger, C. J., and Brennan, Stewart, White, Marshall, and Powell, JJ., joined. Burger, C. J. and Stewart, J., filed concurring opinions. Rehnquist, J., filed a dissenting opinion. Stevens, J., took no part in the case.

32. *Id.* at 761.

33. *Id.*

34. *Id.*

35. *Id.*

36. *Id.* at 761–62.

37. *Id.* at 762.

38. *Id.* at 762.

39. *Id.* at 763.

40. *See* chapter 4, discussion of R. Posner.

41. *Id.* at 763–64.

42. *Id.* at 765.

43. *Id.* at 767–68.

44. *Id.*

45. *Id.* at 769.

46. *Id.* at 769–70.

47. *Id.* at 771, n. 24.

48. *Id.*

49. *Id.*

50. *Id.* at 771 and n. 24.

51. *Id.* at 772–73.

52. *Id.* at 773, n. 25.

53. *Id.* at 773.

54. *Linmark Associates, Inc. v. Willingboro*, 431 U.S. 85, n. 6 at 92.

55. 425 U.S. at 776.

56. *Id.* at 777.

57. *Id.* at 777, quoting 418 U.S. 323, 340 (1974).

58. *Id.* at 777.

59. *Id.*

60. *Id.*

61. *Id.*

61. *Id.* at 778. Stewart also pointed out that courts have referred to the competing First Amendment associational rights of labor and the economic dependence of employees on their employers. Id. at 779, n. 4, and cases cited therein.

63. *Id.* at 779.

64. *Id.*

65. *Id.*

66. *Id.* at 779–80.

67. *Id.* at 780.

68. *Id.*
69. *Id.*
70. *Id.* at 781.
71. See Chapter 3.
72. 425 U.S. at 781.
73. *Id.* at 781–90.
74. *Id.* at 790.
75. *Id.* at 784.
76. *Id.*
77. *Id.* at 785–86.
78. *Id.* at 787–88.
79. *Breard v. City of Alexandria*, 341 U.S. 622, 650 (1951) (dissenting).
80. 431 U.S. 85 (1977). All members joined the opinion except Justice Rehnquist, who took no part in the consideration or decision of the case.
81. *Id.* at 87–88.
82. *Id.* at 95.
83. *Id.*
84. *Id.*
85. *Id.* at 96.
86. *Id.* at 97.
87. *Id.* at 98.
88. *Carey v. Population Services International*, 431 U.S. 678 (1977).
89. *Id.* at 681.
90. *Id.* at 700.
91. *Id.* at 701.
92. *Id.* at 711–12.
93. *Id.* at 712 and n. 6, 712.
94. *Id.* at n. 6.
95. *Id.* at 703, 716–17.
96. *Id.* at 702.
97. *Id.* at 717.
98. *Bates v. State Bar of Arizona*, 433 U.S. 350 (1977).
99. *Id.* at 354 and 385.
100. *Id.*
101. *Id.* at 385.
102. *Id.*
103. *Id.* at 354.
104. *Id.* at 353.
105. *Id.* at 363–64.
106. *Id.* at 364–65.
107. *Id.* at 365.
108. *Id.*
109. *Id.* at 366.
110. *Id.* at 367–68.
111. *Id.* at 368–71.
112. *Id.* at 371.
113. *Id.* at 375.
114. *Id.* at 377.

115. *Id.*

116. *Id.* at 378.

117. *Id.* at 376.

118. *Id.* at 377.

119. *Id.* at 378.

120. See *Virginia State Board of Pharmacy* v. *Virginia Citizens Consumer Council*, 425 U.S. 748, 769 (1976).

121. 433 U.S. at 372.

122. Justice Stewart, concurring in *Virginia State Board of Pharmacy v. Virginia Citzens Consumer Council*, 425 U.S. 748, 780. (1976).

123. *Id.* at 372–73.

124. *Id.* at 373–74.

125. *Id.* at 374–75.

126. *Id.* at 379.

127. *Id.* at 380–81.

128. See, e.g., *Bigelow v. Virginia*, 421 U.S. 809, 815–16 (1975).

129. 433 U.S. at 381.

130. *Id.* at 381–82.

131. *Id.* at 383–84.

132. *Id.* at 404.

133. 436 U.S. 447 (1978).

134. *Id.* at 449–54.

135. *Id.* at 456.

136. *Id.*

137. *Id.* at 456. The securities regulation cases cited by him were *SEC v. Texas Gulf Sulphur Co.*, 401 F.2d 833 (CA2 1968), *cert. denied*, 394 U.S. 976 (1969), and *Mills v. Electric Auto-Lite Co.*, 396 U.S. 375 (1970).

138. *Id.*

139. *Id.*

140. *Id.*

141. *Id.*

142. *Id.* at 457–58.

143. *Miami Herald Publishing Co. v. Tornillo*, 418 U.S. 241, 258 (1974).

144. *Id.* at 459–60.

145. *Id.* at 460–61.

146. The Court pointed out, for example, that the attorney spoke to the young accident victims when they were still distressed. *Id.* at 467. Indeed, one of them lay in traction in the hospital room. *Id.* The attorney used a concealed tape recorder to obtain evidence of one of the victim's consent to his representation. *Id.* Justice Marshall noted that the attorney pursued one person for representation, although this might create a conflict with the other woman's interests. *Id.* at 469–70.

147. *Id.* at 476; The research he cited, *id.* at 476, was J. Auerbach, *Unequal Justice* 42–62, 126–29 (1976).

148. *Id.* at 476.

149. 436 U.S. 412 (1978).

150. *Id.* at 437–38 and n. 32.

151. *Id.* at 435–36.

152. *Id.* at 432.

153. *Id.* at 441–42.

154. *Id.* at 445.

155. 440 U.S. 1 (1979).

156. *Id.* at 10.

157. *Id.* at 16.

158. *Id.* at 19. Justice Marshall joined in his dissenting opinion.

159. *Id.* at 21.

160. *Id.* at 22.

161. *Id.* at 23–24.

162. *Id.* at 24–25.

163. 447 U.S. 557 (1980).

164. *Id.* at 558.

165. *Id.* at 559.

166. *Id.*

167. *Id.*

168. *Id.* at 563.

169. *id.*

170. *Id.* at 564.

171. *Gertz v. Robert Welch, Inc.*, 418 U.S. 323, 340 (1974).

172. 447 U.S. at 564, n. 6.

173. *Id.* at 566. It has since been modified. See discusssion of *Board of Trustees of the State University of N.Y. v. Fox*, below, at conclusion of this chapter.

174. *Id.* at 563.

175. *Id.* at 564.

176. *Id.* at 566.

177. *Id.* at 567.

178. *Id.* at 568.

179. *Id.* at 569.

180. *Id.*

181. *Id.*

182. *Id.* at 570.

183. *Id.* at 571, n. 13. "We have observed that commercial speech is such a sturdy brand of expression that traditional prior restraint doctrine may not apply to it. *Virginia State Board of Pharmacy v. Virginia Citizens Consumer Council*, 425 U.S. at 771–72, n. 24." *Id.*

184. *Id.* at 573.

185. *Id.* at 574–75.

186. *Id.* at 576.

187. *Id.* at 576–77.

188. *Id.* at 564 and 565, n. 7.

189. *Id.* at 578.

190. *Id.* at 589. *Lochner v. New York*, 198 U.S. 45 (1905).

191. See Chapter 3, discussion of "economic due process."

192. 453 U.S. 490 (1981).

193. *Id.* at 512–17.

194. *Id.* at 507–12.

195. *Id.* at 508–11.

196. *Id.* at 521, n. 26.

197. *Id*. at 534, n. 12.

198. *Id*. at 536–40.

199. *Id*. at 540, quoting *Lehman v. City of Shaker Heights*, 418 U.S. 298, 319 (1974) (Brennan, J., dissenting).

200. *Id*. at 541, 555, and 569.

201. 455 U.S. 191 (1982).

202. *Id*. at 205.

203. *Id*.

204. *Id*. at 203.

205. *Id*.

206. *Id*.

207. *Id*. at 206.

208. *Id*.

209. *Id*. at 205.

210. 463 U.S. 60 (1983).

211. *Id*. at 61.

212. *Id*. at 69.

213. *Id*. at 71.

214. 431 U.S. 678 (1977).

215. 463 U.S. at 71.

216. 431 U.S. at 701.

217. *Id*. at 701, n. 27, quoting *Virginia State Board of Pharmacy v. Virginia Citizens Consumer Council*, 425 U.S. at 765.

218. 463 U.S. at 71–72, citing to *Carey* at 701, n. 28.

219. *Id*.

220. *Id*. at 73.

221. *Id*.

222. *Id*.

223. *Id*. at 66, n. 13.

224. *Id*. at 66–67 (footnotes and citations to cases omitted).

225. *Id*. at 80–84 (Stevens, J., concurring).

226. 471 U.S. 626 (1985).

227. *Id*. at 639.

228. *Id*. at 630.

229. *Id*. at 631. The advertisment asserted that the device allegedly caused damage, such as "serious pelvic infections," and asserted that the law firm was representing women in such cases. *Id*.

230. *Id*. at 639.

231. *Id*. at 643.

232. *Id*. at 643–44.

233. See also discussion in chapter 4 of R. Posner.

234. *Id*. at 645.

235. *Id*.

236. *Id*. at 646.

237. *Id*. at 633–34.

238. *Id*. at 650.

239. *Id*. at 650–52.

240. *Id*. at 651.

241. *Id.* at 651–52, n. 14.

242. *Id.* at 651.

243. *Id.* quoting *West Virginia State Board of Education v. Barnette*, 319 U.S. 624, 642 (1943).

244. *Id.* at 651.

245. *Id.* at 653.

246. *Id.* at 656–58.

247. *Id.* at 657, n. 1.

248. *Id.* at 658 and 658, n. 2.

249. See discussion in chapter 2.

250. 478 U.S. 328 (1986).

251. *Id.* at 345–46.

252. *Id.* at 346.

253. *Id.* at 340–44.

254. *Id.* at 351.

255. *Id.*

256. 108 S. Ct. 1916 (1988).

257. *Id.* at 1919.

258. *Id.* at 1922–23.

259. *Id.* at 1925 (O'Connor dissenting).

260. *Id.* at 1929–30.

261. The Iowa court (in *Committee on Professional Ethics v. Humphrey)* subsequent to the *Zauderer* case (*Zauderer v. Office of Disciplinary Counsel*, 471 U.S. 626 [1985]) upheld restrictions on TV advertisements of attorneys, owing to the special nature of that media. In 1986 the U.S. Supreme Court dismissed an appeal for lack of a substantial federal question. 106 S. Ct. 1627. Said dismissal, under *Hicks v. Miranda*, 422 U.S. 332 (1975), is deemed a holding on the merits as to those issues correctly before the court. The first state opinion is at 355 N.W.2d 565 (1984). The Supreme Court vacated and remanded the case to the Iowa court in view of *Zauderer*. The second *Humphrey* case is at 377 N.W.2d 643 (1985). *See*, W. Ward Reynoldson, *The Case Against Lawyer Advertising* 75, ABA Journal 60–61 (Jan. 1989).

262. Fein, *A Court That Obeys The Law*, vol. XLI, no. 18, National Review at 50 (Sept. 29, 1989).

263. 109 S. Ct. 3028 (1989).

264. *Id.* at 3030.

265. *Id.*

266. *Id.*

267. *Id.*

268. *Id.* at 3030–31.

269. *Id.* at 3031, n.1.

270. *Id.*

271. *Id.* at 3032.

272. *Id.*

273. *Id.*

274. *Id.*

275. *Id.*

276. 447 U.S. at 564.

277. 471 U.S. at 644, 651 n. 14.

278. 455 U.S. at 203 and 207.

279. 108 S. Ct. at 1921.

280. 107 S. Ct. at 2981 n. 16.

281. 109 S. Ct. at 3033.

282. *Id.*

283. *Id.*

284. *Id.*

285. *Id.*

286. *Id.*

287. *Id.* at 3034

288. *Id.*

289. *Id.*

290. *Id.*

291. *Id.*, quoting *Posadas* 478 U.S. at 344.

292. *Id.*

293. Citing *Metromedia*, 453 U.S. 513.

294. Quoting *San Francisco Arts & Athletics*, 483 U.S. at 539.

295. *Id.* at 3034–35

296. *Id.* at 3035, quoting at end, *Ohralik*, 436 U.S. at 456.

297. *Id.* at 3038, n. 1.

298. Slip opinion at 13, no. 9 (1988).

299. *Id.*

300. *Id.* at 15.

301. *Id.* Riley slip opinion at 14. The Court was citing to *Wooley v. Maynard*, 430 U.S. 705, 714 (1977), which in turn quoted *West Virginia Board of Education v. Barnette*, 319 U.S. 624, 637 (1943)

302. *Board of Trustees of State University of N.Y. v. Fox* 109 S. Ct. at 3035.

303. *Id.* at 3038.

304. *Id.* at 3035.

305. *Id.* at 3036. See also *Dunn & Bradstreet, Inc. v. Greenmoss Bldrs., Inc*, 472 U.S. 749, 790 (1985) (Brennan, J., dissenting).

306. See chapter 5 discussion of the *Lowe* Case.

2

SEC Speech

In chapter 1 we described the commercial speech doctrine as developed by the Supreme Court. Now let us examine the judicial application of the First Amendment to regulation by the Securities and Exchange Commission (SEC). We will ascertain whether the commercial speech doctrine fits SEC speech, and if it does not, what alternative analysis may be developed by the courts.

The SEC regulates corporate and individual disclosure in connection with the purchase and sale of securities, and in regard to the governance of the publicly held corporation.[1] Under the Securities Act of 1933 the commission has established a structure of mandatory disclosure for the offer and sale of securities by corporations and controlling shareholders.[2] Pursuant to that regulatory system, corporations prepare elaborate disclosure documents called prospectuses and registration statements.[3] The Securities Exchange Act of 1934 requires the commission to establish a system of mandatory disclosure for proxy statements in connection with meetings of shareholders.[4] Requirements are established for routine meetings as well as extraordinary meetings that involve proxy contests and major mergers and reorganizations. The commission also has established a complex system of mandatory financial and accounting disclosure for various classes of publicly held coporations.[5] Pursuant to this structure, corporations prepare annual reports on Form 10K and periodic reports on Forms 8K and 10Q. The purpose of mandatory disclosure is to winnow out the false from the true. A related purpose is to produce a complete and informative description of the business. It is a modern form of censorship designed by a concerned government to protect the investor from misrepresentation and lies. It differs from older forms of censorship that flatly banned publication in the important sense that mandatory disclosure requires the dissemination of information, sometimes more information than would be disclosed in the absence of the regulation.

Another central element in the disclosure system is civil and criminal fraud prosecution. The commission has the power under a number of antifraud rules and statutes, such as Rule 10b–5[6] and Rule 14a–9,[7] to seek an injunction and ancillary equitable relief in court against corporations and individuals who have committed fraud in connection with proxy voting or the purchase and sale of securities. The commission, as discussed below in some detail, has the power to require registration and disclosure by investment advisors. In certain cases the commission has administrative powers to punish transgressors.[8] In virtually all cases the Justice Department may pursue egregious cases criminally. The essential difference between the two regulatory structures is that mandatory disclosure rules specify the information that must be disclosed. The antifraud statutes and regulations permit the government to prosecute lies and misrepresentation wherever it finds them, even in the absence of a particular disclosure rule mandating a specific disclosure. (The government also is empowered to seek civil and criminal penalties against people who have violated the manadatory disclosure rules.)

The question in SEC regulation is whether some or all of speech governed by the SEC is speech that receives some First Amendment protection. It is now traditional doctrine that commercial speech (at least truthful commercial speech) receives such protection. Commercial speech, as we have seen, is the advertisement of particular products or services for business gain.[9]

Fraud prosecution involves a kind of after-the-fact-of-publication litigation. It can operate without the presence of mandatory disclosure rules. A "simple" form of fraud prosecution would involve a suit by, let us say, an aggrieved buyer against a seller of securities to her. She would allege deceit, materiality of the lie, reliance, and harm. Is the misrepresentation commercial speech?

A somewhat more complicated fraud case might be involved when a publicly held corporation, not engaged in buying or selling its securities, issues a misleading press release, an area not necessarily covered by specific disclosure rules. It runs the risk that the commission may seek to enjoin the statement on grounds of fraud. The court may add ancillary remedies to the naked injunction. Such forms of relief may involve, for example, replacement of the old board with a new board acceptable to the SEC. The Justice Department may pursue the corporation and offending officers criminally.

A famous branch of fraud prosecution involves insider trading. The paradigm case is a transaction in which a corporate insider trades in corporate stock without disclosure of material facts. The insider does not lie or misrepresent. It is a silence case in which the courts generally hold that the insider has a duty to disclose to the shareholders, or refrain from trading.

Consider a publicly held toothpaste corporation. When it advertises toothpaste, that is clearly commercial speech. It receives a limited form of First Amendment protection. Now assume that some shareholders want to expand the business to include gambling casinos. The shareholders organize a proxy contest to change corporate policy and, ultimately, to unseat the incumbent board. The latter responds with proxy material and solicitation of its own. The proxy material is subject to mandatory disclosure regulation, as well as possible criminal or civil fraud prosecution. The commission also has certain administrative powers to help assure truth in disclosure. Certainly the toothpaste ad is commercial speech. There is not a clear fit, however, with commercial speech for the proxy material. That material relates to corporate governance and changes in corporate governance. Likewise, prospectuses issued in connection with sales of toothpaste corporation common stock do not comfortably fit within the commercial speech definition. Investment advice about particular corporations, issued by an investment advisor, also does not easily fit the definition. That advice is frequently in the form of market letters about a corporation, not the advertisement of the investment advisor's services. The latter would be traditional commercial speech. Is, then, corporate financial and business speech fully protected by the First Amendment? Is it commercial speech? Alternatively, will it, should it, be placed in some special third category of SEC speech that is not protected, or barely protected, by the First Amendment?

THE LOWE CASE

First Amendment litigation in the SEC area achieved significance in the modern era with the case of *Lowe v. SEC* in 1985. The issue was whether "petitioners may be permanently enjoined from publishing nonpersonalized investment advice and commentary in securities newsletters because they are not registered as investment advisers under section 203(c) of the Investment Advisers Act of 1940."[10]

On May 11, 1981, the commission, after an administrative proceeding before an Administrative law judge, revoked the registration of the Lowe Management Corporation.[11] Among other misdeeds, Mr. Christopher Lowe had been convicted of appropriating funds of a client. About one year later the commission sought an injunction in a federal district court against the Lowe publication of investment newsletters.[12] These publications constituted investment advice, the commission argued, hence they were in violation of section 203(a) because the petitioners were not registered or exempt from registration under the 1940 Act.[13] The commission did not allege or prove that the financial information and data in the market letters were false or misleading in any respect.[14]

The district court in *SEC v. Lowe*,[15] pointed out that the SEC took the position that the investment advice should be categorized as commercial speech.[16] Therefore, it would be subject to a considerable degree of regulation.

The court (writing before the Justice Scalia opinion in the *Board of Trustees of the State University of New York v. Fox* case) argued that the SEC publication ban violated the fourth prong of the *Central Hudson Gas* test:

> Given the disclosure mechanisms available to the SEC to put subscribers on their guard against interested investment advice, the censorship that the SEC would impose on Lowe is more extreme than necessary to effectuate the congressional goal of a confident and informed investing public.
>
> Prepublication restraints are ordinarily justifiable only where the non-protected character of the content is ascertainable with "relative certainty" prior to dissemination. *See* L. Tribe, American Constitutional Law 730 (1978). Even in the context of commercial speech speculative assessments may not be relied upon to curb first amendment exercise where the less drastic alternative of disclosure exists.[17]

Chief Judge Weinstein then questioned whether the market letters constituted commercial speech. He suggested that the Supreme Court has limited the concept to product or service advertising. He emphasized that

> [i]nvestment advisory material disseminated to the public is not commercial advertising of a product or a service. Such publications are not the words of a seller peddling his own wares or services, but those of an apparently detached observer commenting on the value of [choices] offered or held by others. To be sure the investment publisher has a financial motivation to disseminate his analyses and recommendations, but so may the literary publisher or political pamphleteer.[18]

The judge then made an important observation about the fuzziness of attempted definitions of ideological and political versus nonpolitical speech, or commercial speech. He stated:

> Recommendation of particular securities is somewhat dissimilar from "[i]deological expression, be it oral, literary, pictorial, or theatrical, [that] is integrally related to the exposition of thought—thought that may shape our concepts of the whole universe of man" [Quoting from *Virginia State Board of Pharmacy*, 425 U.S. at 779 (Stewart, J., concurring)]. But there is no clearly defined perimeter that circumscribes the universe of ideological thought. Economic discussion addresses issues of public concern and qualifies as ideological debate. See, e.g., P. A. Samuelson, Economics, passim (11th ed. 1980) (Particularly chapter 42, "Winds of Change: Evolution of Economic Doctrine"); A. Alchien & W. R. Allen, Exchange and Production: Competition, Coordination and Control, Preface (2d ed. 1977); H. G. Manne, The Economics of Legal Relationships 1–3 (1975). The state of the nation's economy and finances is often an issue uppermost in the minds of voters, and politicians regularly point to the performance of the stock markets as an index of public confidence in their office. There exists moreover, no sharp demarcation in the range of economic observation that

runs from comment on economic policy to prediction of the performance and recommendations of specific securities.[19]

The judge did concede that market letters may not get identical protection with political speech. He concluded with the observation that since, in his opinion, newsletters are not commercial speech, and are closely related to matters of important economic concern, there are "unanswered questions concerning the conditions, if any, under which an absolute restraint may constitutionally be imposed upon them."[20]

He then reached a result designed to uphold the constitutionality of the Advisers Act. He held that the Act must be interpreted to permit the defendants to register and publish so long as they provide all information required by the SEC. [21] He concluded that the act could not be construed to ban registration to publishers because of past misconduct. In that manner the Act, as so construed, would not violate the First Amendment. The commission, however, may bar them from personal investment advice, such as personalized advice by letter or phone. The impersonal publication and dissemination of market letters are protected by the First Amendment from a flat ban, as distinguished from mandatory disclosure requirements. Personal professional advice is not, since it involves "delegations of trust and responsibility."[22]

A divided panel of the Court of Appeals for the Second Circuit reversed.[23] To begin with, the majority rejected the district court's interpretation of the Advisers Act as distinguishing between personal and impersonal advice.[24] It argued that the Act was intended to apply in the same manner to both. The key statutory issue was to determine if the Lowe newsletters were subject to the registration requirements or were "bona fide newspapers," and hence statutorily exempt from registration requirements.[25] The court majority relied on a then fourteen-year-old decision in the second circuit, *SEC v. Wall Street Transcript Corporation.*[26] That court construed the exemption as meaning "those publications which do not deviate from customary newspaper activities to such an extent that there is a likelihood that the wrongdoing which the Act was designed to prevent has occurred."[27] That court found that "[m]ost of its published material consists of reprinted reports assessing various securities issues."[28] It therefore held that "[t]his characteristic emphasis on particular issues and companies at the very least raises doubt about whether the *Transcript* is outside the exclusion—a suspicion which we believe that the SEC should be allowed to investigate."[29]

The Lowe court held that under the test of *Wall Street Transcript*, "it is equally clear that Lowe's publications are not engaged primarily in 'customary newspaper activities,' but rather in the activities that the Investment Adviser Act is intended to regulate."[30] That activity was "the business of advising others . . . as to the value of securities or as to the advisability of investing in, purchasing or selling securities.[31]

The majority also relied on the *Wall Street Transcript* case for its First

Amendment conclusions.[32] That earlier decision, decided well before the later Supreme Court commercial speech cases, had distinguished between commercial activities and social, political, or religious expression.[33] That older case had also, in turn, relied on remarks by Justice Harlan in *Curtis Publishing Co. v. Butts*. Justice Harlan had said: "A business 'is not immune from regulation because it is an agency of the press. The publisher of a newspaper has no special immunity from the application of general laws.... Federal securities regulation, mail-fraud statutes, and common-law actions for deceit and misrepresentation are only some examples of our understanding that the right to communicate information of public interest is not 'unconditional.' "[34]

The *Wall Street Transcript* approach could be interpreted as relying on the notion of regulatable economic activity, that is, regulated transactions in securities as the basis for regulation of speech that, at best, is merely incidental to the regulated activity. (This is similar to Justice Rehnquist's analysis in the *Posadas* case.) The court majority in Lowe held that the *Wall Street Transcript* decision still was good law.[35] The court majority also construed the Supreme Court commercial speech cases as supportive of the same result as the rationale of the *Wall Street Transcript* case.[36]

The court majority also cited a 1977 Seventh Circuit case, *Savage v. Commodity Futures Trading Commission*,[37] which held that "the publisher of the Commodity Exchange Bulletin, a newsletter containing views on the commodity market, was not entitled to registration under the Commodity Futures Trading Commission Act as a commodity trading adviser in view of his previous convictions for securities fraud and mail fraud arising out of the operations of a securities conmpany."[38]

The court majority rejected the appellees' argument that *Savage* was distinguishable, since the publisher erroneously contended that his newsletter received only commercial speech protection.[39] Appellees argued that their newsletter was not commercial speech but more, or fully, protected speech. The court in the Lowe case contended that the Supreme Court cases had not limited commercial speech to the advertisement of products or services.[40] It cited to the *Central Hudson* opinion, which defined commercial speech as "expression related solely to the economic interests of the speaker and its audience."[41] It also cited *Friedman v. Rogers*: "[b]y definition commercial speech is linked inextricably to commercial activity."[42]

The court then interestingly stated: "Thus, although we think it preferable to analyze this case as one involving the permissible regulation of economic activity, we believe that the Investment Advisers Act withstands constitutional scrutiny under First Amendment doctrine relating to commercial speech as well."[43] The reference to economic activity is the kind of analysis later developed in the *Wall Street Publishing Institute* case discussed below.

The court majority addressed the Lowe argument that the ban amounted to an impermissible prior restraint. The court used two arguments to rebut the contention. First, it analogized the ban to the licensing of professionals. Historically, the government has been permitted to deny a professional license for prior criminal conduct.[44] Second, the court relied on the *Friedman* case, and asserted that since Lowe's past deceptive conduct proves that his market letters are inherently subject to deception, they may be banned under traditional commercial speech doctrine.[45]

The court majority limited its holding to a prohibition against publishing advice about specific securities. Lowe was left free to publish his views on "matters of current interest, ... the trend in interest rates, ... whether the next election will affect market conditions."[46]

Judge Brieant wrote what I believe was a most penetrating and persuasive dissent.[47] He agreed with the district court that the Act should be construed so as to prohibit a ban on publishing, to avoid a violation of the Constitution. He took issue with the court majority conclusion that commercial speech included the market letters at issue. He examined the Court commercial speech cases and correctly noted that "examination of the characteristics of commercial speech which have caused the Supreme Court to accord to it a lesser degree of First Amendment protection demonstrate that since 1976 all speech so considered has been inextricably intertwined with advertising."[48] The central reason given by the Court for granting limited protection to commercial speech is the supposed ease of verifying the informational content of advertising and the alleged hardiness of such speech. Investment advice, however, involves opinion, in the sense used by the Supreme Court, about important economic issues. The market letters at issue comment on general economic trends as well as individual securities. Market letters "do not differ in principle from well-known periodicals such as Barron's, Forbes, or Consumer Reports."[49]

Even if the speech is commercial speech, the dissent argued that the injunction violated the third and fourth prongs of the *Central Hudson* test.[50] One of Brieant's reasons for that conclusion was that it would be difficult to frame a workable injunction that barred comment on specific stocks, yet permitted virtually all other financial and economic commentary on events that impact on the market for stocks and securities in general. This difficulty amounts to "impermissible prior restraint on publications which have not yet been found to constitute 'investment advice.' "[51]

The Court granted certiorari to consider the question whether an injunction violated the First Amendment. As the Court put it, "petitioners contend that such an injunction strikes at the very foundation of the freedom of the press by subjecting it to license and censorship."[52] Petitioners agreed that "person to person communication in a commercial setting may be subjected to regulation that would be impermissible in a public forum."[53] Lowe, however, was disseminating "impersonal investment advice."[54]

As noted above, there is an exception in the statute for the "publisher of any bona fide newspaper, news magazine or business or financial publication of general and regular circulation." The Court held that the petitioner's market letters fell within that statutory exception.[55] Hence the Court, it felt, legitimately avoided the constitutional issue. As a result, the Court removed from the registration provisions of the Act every publicly disseminated stock advice and market letter.

Justice White wrote a concurring opinion in which then Chief Justice Burger and Justice Rehnquist joined. He concluded that the newsletters did not fall within the exemption. He emphasized that "[o]ne does not have to read the Court's opinion very closely to realize that its interpretation of the Act is based on a thinly disguised conviction that the Act is unconstitutional as applied to prohibit publication of newsletters by unregistered advisers."[56] Therefore, his concurring opinion addressed the First Amendment issue.

The justice, at the outset, recognized that at issue was the power of the government to regulate entry into professions or occupations. He argued that the power to regulate is not lost despite the presence of speech in the practice of the vocation. The justice quoted the Court in *Giboney v. Empire Storage & Ice Co.*: "it has never been deemed an abridgment of freedom of speech or press to make a course of conduct illegal merely because the conduct was in part initiated, evidenced, or carried out by means of language, either spoken, written, or printed."[57]

The power of government to license the vocations, however, "has never been extended to encompass the licensing of speech per se or of the press. ...At some point, a measure is no longer a regulation of a profession but a regulation of speech or the press; beyond that point, the statute must survive the level of scrutiny demanded by the First Amendment."[58]

Justice White drew the line between regulation of a profession and censorship of speech as follows:

One who takes the affairs of a client personally in hand and purports to exercise judgment on behalf of the client in the light of the client's individual needs and circumstances is properly viewed as engaging in the practice of a profession. ...Where the personal nexus between professional and client does not exist, and a speaker does not purport to be exercising judgment on behalf of any particular individual with whose circumstances he is directly acquainted, government regulation ceases to function as legitimate regulation of professional practice with only incidental impact on speech; it becomes regulation of speaking or publishing as such, subject to the First Amendment's command.[59]

Therefore, the attempted ban on impersonally distributed market letters constituted a "direct restraint on freedom of speech and of the press subject to the searching scrutiny called for by the First Amendment."[60]

The government contended that the speech in question was merely commercial speech. Petitioner asserted that the newsletters were "not commercial speech, as it does not propose a commercial transaction between the speaker and his audience."[61]

Justice White did not believe it necessary to decide whether the speech was fully protected or commercial speech.[62] The ban violated the First Amendment in either case. A flat prohibition on truthful speech is "presumptively invalid"[63] as applied to fully protected speech. Even if it were commercial speech, the ban falls because it is too far reaching. The government argued that since petitioner had engaged in prior misconduct, he might in the future publish misleading speech. The justice argued:

Our commercial speech cases have consistently rejected the proposition that such drastic prohibitions on speech may be justified by a mere possibility that the prohibited speech will be fraudulent. . . . It cannot be plausibly maintained that investment advice from a person whose background indicates that he is unreliable is *inherently* misleading or deceptive, nor am I convinced that less drastic remedies than outright suppression (for example, application of the Act's antifraud provisions) are not available to achieve the government's asserted purpose of protecting investors.[64]

The justice also pointed out that he would not foreclose in the future the use of the Act's reporting provisions to mass market letters.[65] In that manner he approved of the use of mandatory disclosure in regulating the truthfulness of financial advice.

Troubling questions are raised by this case. It is clear that the market letters do not comfortably fit the usual definition of commercial speech for the reasons already advanced. Hence even disclosure regulations well short of outright ban may face severe constitutional problems. If we endeavor to solve the definitional problem by expanding the definition of commercial speech to include the market letters because of their economic content, we create considerable perplexity. The Supreme Court, as noted in the previous chapter, has concluded that speech does not become commercial speech merely because of economic motivation or economic subject matter. The reason is fairly apparent. Much of fully protected speech is economic in motivation or content. A few days spent in reading the first page of the *New York Times* will confirm that obvious fact. Hence the district court, and the dissent in the Second Circuit, limited commercial speech to the advertisement of a specific product or service for business gain, or to speech that promoted a commercial transaction, such as an employment advertisement. Naturally there can be considerable room to reasonably disagree about the definition at the boundary, but the point is eminently reasonable. Too broad a definition threatens to reduce much of core political speech to commercial speech. Indeed, it was this concern (i.e., a fear that the definition might be broadened), that, in part, led Justice Rehnquist to his many dissents from commercial speech case holdings.

This case signals that much of SEC-regulated speech may not comfortably fit the rubric of commercial speech. Proxy speech is not an advertisement for product or services. The prospectus relating to the sale of securities is not a comfortable fit with an advertisement definition. Corporate speech about pending mergers is not an advertisement. The list can be expanded. This issue will be examined again below.

LONG ISLAND LIGHTING CO. v. BARBASH

Another case, *Long Island Lighting Co. v. Barbash* is extremely important in the SEC–First Amendment area.[66] The Long Island Lighting Company (LILCO), a state-regulated public utility, brought suit to enjoin alleged violations of section 14(a) and rules thereunder governing proxy solicitations. The trial court granted summary judgment dismissing the complaint.[67] The corporation's nuclear power plant was the subject of considerable controversy concerning safety. John W. Matthews, a political figure in Nassau County, demanded a special shareholders' meeting to affect company policy on this issue.[68] Another defendant in the case was a group called Citizens to Replace LILCO. On October 15 this group published a newspaper advertisement accusing the management of mismanagement, and of passing unnecessary costs of construction of the plant onto ratepayers.[69] The advertisement called for a public authority to take over LILCO as a producer of utility power.[70] Matthews had commenced a proxy contest designed to eject the incumbent board.

LILCO argued in court that defendants had "published a materially false and misleading advertisement in *Newsday*, a Long Island newspaper, and ran false and misleading radio advertisements throughout the New York area."[71] The complaint sought an injunction banning defendants' solicitation of proxies until appropriate proxy filings were made with the SEC and the misleading statements were corrected. LILCO contended that the newspaper advertisement was, in reality, a solicitation under the proxy rules, hence subject to proxy regulation.

The trial court had ordered a truncated discovery procedure for the LILCO attorneys. The appeals court held that LILCO was entitled to additional discovery "for the purpose of attempting to establish that the defendants' advertisement was, in the language of Rule 14a–1, 17 C.F.R. Sec.14a–1(f)(1)(iii), a 'communication to security holders under circumstances [reasonably] calculated to result in the procurement, withholding or revocation of a proxy.' "[72] The court held that the trial court erred in deciding that "the proxy rules cannot cover communications appearing in publications of general circulation and that are indirectly addressed to shareholders."[73]

The issue, the court asserted, is whether the communications in question are " 'reasonably calculated' to influence the shareholders' votes."[74] The court concluded that after reversal and remand to the trial court, and its determination of whether the advertisement constituted proxy solicitation, the court could consider the impact of the First Amendment.

Judge Winter dissented.[75] He argued that if the First Amendment protects the advertisements, further discovery would be prohibited. Judge Winter then determined that in his opinion, the newspaper advertisement was not proxy solicitation. Hence he would avoid the issue of the impact of the First Amendment on the proxy rules that would arise if the trial court on remand concluded that the ad was indeed proxy solicitation. Judge Winter argued that where advertisements criticize corporate behavior, are on their face directed to the public, do not mention the use of proxies, and debate issues of genuine public concern, they are not proxy solicitation.

The judge cited the Lowe case as an example of statutory construction that legitimately avoided a conflict between the First Amendment and SEC regulation. He pointed out that in the Lowe case, "the congressional purpose of protecting the public...was far more deeply implicated...than are the purposes of federal proxy regulation implicated by the advertisement at issue in the present case."[76]

This, I submit, is a significant case. It illustrates the free-speech dilemma created by proxy regulation, particularly where proxy contests are involved. The latter, of course, directly involve contests for corporate control that are analogous to campaign battles in the political arena. Material contained in newspaper advertisements about corporate policy not relating to shareholder meetings and proxies are concededly fully protected by the First Amendment. But the SEC would contend that materials on similar issues directed to shareholders and their meetings, at best, would receive commercial speech protection. The distinction is not entirely clear unless we can comfortably fit proxy speech within the rubric of commercial speech or a similar concept. Because proxy speech relates to the governance of the corporation, not the advertisement of a specific product or service, the fit with commercial speech is not an easy one.

The difficulty in distinguishing proxy speech from fully protected speech is compounded by the *First National Bank of Boston v. Bellotti case*.[77] In that litigation the Court held that corporate speech to the public, even about matters not necessarily directly affecting the business of the corporation, is fully protected by the First Amendment. The Court held that the protection is not lost because the speaker or writer is a business corporation. Because so-called external speech is fully protected, it appears somewhat problematical that internal corporate governance speech is not fully protected. The senior management usually determines the content of external speech, for example, the corporation's position about the institution of an income tax in a state where executives reside. Hence choice of which contesting team of management will prevail (a choice determined by a proxy contest) directly affects the ultimate external speech. Surely, then, logic should suggest that both modes of speech should be protected to the same degree.

WALL STREET PUBLISHING INSTITUTE CASE

If it is ultimately conceded that SEC-regulated speech does not fit the commercial speech definition, what flows from this? A recent case in the U.S. Court of Appeals, District of Columbia Circuit, has considered this very issue.[73] The SEC sought an injunction against the publisher of a market letter under the so-called antitouting section of the Securities Act of 1933. That section essentially forbids the newspaper discussion of a company security where the corporation has paid for the discussion, without full disclosure of the payment.[79] In the instant case the SEC alleged that the publisher received glowing articles on a company from the company itself, and published the pieces without change. The practice, described as "free text," constituted, according to the SEC, consideration described by the statute.[80] The commission sought an injunction requiring disclosure of the "free text" practice.

The commission characterized the articles as commercial speech. The publisher argued that the market letters were fully protected speech.

The court's analysis of this dispute is worthy of full quotation:

> The SEC's position is difficult to reconcile with the contours of the commercial speech doctrine as drawn in Supreme Court opinions. . . . Later, in *Bolger v. Youngs Drug Products Corp* . . . the Court reiterated the "speech which does no more than propose a commercial transaction" formulation and characterized this language as describing the "core" of commercial speech, thereby suggesting that commercial speech encompasses a somewhat broader area. Then the Court identified three characteristics of commercial speech, while being careful to note that none is necessary or sufficient for speech to be classified as commercial. According to the Court, speech that is *concededly* an advertisement, refers to a specific product, and is motivated by economic interest may properly be characterized as commercial speech. . . .
>
> Under the broader formulation of *Youngs Drug*, we are not convinced that the feature articles under consideration here are commercial speech. The articles are not "conceded" to be advertisements, and in fact, are not in advertisement format. Generally two or three pages long, they are indistinguishable from run-of-the-mill newspaper or magazine stories. Furthermore, while most of the articles specifically mention the company's stock along with its price history, not all do this, and in none is the reference to the company's stock particularly prominent. So, it would be difficult to draw a doctrinal line between these articles and any article that focuses on a particular company.[81]

The court concluded that there was not "a clear fit between the commercial speech doctrine and the publications that the SEC here seeks to regulate."[82] The court, however, announced a new doctrine: "We believe instead that the government may have the power to regulate *Stock Market Magazine*, not because the articles are 'commercial speech' but rather because of the federal government's broad powers to regulate the securities industry."[83] The Court, however, ruled that Section 17(b) couldn't support mandatory disclosure based on use of free text. (That would interfere with content.) But the injunction could require disclosure when consideration was paid in methods other than free text.

The court conceded that since the Supreme Court's opinion and decision in *Lowe*, there is some First Amendment protection in the securities field. The court asserted: "Speech relating to the purchase and sale of securities, in our view, forms a distinct category of communications in which the government's power to regulate is at least as broad as with respect to the general rubric of commercial speech."[84] The court then proceeded to reject the application of the second through the fourth prongs of the *Central Hudson* test: "In areas of extensive federal regulation-like securities dealing, we do not believe the Constitution requires the judiciary to weigh the relative merits of particular regulatory objectives that impinge upon communications occurring within the umbrella of an overall regulatory scheme."[85] Even if the court did balance the governmental interests, it would apply the liberal *Zauderer* test in areas of mandated disclosure, not the more rigorous *Central Hudson* test.[86] That test, as described in the preceding chapter, was more liberal because of the argument that the First Amendment "looks" more kindly on regulation that requires more disclosure than the subject might voluntarily provide.

There is support for this analysis in some dicta in Supreme Court cases on commercial speech. For example, in *Ohralik v. Ohio State Bar Association*, the Court said:

Moreover, "it has never been deemed an abridgment of freedom of speech or press to make a course of conduct illegal merely because the conduct was in part initiated, evidenced, or carried out by means of language, whether spoken, written, or printed." *Giboney v. Empire Storage & Ice Co.*, 336 U.S. 490, 502 (1949). Numerous examples could be cited of communications that are regulated without offending the First Amendment, such as the exchange of information about securities, *SEC v. Texas Gulf Sulphur Co.*, 401 F.2d 833 (CA2 1968), cert. denied, 394 U.S. 976 (1969), corporate proxy statements, *Mills v. Electric Auto-Lite Co.*, 396 U.S. 375 (1970), the exchange of price and production information among competitors, *American Column & Lumber Co.* v. *United States*, 257 U.S. 377 (1921), and employers' threats of retaliation for the labor activities of employees, *NLRB v. Gissel Packing Co.*, 395 U.S. 575, 618 (1969). See *Paris Adult Theatre I v. Slaton*, 413 U.S. 49, 61–62 (1973). Each of these examples illustrates that the State does not lose its power to regulate commercial activity deemed harmful to the public whenever speech is a component of that activity. Neither *Virginia Pharmacy* nor *Bates* purported to cast doubt on the permissibility of those kinds of commercial regulation.[87]

The difficulty with the SEC speech as a separate category is twofold.[88] First, in the realm of federal regulation, speech is not an incidental component of the economic activity that is presumably regulated. Indeed it is speech about securities transactions that is the core of federal securities governance. As the court itself recognizes, "requiring disclosure of a material fact in order to prevent investor misunderstanding is the very essence of federal securities regulation."[89]

Second, the approach is overly broad. Because the Congress regulates taxes, shipping, and numerous other economic areas, the court's theory would authorize curtailment of incredibly diverse realms of speech.

The court may have been hinting, however, at the theory advanced in the *Posadas* case.[90] There, Chief Justice Rehnquist authored an opinion that permitted a ban on casino advertising, since the government could have forbade the gambling. The speech restriction was, arguably, the lesser restriction. Therefore, because the Congress could ban trading in defined risky securities, or ban the corporate sale of securities in defined risky underwritings, perhaps the Congress can ban or regulate speech about the transactions, rather than ban the activity itself. Many state regulatory schemes, popularly called merit regulation, do indeed ban specified underwritings within their borders.

Justice Brennan's objections to this argument were described in the previous chapter. Further, this argument is also subject to an overreach objection. Because vast areas of economic activity can be banned, or severely regulated, the Rehnquist approach would validate a potentially enormous restraint of speech.

This chapter considered leading cases on the SEC and the First Amendment. The cases underscore the difficulty in fitting much SEC speech into the class of commercial speech. The cases also suggest creating a third category of speech, SEC speech, to supplement the categories of fully protected speech and commercial speech. We will have to examine modern legal scholarship on the purposes of the First Amendment to find the appropriate intellectual structure in which to place these attempts at definition. One theoretical approach is to use certain powerful economic models and arguments to correctly define the categories. These are considered in chapter 4. In chapter 3 other theoretical work, not necessarily based on economic approaches, that have addressed these issues is scrutinized. Finally, in chapter 5 some ideas that will help in considering these perplexing issues are suggested.

NOTES

1. *See* M. Budd and N. Wolfson, *Securities Regulation* 1–24 (1984).

2. *See* W. Painter, *Business Planning, Problems and Materials* 378–86 (2d ed. 1984).

3. *See, generally,* Schneider, Manko, and Kant, *Going Public: Practice, Procedure, and Consequences,* 27 Vill. L. Rev. 1 (1981).

4. *See* Budd and Wolfson, *Securities Regulation,* 453–62 (1984).

5. *See* Schneider and Shurgel, "Now That You Are Publicly Owned,... Business Lawyer 1631 (1981).

6. 17 C.F.R. Sec.204.10b–5 (1987).

7. 17 C.F.R. Sec.240.14a–9 (1987).

8. Section 15 (C) (4) of the Securities Exchange Act of 1934 permits the SEC to issue an order requiring a person who failed to comply with sections 12, 13, 14, or

15 (d) of the Securities Exchange Act of 1934 to comply with such provisions, on terms specified by the commission.

9. Judge Brieant, dissenting in the Court of Appeals of the Second Circuit opinion in *SEC v. Lowe*, stated it well:

Our attention is directed to the several recent articulations of what constitutes "commercial speech" which are said to establish that "commercial speech" is not confined to advertising, but extends to all "expression related solely to the economic interest of the speaker and its audience. "Central Hudson Gas and Elec. Corp. v. Public Service Comm., 447 U.S. 557,561.... Consideration of the Supreme Court's attempts at redefinition since Virginia Pharmacy Board v. Virginia Citizens Consumer Council, 425 U.S. 748 ... convices me that the concept of commercial speech has now been confined to naked advertising and closely related methods of commercial solicitation.... Each recent Supreme Court commercial speech case has arisen in the context of service or product *advertising*.... That each of the cases in which the court has sought to clarify the "commercial speech" doctrine has arisen in the context of attempts to regulate or prohibit advertising, while significant, does not, standing alone, demonstrate conclusively that commercial speech is restricted to advertising and equivalent economic promotional activities. However, examination of the characteristics of commercial speech which have caused the Surpreme Court to accord to it a lesser degree of First Amendment protection demonstrate that since 1976 all speech so considered has been inextricably intertwined with advertising. SEC v. Lowe, 725 F.2d 892, 904–5 (1984) (Brieant, J., dissenting), rev'd, 105 S. Ct. 2557 (1985).

10. *Lowe v. SEC*, 472 U.S. 181, 183 (1985).

11. *Id.*

12. *Id.*

13. *Id.*

14. *Id.* The district court denied the SEC argument that the publications were fraudulent because of failure to disclose Lowe's criminal record or the revocation of the investment registration. The court argued that SEC had failed to pass any rules demanding such disclosure. *SEC v. Lowe*, 556 F.Supp. 1359, 1370 (E.D.N.Y. 1983).

15. *SEC v. Lowe*, 556 F.Supp. 1359 (E.D.N.Y. 1983), *rev'd*, 725 F.2d 892 (1984), *rev'd*, 472 U.S. 181 (1985).

16. *Id.* at 1365.

17. *Id.* at 1366.

18. *Id.*

19. *Id.* at 1366–67.

20. *Id.* at 1367.

21. *Id.* at 1369.

22. *Id.* at 1365 and 1371.

23. *SEC v. Lowe*, 725 F2d 892 (2d Cir. 1984), *rev'g* 556 F.Supp 1359 (1983), *rev'd*, 472 U.S. 181 (1985).

24. *Id.* at 896.

25. *Id.* at 898.

26. 422 F2d 1371 (2d Cir.), *cert. denied*, 398 U.S. (1970).

27. *Id.* at 1377.

28. *Id.* at 1378.

29. *Id.*

30. 725 F2d at 898.

31. *Id.* The court was quoting from 15 U.S.C. Sec.80b–2 (11).

32. *Id.* at 899.

33. *Id.*
34. *Curtis Publishing Co. v. Butts*, 388 U.S. 130 (1967) (citations and footnotes omitted). The court of appeals quoted the *Curtis* remarks. 725 F2d at 899.
35 725 F2d at 899.
36. *Id.*
37. 548 F2d 192 (7th Cir. 1977).
38. 725 F2d at 900.
39. *Id.*
40. *Id.* at 900–901.
41. *Central Hudson Gas & Electric Corp. v. Public Service Commission*, 447 U.S. 557, 561 (1980).
42. *Friedman v. Rogers*, 440 U.S. 1, 10, n.9 (1979).
43. 725 F2d at 901.
44. *Id.*
45. *Id.*
46. *Id.* at 902.
47. *Id.* at 903 (Brieant, J., dissenting).
48. *Id.* at 905.
49. *Id.* at 906.
50. *Id.* at 907.
51. *Id.* at 910.
52. *Lowe v. SEC*, 472 U.S. 181, 189 (1985).
53. *Id.*
54. *Id.*
55. *Id.* at 204.
56. *Id.* at 226 (White J., concurring).
57. *Id.* 228 (quoting Giboney, 336 U.S. at 502, 1949).
58. *Id.* at 229–30.
59. *Id.* at 232.
60. *Id.* at 233.
61. *Id.* at 234.
62. *Id.*
63. *Id.* at 235.
64. *Id.* (Footnote omitted.)
65. *Id.* at 236.
66. 779 F2d 793 (2nd Cir. 1985), *rev'g* 625 F.Supp. 221 (1985). Chief Judge Weinstein, for the district court, held that the advertisement, critical of the utilities record and advocating public ownership, was not a "proxy solicitation" within the meaning of the SEC regulations. *Long Island Lighting Company v. Barbash*, 625 F.Supp. 221, 224 (E.D.N.Y. 1985). He argued that a communication must be aimed directly at shareholders by "parties intimately involved in the proxy fight" to constitute proxy material subject to SEC regulation. *Id.* He granted a summary judgment dismissing the complaint.

At the same time as the ad was published, certain parties were in the process of conducting a proxy fight to change the utilities board so as to get a majority in favor of public ownership. The judge did not find a close enough connection between the sponsors of the newspaper ad, and their purposes and tactics, and the proxy group to hold the ad a proxy statement.

Because he found the ad outside the SEC proxy rules, he was free to apply the First Amendment without fear of chilling SEC regulation. He found the ad fully protected by the First Amendment. *Id.* at 225.

He did assert that even if the sponsors of the ad did conspire to use the ad to influence the proxy fight, an assumption of fact he asserted had no basis in the record, that fact would be irrelevant, and the First Amendment would fully protect the ad. *Id.* at 226. He distinguished messages aimed at shareholders from messages aimed at the "general public." *Id.* The former he thought were subject to SEC regulation without as much concern with the First Amendment. *Id.*

The obvious conundrum is that shareholder issues are often public issues. The relation is based on the frequent impact of corporate action on the public, whether in the local community or the larger society. Line drawing here is fundamentally suspect. Where shareholders debate matters of corporate policy that are of public interest, the First Amendment should apply to its fullest extent. Otherwise, we arbitrarily make shareholders a second-class group.

67. *Id.* at 795.

68. *Id.* at 797 (Winter, J., dissenting).

69. *Id.*

70. *Id.*

71. *Id.* at 794.

72. *Id.* at 795.

73. *Id.*

74. *Id.* at 796. The court was quoting from Rule 14a–1, 17 C.F.R. Sec. 240. 14a–1 (f) (1) (iii).

75. *Id.* at 797–99 (Winter, J., dissenting).

76. *Id.* at 799.

77. 435 U.S. 765 (1978). See, however, the later *Austin* discussed in Chapter 5.

78. *SEC v. Wall Street Pub. Institute., Inc.* 851 F.2d 365 (D.C. Cir. 1988), *cert. denied*, 398 U.S. 958 (1989).

79. Sec. 17(b), Securities Act of 1933, 15 U.S.C. Sec 77q(b).

80. 851 F.2d 365, 367 (D.C. 1988).

81. *Id.* at 372.

82. *Id.*

83. *Id.*

84. *Id.*

85. *Id.*

86. *Id.*

87. 436 U.S. 447, 456 (1978). In 1988 the Court in *Riley v. National Federation of the Blind*, as discussed in the previous chapter, in dicta called securities disclosure the domain of commercial speech. Slip opinion, 13 n. 9 (1988).

88. There was a somewhat related thought expressed in court of appeals opinion in *SEC v. Lowe. SEC v. Lowe*, 725 F.2d 892 (1984), *rev'd*, 105 S. Ct. 2557 (1985). The court cited the previous quoted passage in *Ohralik*. The court then stated "[W]e believe that the provisions of the Investment Advisers Act at issue here are precisely the kind of regulation of commercial activity permissible under the First Amendment." *Id.* at 900.

In any event, the court argued that the Supreme Court commercial speech cases did not limit "commercial speech solely to product or service advertising." *Id.*

The court relied on the *Wall Street Transcript* case, which held that the Advisers
Act, when construed not to exempt market letters as bona fide newspapers, does not
violate the First Amendment. *SEC v. Wall Street Transcript Corp.*, 422 F.2d 1371 (2d
Cir. 1970), *cert. denied*, 398 U.S. 958 (1970). *Id.* at 898.

Judge Brieant, dissenting, called that case "as dead as Marley" because it predated
Virginia State Board of Pharmacy v. Virginia Citizens Consumer Council, 425 U.S.
748 (1976), and the subsequent line of Court commercial speech cases. *Id.* at 904
(Brieant, J., dissenting).

   89. 851 F.2d 365, 374, n. 9.

   90. *Posadas de Puerto Rico Association v. Tourism Co.* 478 U.S. 328 (1986).

3

Scholarly Evaluation of the Commercial Speech Doctrine

INTRODUCTION

In this chapter we begin the discussion of some of the more influential modern scholarly commentators on the Court's commercial speech doctrine. Although categories can be misleading, it is fair to say that the commentators may be divided between exponents of modern economic analysis and thinkers who work in more traditional modes of legal discourse. In chapter 4 the former are discussed.

In this discussion it is impossible to proceed in depth without analyzing the principal reasons usually given for the First Amendment principle as it applies to political, artistic, or otherwise fully protected speech.[1] These principles usually are presented as (1) the market for truth (i.e., discussion as a process for achieving truth) (2) the necessary relation between free speech and democracy, and (3) speech as essential for self expression, human dignity, or autonomy. Thomas Emerson has added a fourth, free speech as a vehicle for mediating peaceful change.[2] The latter is closely related to number two above.

An initial question is our ability to distinguish the merits of protecting speech from government regulation, as contrasted to protecting conduct. If we cannot accomplish that philosophical goal, First Amendment theories based on the preeminent position of speech are in grave difficulty. Proof of the similarity of conduct and speech, however, does not necessarily mean that we protect speech less than currently protected. If the reasons for protecting certain kinds of conduct *and* speech are powerful, we can continue to justify full protection of speech, as a correct philosophical measure.

John Milton argued for the truth-making value of the market for ideas in the seventeenth century: "Let [truth] and falsehood grapple; who ever knew Truth put to the worse in a free and open encounter."[3] We are no longer so certain about that assumption in the twentieth century. Our belief in the inevitability of truth emerging from calm rational discourse has faltered. Slavery prevailed in the United States until the 1860s, and was put down by force, not discussion. Thereafter, racism prevailed until recent years, and many believe today as well. Anti-Semitism perseveres despite rational debate to the contrary. There is psychological evidence in less transcendental areas contrary to Milton's simple naivete. For example, "there is substantial evidence in the psychology literature that individuals tend to overweigh recent data in making forecasts and judgments."[4] Without even getting into the subtleties of defining the nature of truth, and distinguishing opinion from fact, it is apparent that few today would share Milton's naive optimism.

There are additional, more persuasive arguments for the market in truth theory. Perhaps the most powerful point is the danger of entrusting government bureaucrats with a monopoly over defining the truth. Government agents have biases, personal limitations, and self-interest, and will distort the truth to accomplish their own, often sinister ends. Hence this popular argument maintains that we must protect speech from government interference. Moreover, given the complexity of the issues, the government is prone to error, even if well motivated.[5]

The point I want to emphasize here, one made eloquently by Messrs. Coase and Director (see chapter 4), is that the same arguments can be made (and often have been made) for a free market for goods and services. As Coase put it, "in all markets, producers have some reasons for being honest and some for being dishonest; consumers have some information but are not fully informed."[6] The Adam Smithian, invisible hand hypothesis, to put it crudely, assumes that a free market in goods and services will result in satisfied consumers and, ultimately, honest and efficient producers. This is identical to the argument for truth in ideas resulting from the free competition of the spoken and the written word.

When the public and the politicians find "market failure" in the market for goods and services, they regulate in the hope that regulators will more often than not make the correct decisions about the products and services regulated. (I ignore here the more cynical assumptions of the public choice literature on the motives for regulation.) The argument advanced is that the costs of regulation are less than the benefits derived therefrom. Thus, where the safety of goods is at issue, the argument is that the consumer cannot distinguish the safe from the harmful, but government-appointed experts can do so without fear of industry influence. The identical approach conceptually applies to the market for ideas. Where there are market failures, perhaps government regulation is a better method than free competition. A market-failure argument might involve the argument that in area X (e.g., evolution versus creationism), the complexity of the dispute cannot be mastered by the consumer of ideas, hence government experts (e.g., school officials) should be appointed to distinguish the true from the false. The difference between the principle of protecting speech from regulation, as contrasted with conduct, is not at all clear in the context of the market- for-truth argument.

The second principle is the close association of free discussion with the democratic polity. People must be free to speak in order to partake in the democratic process, and people must be free to listen in order to be informed members of the electorate. If, however, the majority by vote, limit the right to speak, by what independent principle do we forbid the restriction? Democracy? That is a principle of majority rule. Human dignity? That is a separate principle we shall soon consider. Truth-seeking? We have already considered the strengths and weaknesses of that principle.

On the subject of conduct versus speech, the primacy of speech as a vehicle for democratic process is less than conclusive. Commonsense perception of the daily political influence game reveals that U.S. polity is not run by rational voting based on the weighing of intellectual discussion points. Economic influence, threat by interest groups, occupational self-interest, economic greed, occupation of buildings by student groups, and hunger strikes by committed individuals and groups are greater influences than academic, reasoned, political free speech debate. If we make a normative statement and assert that a democracy should be run by calm, rational, intellectual debate, we are appealing to a principle independent of democracy. We appear to be appealing to the Miltonic truth principle, discussed above, or to a desire to rid democracy of individual and group power and economic self-interest.

A third principle is the self-expression argument. Here the conflation of conduct and speech is apparent. Self-expression includes the right to choose my occupation, food, home, clothing, number of children, and spouse or companion. Government interference with these modes of conduct is as serious an infringement of autonomy as interference with my right to free speech. There does not appear to be any independent principle to justify greater protection of one or the other unless we rather arbitrarily assert that intellectual discourse is the highest end of man or woman.

Perhaps we can find so-called market failure in one or the other markets for goods, services, or speech that justifies regulation. To distinguish speech from conduct, we must be able to make the case that the government has a lesser ability to regulate speech than conduct. Perhaps, in this regard, we can demonstrate that government commits less error in regulating toothpaste consumption, or job entry in the professions, than in regulating certain speech. (As we shall see in chapter 4 Judge Richard Posner makes such an argument in constructing an economic rationale for regulating commercial speech.) But the nature of this demonstration will be similar to all of the disputes over the advisability of economic regulation of conduct versus a free-market approach. The question always is, does the cost of regulating drugs, securities transactions, and licenses for medical practice outweigh the net benefits, if there are any, of less or no regulation?

With this as an introduction, I propose to consider some of the more modern influential scholarly analyses of the commercial speech doctrine. It is impossible to consider all of the almost countless articles on this topic, but I have selected a group of some of the more influential and representative modes of analysis.

SELF-REALIZATION

In an often cited article Martin H. Redish, in 1971, long before the development of the Court commercial speech doctrine, argued for full First Amendment protection of commercial speech.[7]

He began by asserting that commercial advertising performs a serious service in assisting the consumer. He quotes the famous British economist Pigou to the effect that advertising informs "people of the existence of articles adapted to their tastes."[8] He quotes the economist Stigler that it is "an immensely powerful instrument for the elimination of ignorance—comparable in force to the use of the book instead of oral discourse to communicate knowledge."[9] Advertising does more, however, than provide information about new products or services. It also can further the buyer with intelligent bases for selecting among competing goods.[10]

Redish concedes that advertising does not always coolly and rationally inform. Perhaps more often than not it attempts to persuade through use of techniques of entertainment. Again he quotes Stigler: "The use of entertainment to attract buyers to information is a comprehensible phenomenon. The assimilation of information is not an easy task for most people."[11] Redish might have added that much that passes for political information is presented currently in the form of entertainment. Consider the political advertisements of the 1988 presidential campaign.

Next he turns to the philosophy of Alexander Meiklejohn.[12] He uses him as a vehicle for comparing what he believes is an overly narrow Meiklejohn definition of First Amendment expression with the expansive value of "individual self-realization."[13] The latter concept includes development of individual happiness, as well as the individual's control over his or her destiny. The construct is not derived from nonexistent intent of the founders. It is a "logical one," derived from axioms and assumptions about the proper goals and processes of democracy.[14] Properly interpreted, Redish argues, the notion of self-realization includes commercial speech.

Meiklejohn based the free-speech doctrine on the goals of democratic self-government. As Redish accurately puts Meiklejohn's basic point: "The continued functioning of our system of self-government rests upon the right of the electorate to be informed about matters which might in some way aid them in the voting booth. The First Amendment right, then, is located with the listener, rather than the speaker."[15]

Meiklejohn would give political speech absolute protection. He would deny First Amendment protection to "private" speech.[16] Private speech, which certainly includes, in his opinion, commercial speech, would not be protected by the First Amendment because it has no direct relation to the political process. Without doubt, as he defines the political process, he would be right. He defines it as a sort of small New England town meeting in which voters speak and other voters have the right to listen to such speech under the protection of the First Amendment.[17]

He defined free speech, also, as political speech not motivated by profit. Therefore, he believed that radio should not be protected because "[i]t is not engaged in the task of enlarging and enriching communications. It is engaged in making money."[18]

His theory would probably exclude literature, the arts, and academic study, except where it directly involved the political process as he defines it. Redish points out that ultimately he agreed that literary works, education, philosophy, and the sciences should be included as protected speech.[19] However, because much of these areas frequently do not involve election campaigns and campaign issues, the Meiklejohn inclusion does not rest easy with the Meiklejohn theory of protected free speech as political speech.

Redish will not buy into the Meiklejohn definition of the acceptable justification for protected speech. He argues that another, or perhaps "better," purpose of free-speech protection is the development and satisfaction of the personal capacities of the individual. This is facilitated, to be sure, by participation in the political arena. But Redish argues that such development also can be fostered by private decision making. Frequently there is a close relation between the two. As he puts it: "Sharp distinctions in the application of the first amendment between the political and private sectors take on an air of irrationality with the recognition that much political activity is directed to the betterment of the individual's material welfare."[20]

Redish emphasized the self-realization value, particularly of the listener, inherent in commercial speech. He argued that commercial speech aids the consumer in his or her selection of goods and services, all of which make for the good life.[21]

In a later work Redish defined his self-realization value as including both "the development of the individual's powers and abilities" and the "individual's control of his or her own destiny through making life affecting decisions."[22] He further argued that both prongs of his definition included actions in the private personal arena as well as the public governmental arena.[23] As he put it, "free speech aids all life-affecting decisionmaking, no matter how personally limited."[24]

Redish argues that the "intrinsic" purpose of the democratic process is to achieve individual "control of their own destinies" in the private and the public domain.[25] The "instrumental" value of the democratic system is "development of the individual's human faculties" in both the public and the private domain.[26] He argues that free speech fosters both such values. Hence the free-speech principle applies in the world of commercial speech as well as in the arena of campaign speech. It applies in the former, since untrammeled commercial speech facilitates the self-realization, as defined, of the listener or consumer of commercial speech.

Redish points out that Meiklejohn would concede that in a society where all personal decisions, such as use of a shampoo, were subject to the political process, the Meiklejohn principle would apply full First Amendment protection to individuals' speech about shampoo and so on. Yet in a society that, because of "moral concern about individual autonomy" or whatever the reason, cedes political power over private decisions, Meiklejohn would remove First Amendment protection from such private speech.[27] This is an untenable position, Redish argues, since individuals have less right to information when they have direct control over decisions than when they have indirect control in a society where all private decisions are politicized.[28]

Redish has made some good points. But I don't think he is successful in claiming that he has identified a unitary and unifying principle of free speech. For example, the value of achieving or maximizing my individual dominion over the political or commercial process is not necessarily the same as individual self-satisfaction or self-development. It is plausible to assert that many a man or woman prefers less, rather than more, intellectual discourse, political involvement, power, and the responsibility of power and dominion. Those same individuals may prefer more, rather than less, soccer, food, housing, sex, and congenial pubs. Free speech may maximize some or all of those values, but the values are different. Further, he concedes that "no value . . . is fostered exclusively by speech, rather than conduct."[29] Hence free markets in goods and services may foster those same values. (Even intellectual discourse is facilitated by private ownership of publishing houses.) Indeed, as Aaron Director and Ronald Coase suggested in earlier works (see chapter 4), perhaps most men and women are far more concerned with the non-speech values, such as the freedom to work, bear children, and choose their food than with political debate or academic discourse.

The 1971 Redish article gave greater constitutional value to informational advertising than to emotional or entertainment modes of advertising. In his later work Redish rejected that distinction. He argued that his principle of self-fulfillment required freedom to receive, consider, accept, or reject both kinds of input.[30] This appears a reasonable point, if we accept the analogy to political debate. The First Amendment certainly protects the appeal in political campaigns to emotion rather than to information or reason.

In his 1984 book on freedom of expression he critiques the first Supreme Court decision that directly adopted First Amendment protection for commercial speech.[31] That opinion noted the economic benefits to the poor and the sick of advertising prescription drug prices. On a more fundamental level it approved of the ability of advertising to help rationally allocate resources in a capitalist society. Redish objects that such economic goals bring the Court "closer to the logic of the economic due process cases than it does to traditional first amendment doctrine."[32]

This objection is a bit surprising in light of Redish's enumeration of the economic values of advertising. Those economic values, carefully recited by him as the policy premise for his commercial speech article, are identical to the allocation of resources argument of the Court.

If the Court is correct in its analysis of the value of advertising, then Redish's goal of individual fulfillment as well as his argument that "sharp distinction ... between the political and private sectors take on an air of irrationality" are both met.

That is, the individual consumer, aided by advertising, rationally fulfills himself or herself (the Redish private sector fulfillment) and at the same time assists in the rational allocation of resources. The latter is a political (i.e., public) as well as economic goal, presumably sought after by citizens in a free-enterprise economy.

Redish consistently maintains that protection of commercial and political speech protects the same fundamental value, individual development. Hence they should receive the same level of constitutional protection. The Court in *Virginia Pharmacy*, however, argued that the truth of commercial speech is more readily verifiable by its disseminator than is political commentary. Further, advertising is arguably more resistant to regulation than is political speech. He concedes that if the Court is correct in its assertions, it may indeed give less protection to commercial speech.[33]

He disputes the premise that commercial speech usually is more easily verifiable than political commentary. He gives no citation, however, as a basis for his skepticism.[34] Next he points out that magazines and newspapers (presumably political expression) are robust (i.e., resistant to regulation), since they are published for profit. Further, he argues that although the robust commercial disseminator may continue to publish, it will alter the message to comply with the government censor.[35]

In the end he appears to blink. He concedes that there is justification for government review of possibly false commercial speech, but not review of political speech. The reason is that those in power would use the censor power to defeat the political opposition. He believes that such sinister motive is not present with respect to the regulation of commercial speech. Thus, in the end, he adopts the premise that political speech involves values far more important to society and the individual than those of commercial speech.[36]

Redish, in his book *Freedom of Expression*, emphasizes that his argument is formal or logical, not historical. His justification is that few scholars rely on the intent of the founding fathers. This is because, "as Judge Bork states,'[t]he framers seem to have had no coherent theory of free speech.' "[37] Indeed, to the extent a historical consensus existed, Redish correctly points out that it was an extremely restricted view.

COERCIVE REGIME OF CORPORATE PROFIT-SEEKING

Another "logical" argument that is frequently cited in the literature is the analysis of C. Edwin Baker.[38] Baker's First Amendment theory begins with the following proposition: "As long as speech represents the freely-chosen expression of the speaker while depending for its power on the free acceptance of the listener, freedom of speech represents a charter of liberty for noncoercive action."[39]

The next step is the crucial one. Baker assumes that the speech of commercial corporations is coercive. He offers no proof except for anecdotal observations about the impersonal nature of the corporation, the separation of individual work from the home (the good old feudal times) and its removal to the workplace of today (i.e., the corporate office), and the observation that the profit motive results in useless production of wants.[40] Obviously he doesn't think much of capitalism. Thus he concludes, or rather assumes, that the profit motive, combined with the modern corporation, produces speech that is driven by the coercive exigencies of Adam Smithian greed.

Hence not merely corporate advertisements for products or service are not protected by the First Amendment. All corporate speech about political issues that impact directly or indirectly on the corporation also are not protected by the First Amendment.[41]

No other drive has this coercive impact. The drives of domination, envy, sex, fear, sexism, hubris, racism, and religious zealotry do not carry with them the coercive taint that inherently resides in corporate lust for the bottom line.

Corporate lust for profit is coercive because it is divorced from the self-expression of the speaker. Sometimes this is due to the fact that corporations systematically take positions divorced from the desires of all corporate employees and shareholders. This is an empirically dubious proposition, but Baker takes it as a given. Even if this divorce is lacking, there is something inherently suspect in the corporate profit motive.

These assumptions create some apparent difficulties that must be surmounted. His position threatens to delegitimate the modern corporate-owned newspaper, such as the *New York Times*, the television news, the cinema industry, and the magazine world. Baker's response is to assume, not demonstrate, that corporate word and image producers are a breed apart from all other corporations.[42] They somehow can surmount the profit motive so as to provide the absolutely essential societal need to check the excesses of government, something demanded by the free-press clause of the First Amendment.

All other non-profit organizational interests can organize and speak freely. He includes labor unions as part of the protected group of organizations. Their drive for wage maximization is assumed to be self-expressive and voluntary, as distinguished from corporate self-interest. He also includes books written for profit, and most organizations not run for a profit, nontraditional communes, and political groupings. I assume he also excludes from the evil of coercive self-interest the law professor who writes a tenure piece to obtain a permanent job contract with a university.

He also would protect the speech of individual or small-business proprietors. Their self-interest in a profit is not sufficiently divorced from their internal self-expression so as to remove their speech from the full protection of the First Amendment.

This is a form of analysis that may not hold up even if we grant the assumptions of the author about corporate greed. To begin with, we have to assume that the modern corporation creates a coercive structure different from all other groups in society. We also have to assume that the drive for profit is inherently coercive only in the form of modern corporate structure. Individual, union, and commune self-interest are, on the other hand, valid forms of self-expression.

This is basically incoherent, unless we simply take as a given that corporate structure and its speech are inherently evil.

There are other bodies of analysis that make claims about economic power and free speech. For example, the theory of public choice (see discussion of Fred McChesney in chapter 4) views virtually all of American society as driven by economic self interest. Hence Fred McChesney analyzes First Amendment doctrine as simply the product of successful economic pressure group lobbying and judicial manipulation. Public choice theory uses economic analysis to formalize and make rigorous the foregoing insight.

Marxist analysis, and its progeny, views American capitalist society as the product and playground of economic elitist interest groups. Critical legal studies view law as, in large measure, the product of such powerful elitist hierarchical groups.

The Marxist and the public choice theorists would view virtually all of American society as controlled by coercive capitalist forces. Baker, however, must draw a sharp line between the publicly held shareholder corporation, and other large business forms, and the "good guys" in capitalist society. He believes that it is necessary, for example, to exempt out from his analysis the giants of the communications industries. These corporate giants are assumed to be free of the evils of coercive, as distinguished from noncoercive, greed. If not, then because of the pervasive presence of publishing and cinema corporate megagiants, First Amendment protection would be stripped from virtually all that passes as artistic or political speech in America.

He writes: "Market necessity and the actual business of the speaker determine the specific attitudes or desires which the advertiser must attempt to stimulate, reinforce, or focus upon."[43] This is code for the conclusion that corporate capitalist drives (as distinguished from other motives or interests) are beyond the redemption of free choice. Next he writes: "The communications industry needs only to stimulate a desire for communicated expression—a desire of constitutional status."[44] This is code for the conclusion that corporate communication business greed is protected.

He further writes: "Except for the stimulation of a desire for expression, the market structure does not require that the press be concerned with promoting any specific attitudes or values."[45] Note that here he seems to postulate a free-floating freedom of expression that is assumed to be divorced from market pressure, economic self-interest, competition, or all of the other indicia of a free-market economy. He thus makes the entreme statement that market forces and profit drives do not influence the production or presentation of news, movies, and art.[46]

Although he frequently protests that he is not making content-driven discrimination when he distinguishes market forces from other drives, it is clear that indeed he is making such discriminations. In essence, he believes that corporate speech creates cheap wants and desires that diminish the true self. This is a metaphysical given for him, such as for others the axiom that Jews are evil and therefore their speech will destroy a good Aryan or Christian or Islamic society; atheists are evil, and therefore their speech will create a false, godless society; gays are evil, and therefore their speech will inevitably corrupt the listener. Hence he would remove First Amendment protection from commercial speech.

Virtually all opinions on the evils of corporate America would receive First Amendment protection. All interest groups (i.e., groups with direct or indirect economic interest in a free enterprise economy) that disagree with him would be banned from the marketplace of ideas. It is a transparent effort to tilt the marketplace of ideas against modern free enterprise and to introduce a form of censorship that will ultimately result in the victory of a noncapitalist society.

Next he falls back on a questionable version of original intent, and argues that the First Amendment was designed to give special protection to the press.[47] But Baker recognizes that unless he can demonstrate that media giant corporations are free of the coercive impact of greed, he is, in effect, adopting an original intent theory that legitimates unacceptable domination, in his terms and in his universe, of pervasive coercion. Hence he assumes that corporate media giants are freely self-expressive speakers, unlike all other giant corporations. I say assumes because nowhere does he develop data or theory (as distinguished from axiomatic assumptions) to account for the supposed difference. It is here that he perfectly fits the Coase argument (see discussion of R. H. Coase in chapter 4) that intellectuals have an obvious self-interest in protecting their business, that is, production of speech (books, movies, newspapers), as well as an interest in removing, or at best a lack of interest in protecting, First Amendment coverage of the commercial speech

of their rivals for power and influence in society, business people who produce non-speech products and services.

COMMERCIAL SPEECH AND ECONOMIC DUE PROCESS

Another influential analysis of the commercial speech doctrine appears in
an often-cited piece by Thomas Jackson and John Jeffries.[48] These authors
accept two principles as dominating judicial construction of the First Amendment. "The first sees the freedom of speech as an essential corollary of
representative democracy as established by the Constitution."[49] As they put
it, the battle among theorists is with respect to the scope of the definition of
political speech and "its exclusivity"[50] as a governing principle. The second
ordering principle most commonly advanced is "the idea of individual self-
fulfillment through free expression, a view most notably expounded by Professor Emerson."[51]

Emerson starts with the premise that "the proper end of man is the real-
ization of his character and potentialities as a human being."[52] Emerson
asserted that "every man—in the development of his own personality—has
the right to form his own beliefs and opinions."[53] This is crucial because
"expression is an integral part of the development of ideas, of mental explo-
ration and of the affirmation of self."[54] "Hence, suppression of belief, opinion
and expression is an affront to the dignity of man, a negation of man's essential
nature."[55] Emerson enumerates four "values" that freedom of expression
maintains: Maintenance of a system of free expression is necessary (1) as
securing self-development,[56] (2) developing information and truth,[57] (3) facilitating democratic decisionmaking,[58] and (4) creating a peaceable community, while permitting disagreement.[59] Emerson argues that each is
essential; however, each is not alone sufficient.[60] Jackson and Jeffries assert
that the first value is the one associated most frequently with Emerson.[61]

A frequent objection to the Emerson thesis is the lack of an acceptable
distinction between speech and action.[62] The human personality can express
itself through action as well as speech. Sexual behavior, choice of clothing,
and life-style are areas that are equally as important in human self-expression
as the freedom to speak. Indeed, it is for this reason, as we shall see in the
next chapter, that the distinguished law and economics scholar Richard Posner
rejects free expression of the self as a component in his economic formula
for the scope of the free speech principle.

Jackson and Jeffries accept both the political speech and the individual self-
fulfillment principles as sound bases for the First Amendment doctrine. They
then dismiss the suggestion that commercial speech could have any connection with the idea of individual self-fulfillment. The only arguments they make
are (1) the bare assertion that "the concept of a first amendment right of
personal autonomy . . . stops short of a seller hawking his wares"[63]; (2) the
statement that "Professor Emerson himself"[64] rejects the notion that com-

mercial speech falls within the protection of the First Amendment; and (3) that the *Virginia Pharmacy* opinion did not rely on the pharmacists' self-expression.[65]

The first "argument" is obviously merely a kind of groan or grunt. Consumers of commercial speech benefit by the receipt of information. The economic advantages of advertising, referred to above by Redish (i.e., dissemination of economic information) are accepted by many reputable economists. Hence consumers of commercial speech enjoy personal fulfillment, unless we arbitrarily exclude consumption of economic speech from the pantheon of individual fulfillment.

The reference to Emerson is hardly conclusive. He was an eminent thinker, but we cannot reason simply by citation of his viewpoint. The mention of the *Virginia Pharmacy* case ignores the argument in the opinion that advertising promotes the spread of economic information, educates the consumer (hence maximizing self-fulfillment), and, therefore, facilitates the rational allocation of resources. Later Jackson and Jeffries address this argument, but in the context of equating protection of commercial speech with the obsolete legal doctrine of economic substantive due process. We will consider that argument in due course.

Jackson and Jeffries also reject the argument that commercial speech falls within the protection of political speech. They accomplish this by erecting an artificial distinction between economic issues and so-called political issues.[66] This can be done only by a kind of Meiklejohn limitation of political to the speech directly concerning political campaigns. Because so much of political debate is directly concerned with the economic interest of various economic pressure groups, the Meiklejohn kind of distinction is unsatisfactory. This analysis also ignores the vast Marxist literature on the left and public choice theory on the right that closely bind the political realm to the economic.

Jackson and Jeffries also refer to the *Virginia Pharmacy* argument that economic speech, commercial advertising, and the like are helpful in facilitating the free flow of economic information, hence educating consumers and facilitating the allocation of resources in a free-market economy.[67] In rebuttal they make the unsupported assertion that "neither commercial advertising nor a free market economy is essential to informed political decisionmaking."[68]

It is apparent that Jackson and Jeffries have failed to adequately address the arguments of the *Virginia Pharmacy* case. The Court was making the fundamental argument that a free-market economy is essential to the existence of a viable free political economy. It is not sufficient, but it is essential. The Court also maintained that First Amendment protection of economic speech makes possible the existence of a free economy and facilitates the performance of that free-market economy. This is an entirely respectable and fundamental mainstream argument in political science. It is based on the commonsense notion that a state-owned and -directed economy is incompatible with political freedom. If the state owns most businesses, including the press, publishing, printing, and television, no one is free to counter the state with speech or book or television effectively. If the state owns or controls most businesses and most of the sources of economic speech about products and services, every aspect of personal and public life is at the mercy of the state. Further, if commercial speech is completely at the mercy of the state, the public will be limited in its understanding and knowledge of the facts and arguments necessary to make the free economic choices necessary in a free economy. We have only to witness the remarkable efforts of people in China and the Soviet Union to recognize this elemental principle, and to free up their societies by limiting the economic power of the state and freeing up speech about the state economy to appreciate its force.

In a concluding section of their article Jackson and Jeffries argue that the protection of commercial speech is merely a disguised reconstruction of the Lochner doctrine of economic due process.[69] That obsolete doctrine used the due process clause to limit the power of the state to regulate economic transactions on grounds of freedom of contract.

The Jackson and Jeffries argument is essentially that the "greater power normally includes the lesser."[70] The state, since the demise of the Lochner doctrine, can regulate economic transactions limited only by the relatively permissive restraints of modern due process doctrine. Hence the state should be able to exercise the lesser power of restricting commercial speech about such transactions.[71]

The Jackson and Jeffries argument asserts that the modern state under post-Lochner doctrine is free to regulate virtually all economic conduct. Because most "political" speech is about economic issues, the Jackson and Jeffries doctrine would justify virtually unlimited regulation of most of what passes for political speech today. They would take the Coasian argument about the equivalence of markets for goods and speech and use it, not like Coase to counsel caution on regulation, but to justify regulation of vast areas of speech that relate to economic activities. In that manner they ignore the existence of the First Amendment, and also ignore the policy arguments against the efficacy of regulating the market of ideas.

The Jackson and Jeffries position, in the words of Justice Brennan, dissenting in the *Posadas* case, would "justify protecting commercial speech less extensively where, as here, the government seeks to manipulate private behavior by depriving citizens of truthful information concerning lawful activities."[72]

As Justice Blackmun put it, when concurring in the judgment in *Central Hudson* case:

Even though "commercial" speech is involved such a regulatory measure strikes at the heart of the First Amendment. This is because it is a covert attempt by the State to manipulate the choices of its citizens, not by persuasion or direct regulation, but by depriving the public of the information needed to make a free choice.... [T]he State's policy choices are insulated from the visibility and scrutiny that direct regulation would entail and the conduct of citizens is molded by the information that government chooses to give them.[73]

NEGATIVE THEORY

Frederick Schauer, in his influential book on the First Amendment, advanced the "negative" theory of the First Amendment.[74] Rather than focusing on the positive values of free speech, he chose to emphasize the evils foregone by adherence to its protection. In this manner he hoped to avoid the inherent difficulty of distinguishing the unique values of free speech from the values of free conduct.

The first argument he makes is that government is more prone to err in the regulation of speech than in the regulation of conduct. He gives as examples the prosecution of Galileo and the discrimination against dissident religious beliefs.[75] The error factor is, as we shall discuss in chapter 4, built into a cost-benefit analysis of Richard Posner, in his economic analysis of the First Amendment.

It is not at all clear, however, that governments commit less error in the regulation of conduct, or that error is more easily perceived in the realm of conduct. The truth or falsity of government regulation of birth control, or abortion, or sexual conduct in general is clouded with as great a possibility of error, or inability to define the nature of those terms, as are matters of so-called political speech.

Schauer's reference to Galileo implies that scientific speech is perhaps too complex to be censored by the government. This argument indicates that the (contrary to Schauer's position) scientific component of advertising (e.g., the efficacy of this or that drug) may not be suitably subject to the censorship of the government.

Next, Schauer suggests a deeper reason for the error factor. He argues that government officials are infected by a conflict of interest or inherent bias in regulating speech that is critical of government.[76] A similar suggestion has been made by Vincent Blasi that speech charging government misconduct merits special First Amendment protection.[77] Similar arguments have been made by another distinguished commentator, Ronald A. Cass.[78]

I doubt that anyone would make light of the bias factor in government officials. This argument is similar to theories of the early Bork and of Meiklejohn. They argued that freedom of political speech was essential to the functioning of the democratic society. Free speech was necessary to check overreaching officials, replace them when appropriate, and preserve the democratic process.

One of the issues in the commercial speech debate is whether conflicts of interest or bias, in Schauer's terms, are unique to noncommercial speech.

McChesney, for example (see chapter 4), and many others (Ralph Nader is a prominent example) have demonstrated how powerful interest groups can influence the legislative and agency regulation of commercial speech to achieve regulatory results congruent with their interest. Government employees readily bow to such pressure, and in the revolving-door structure of government, have a bias in favor of industry in order to lubricate their entry into profitable positions in private industry.

This bias or conflict of interest is not limited to speech regulation. Self-interest, power, desire for conformity, religious belief, and bias may distort government regulation of conduct in the areas of procreation, sex, gender stereotyping, diet, choice of life-style, job, or eligibility for a profession.

Schauer has suggested that line drawing is inherently more complex and unmanageable in the area of speech than in conduct.[79] This, even if true, would not serve to distinguish commercial speech from other speech. Indeed, it is an argument to regulate both equally. But as an argument it is deficient. The complexity of varieties of conduct is immense. For example, one of the arguments made by supporters of the right to choose is that it is impossible to distinguish regulation of abortion from regulation of birth control. Another example is the complexity of distinguishing withholding extraordinary medical assistance to the dying from more traditional aid designed to maintain "meaningful" life. These are but two examples of the subtleties and nuances and difficulties in attempting to distinguish between permitted and forbidden varieties of sexual, occupational, death with dignity, gender, and all other life and death conduct choices.

Schauer also considers whether the profit motive of the speaker delegitimates commercial speech. He rejects that, since he argues that the interest of the listener is paramount.[80] Hence the motives of the corporate speaker are unimportant.[81]

In conclusion, Schauer fails not only to adequately distinguish speech from conduct, but also cannot distinguish political speech from commercial speech.

CHECKING VALUE AND PERIODS OF CONSTITUTIONAL CRISIS

Vincent Blasi first identifies what he believes are the core values of the First Amendment. These include speech about government, particularly speech critical of the government.[82] As he puts it: "The elaborate system of rights and structures set out in the ... American Constitution make sense only in the context of a commitment to limited government. That commitment necessarily entails ... some practical capacity of citizens to challenge and check those who wield power in the name of the state."[83] This is what Blasi calls the "checking value" of First Amendment protection. It is a variant of the negative theory of the First Amendment.

His fear is that an overly expansive definition of the scope of the First

Amendment, one that moves beyond core meaning, may, in periods of societal stress, cause a dilution of First Amendment protection of the core values. Schauer shares this concern.

By now it must be clear, however, that there is no established consensus about a supposed "core" value of the First Amendment, except perhaps at the most uselessly generalized level. Thus few would dispute the Blasi point, one that is really a cliche in the sense of patently true, that free speech necessarily includes criticism of alleged government misconduct. However, if SEC or commercial speech cannot be usefully distinguished from political speech, the Blasi argument on core versus noncore speech and the dilution factor must fail.

A considerable amount of SEC disclosure (i.e., censorship regulation) has been severely criticized over the years by academicians and practitioners (see dicussion in chapter 5). Does this mean that a corporation should be free to disseminate a proxy statement that contravenes an SEC disclosure censorship regulation deemed foolish or worse by the corporation? Blasi would condemn the proxy statement to the ultimate doom of noncore commercial speech. But it is at this point that there is disagreement, and Blasi's reference to the ambiguous term of core value is not very helpful. Most of Blasi's examples of government misconduct are instances of prior anti-Red or anti-left-wing radical regulation. But there are vast areas of government misconduct, bias, and ignorance in the realm of speech regulation of the financial and business world. Blasi assumes that such government action is directed at speech that is non-core. His conclusion, as should now be apparent, is hardly self-evident.

Blasi considers whether the Court should protect commercial speech.[84] Note that he does not reject full protection merely because it is not within his definition of core value. His method is to decide whether protection of commercial speech will chill protection of core speech in times of stress. If it will, then he is against it.

His approach is essentially a psychological guess about how courts will decide in the future. For example, judges are free to examine the truthfulness of commercial speech under current doctrine. That is, the Court applies a middle-of-the-road approach in commercial speech cases, not full protection as in political speech cases. They cannot evaluate truthfulness with regard to so-called political speech. Blasi wonders whether in times of societal crisis the courts will use commercial speech precedent to enter into a dangerous case-by-case judicial scrutiny of the veracity of minority political speech.[85] Therefore, he counsels either no First Amendment protection or full protection to get rid of the case-by-case balancing tradition building up in the Court's middle-of-the-road approach to commercial speech cases.[86]

In the end he opts for no protection. First, he speculates whether total exclusion of commercial speech from First Amendment protection would lead courts to deny protection of some speech that is at the border of commercial speech, based on purpose of the speaker or relative importance of the communication. He points out that if commercial speech is treated the same as political speech, courts would not make such graduations of judgement.[87]

This speculation fails to convince him. The evils of no protection are outweighed, he believes, by the costs of full protection: "On balance I think [granting full protection to commercial speech would mean that] . . . regulatory objectives long considered important and legitimate would be frustrated, engendering in all probability a weakening of public respect for the first amendment quite a bit more severe than that now caused by the Court's middle of the road approach."[88]

This is a mix of empirical guesswork and subjective valuation of regulation. It is surely a matter of dispute as to whether many regulatory objectives are important or legitimate, or so viewed by the public. In any event, Blasi seems to be making a content judgment. That is, certain kinds of government censorship are salutary (I refer to the mention of "regulatory objectives long considered important"), and hence deserve lesser First Amendment security. It is equally pure guesswork whether exclusion of commercial speech from protection will, as he puts it, cause future courts to engage in dangerous evaluation of the worth of the speech or the motivation of the speaker. In the end, we can only guess whether the cost of totally excluding commercial speech from protection is less than or greater than the benefit of preventing some degree, if any (at what probability factor?) of political speech chill in future times of stress.

He attempts to finesse some of these concerns by claiming that the burden of persuasion is on those who would bring commercial speech within the protection of the First Amendment. This is a clever rhetorical flourish that most disputants and advocates in every controversy always love to bring to bear on their side.

ECLECTICISM

Steven Shiffrin rejects the need for a general theory of the First Amendment.[89] He argues that "the structure of first amendment doctrine varies from context to context."[90] He adds that the "nature of social reality is too complex to expect that any single vision, value, or technique could meet the needs of society."[91] He attempts to prove his eclectic approach by disproving the general theories that have been proposed. For example, he rejects the argument that core speech is political and that commercial speech is sharply distinguished from the core area.[92] In this respect he points out that even commercial speech qua advertisement for a product or service has political aspects, and that some so-called commercial speech is even easier to define as political. One of the examples he proffers is the speech regulated by the SEC. He points out that proxy speech and other forms of SEC-regulated speech, where important publicly held corporations are involved, can hardly be distinguished from traditional notions of political speech.[93] This kind of argument had already been made by Chief Judge Weinstein in the case of *SEC v. Lowe*.[94] Next, he endeavors to disprove the self-expression approach. However, the example he uses, that of C. Edwin Baker,[95] is hardly dispositive, since Baker stands for a particular view of individuality that is not shared by many of the other proponents of the self-expression theory.

Shiffrin, in the end, does propose a theory, since a total absence of theory would be an invitation to limitless judicial discretion. As befits his disposition to the eclectic, it is a multifaceted, loosely fitted approach. First, he asserts that "[t]he Court should invoke first amendment scrutiny whenever the government seeks to prevent the truth from being disseminated."[96] Here we can see elements of the Blasi et al. approach that the First Amendment protects against governmental overreaching. Next, Shiffrin argues that the *Virginia Pharmacy* regulation offended the concept of "human dignity."[97] That is, the government regulation banning ads of prices manipulated consumer decisionmaking, and hence was "paternalism."[98] Here we see shards of the First Amendment as self-expression theory. Shiffrin quickly restores his eclectic legitimacy by also asserting that the concept of dignity "will not assist us in resolving most of the most interesting first amendment conflicts,"[99] but are of "enormous importance, particularly in cases like *Virginia Pharmacy*."[100]

Another element he suggest is "government bias in regulating speech."[101] He argues that the marketplace of ideas concept is important in that the First Amendment is needed to prevent a government, with said bias, from dominating the market and repressing the truth.[102] The element is reminiscent of the theories that emphasize, as mentioned above, the repressive nature of government.

Next, he suggests that government bias may be less when the Federal Trade Commission regulates deceptive ads than when government regulates politics or religion.[103] This is, in some sense, reminiscent of the Court notion that truth is easier to verify in commercial areas than in politics.

He considers SEC regulation, and concludes that SEC bias is less than in the case of government regulation of politics. "There do not seem to be grounds for believing that partisan interests have influenced the scope and kind of regulation in such a case, as there would be if a Political Exchange Commission regulated political campaign speeches."[104] He offers no authority for this proposition, which seems to ignore the entirety of the interest theory of regulation, as well as Critical Legal Studies and other neo-Marxist literature. Dean Henry Manne has pointed out that, "[e]ever since George Stigler elaborated the modern 'interest theory' of regulation, scholars have been well-advised in seeking the explanation for a particular regulatory position to ask who would be benefitted most by the rule."[105]

However, lack of bias in this case is unimportant. Despite the absence of bias (which seems to mean less political meat in the mix), he rests on his notion that truth is involved, hence the First Amendment applies.[106] Further, he argues, going back to an earlier argument, that SEC speech is also political.[107] Next, he refers to some of the literature that questions the efficacy of SEC regulation.[108] Finally, he argues, that despite the foregoing, some form of "very strict"[109] scrutiny may be too onerous.

Of course, the *Central Hudson* case was in force at the time, as it is now in modified form, and the traditional four prong test was then applicable to review all SEC-regulated speech.[110] It is not entirely clear that his approach is any different from or similar to that test (or the current Justice Scalia-modified test), since one of the marvels of pure eclecticism is the inability of its critics to define it sufficiently, so as to criticize it.

LAURENCE TRIBE

I could as well have begun this chapter with the Tribe treatise on constitutional law, but instead decided to close with it.[111] His analysis of free speech doctrine and commercial speech will serve as an admirable synthesis in this field. Tribe approves of the inclusion of commercial speech within First Amendment protection. He also approves of the Court's decision to give it limited protection.

To begin with, Tribe disapproves of justifying freedom of speech in purely instrumental terms. He appears to view freedom of speech in part as "an end in itself, an expression of the sort of society we wish to become and the sort of persons we wish to be."[112]

Therefore, he rejects reliance solely on the Milton and Holmes marketplace of ideas concept in which truth and falsehood grapple "in a free and open encounter"[113] and the truth prevails. He questions whether truth will prevail "when the wealthy have more access to the most potent media of communication than the poor."[114] Also, he believes a marketplace approach endangers the right to differ, since it assumes that the real truth will one day emerge, and hence must be supported by the government.[115]

He points out that a closely related theory to the marketplace of ideas theory, but even more restricted in its scope, is the Meiklejohn and Bork theory that free speech is protected to facilitate self-government in a democratic society.[116] This theory would award absolute protection to political speech. However, as Tribe points out, when critics correctly argue that the political category is too narrow, the theory is infinitely expanded to include art, literature, theater and music,[117] and sometimes commercial speech, so long as these categories may indirectly assist the education and knowledge of the voters.[118] So expanded, Tribe points out, the theory tell us little.

Further, when Meiklejohn *et al.* are pressed to articulate the virtues of the democratic polity, they must come up with values that underlie democracy. Those values usually are characterized as personal self-fulfillment.[119]

Tribe's theory for the value of democracy and the First Amendment is based in part on the values of "personal growth and self-realization."[120] Meiklejohn and Holmes were too focused on the intellect and rationality, in the opinion of Tribe. He then quotes Justice Harlan, in *Cohen v. California* opinion, that speech "conveys not only ideas capable of relatively precise, detached explication, but otherwise inexpressible emotions as well."[121] This was the opinion in which the Court upheld, as protected by the First Amendment, the wearing of a jacket bearing the expression "Fuck the Draft" in a courtroom hall.[122]

Tribe then quotes the famous concurrence by Justice Brandeis in *Whitney v. California*: "Those who won our independence believed that the final end of the State was to make men free to develop their facilities. . . . They valued liberty both as an end and as a means. They believed liberty to be the secret of happiness and courage to be the secret of liberty."[123]

Tribe then argues that freedom of speech is not only an end in itself, but also vital for the workings of democratic government. Hence he concluded his discussion with the eclectic assertion that conceptions of freedom of speech must "draw upon several strands of theory" in order to adequately protect free speech.[124]

There are some who do not share Tribe's view that four letter words on jackets implicate any of the purposes of the First Amendment.[125] However, he artfully summarizes the various theories for the First Amendment, and strikes home the dangers of too limited a definition. In the end, he argues for a broad and encompassing theory of self-realization and self fulfillment that clearly encompasses commercial information, whether in the form of information, or of opinion and emotion.

Tribe describes two "ways" in which government can chill speech. First, government can "aim at ideas or information."[126] Second, it can pursue other goals that incidentally limit speech.[127] Tribe asserts that in the first case, the courts use what he refers to as "track one" analysis.[128] There the government must show "that the message being suppressed poses a 'clear and present danger,' constitutes a defamatory falsehood, or otherwise falls on the unprotected side of one of the lines the Court has drawn."[129] In the second case the courts use what he terms "track two." There a government action is constitutional if "it does not unduly constrict the flow of information."[130] Balancing is more permissible in track two analysis than in track one analysis.[131]

He gives as an example of track one analysis the commercial speech cases of *Virginia Pharmacy* and *Central Hudson*.[132] He questions whether the *Posadas* case can be reconciled with his analysis.[133] (see discussion in chapter 1) since it upheld a governmental ban on casino advertising designed to chill the informational (i.e., content) effects of such commercial messages.

Track one analysis is calculated to protect the free flow of ideas and information. Therefore, Tribe approves of the Court's decision in *First National Bank of Boston v. Bellotti* protecting corporate speech despite the corporate nature of the speaker.[134] The crucial value is to protect the rights of listeners to information even where the speaker is a profit-driven entity. Otherwise, we would violate the "norm of viewpoint neutrality"[135] if the government can dictate what speakers may communicate with the public. In another case of corporate speech the Court stated that the test for content-based restriction is that "the government . . . show that the regulation is a precisely drawn means of serving a compelling state interest."[136]

Tribe quotes a commercial speech case to the further effect that when the harm feared from the speech can be averted by further dialogue, government suppression of the speech is unconstitutional.[137] Here Tribe is distinguishing between protected speech (i.e., dialogue, as he sees it), which includes commercial speech, and speech that merely triggers action or causes harm "without the time or opportunity for response."[138]

Tribe explains the landmark *Virginia Pharmacy* case on three ideas.[139] First, the First and Fourteenth Amendments prevent commercial ad bans based on the argument that stupidity is better than knowledge.[140] Second, free-speech protection extends to economic as well as political speech. Third, commercial information facilitates decisionmaking about products, resources, and the economic system. This is important to the proper functioning of democracy.[141]

The crucial issue is the rationalization for giving commercial speech less protection than other protected speech. Tribe advances the by now familiar and dubious argument that the government can more easily verify the truthfulness of the former.[142] This is the error factor used by Judge Posner in his analysis considered in chapter 4. Tribe also mentions that the precise nature of such lessened protection has been less than clearly and precisely defined.[143] He also mentions that the asserted ease of ascertaining truth or falsity before publication has lead the Court to assert that the prior restraint doctrine does not apply.[144]

The *Posadas* case receives careful analysis by Tribe.[145] That case involved the challenge of a Puerto Rican statute that forbade local casinos from advertising gambling facilities to local residents but not from advertising such facilities to residents of the United States or elsewhere. The commonwealth had not banned the gambling activity itself, but desired, so the Court majority assumed, to decrease local resident demand for such activity. Justice Rehnquist, for the Court, concluded that "the greater power to completely ban casino gambling necessarily includes the lesser power to ban advertising of casino gambling."[146]

Tribe points out that the Rehnquist argument hinges on an association with the demise of the Lochner doctrine. That obsolete judicial theory limited the ability of the government to regulate economic activity. The Court used the due process clause of the Fourteenth Amendment to limit government power to reallocate wealth between the economic classes. Rehnquist argues that since the government can regulate or even ban casino gambling to protect potential gamblers, it can limit commercial speech designed to inflame that desire.[147] In the end, this position would decimate the commercial speech doctrine developed by the Court in its pre-*Posadas* opinions. This is similar to the Jackson and Jeffries position described earlier.

Tribe makes a number of arguments in rebuttal. He points out that the First Amendment protects speech. Hence the Constitution protects the marketplace in ideas, even ideas motivated by profit.[148]

Second, he argues that suppression of commercial speech will not protect the less advantaged from the rich and powerful, as presumably non-Lochner governmental power to regulate economic activity will so do.[149] This argument is clearly based on an economic notion that relatively free advertising is advantageous to the consumer on a cost-benefit basis. Scholars such as Coase would argue for the same conclusion with respect to the advisability of regulating economic *activity*, however.

As we will see in chapter 4, Judge Posner finds the Rehnquist kind of argument (i.e., the inextricable relation of advertising and the product advertised) so appealing that he would probably favor a complete reversal of the Court's commercial speech doctrine.

An additional argument for the Tribe positions turns on the impossibility of limiting the Rehnquist approach. Virtually all economic activity is subject to government regulation under minimum rationality review.[150] As I have pointed out elsewhere, virtually all so-called political debate involves economic interest of this or that group. Most so-called political speech relates to economic activity that can be severely regulated. The Rehnquist doctrine would, therefore, permit an enormous wedge for government intrusion into the freedom of speech.

NOTES

1. For an excellent summary and synthesis of the various principles underlying the first amendment, *see* F. Schauer, *Free Speech: A Philosophical Enquiry* 3–86 (1982).

2. T. Emerson, *The System of Freedom of Expression* 7 (1970).

3. J. Milton, *Areopagitica, A speech for the Liberty of Unlicensed Printing* 45, with introduction and notes by H. B. Cotterill (New York 1959).

4. De Bondt and Thaler, *Anomalies, a Mean-Reverting Walk Down Wall Street*, 3 J. Econ. Perspective 189, 193 (Winter 1989).

5. *See* Schauer at 80–85.

6. Coase, *The Market for Goods and the Market for Ideas*, 64 Am. Econ. Rev. Papers & Proceedings 384, 389 (1974).

7. Redish, *The First Amendment in the Marketplace: Commercial Speech and the Values of Free Expression*, 39 Geo. Wash. L. Rev. 429 (1971).

8. *Id.* at 432. Quoting Pigou, *The Economics of Welfare* 196 (4th ed. 1962).

9. *Id.* at 433. Quoting Stigler, *The Economics of Information*, 69 J. Pol. Econ. 213, 220 (1961).

10. *Id.* at 433.

11. *Id.* at 433. Quoting Stigler, *The Economics of Information*, 69 J. Pol. Econ. 213, 222 (1961).

12. Meiklejohn, *Political Freedom* (1965); Meiklejohn, *The First Amendment Is an Absolute*, 1961 Sup. Ct. Rev. 245.

13. M. Redish, *Freedom of Expression* 11 (1984).

14. *Id.* at 13, n. 27.

15. *Id.* at 435.

16. *Id.* at 436.

17. Meiklejohn, *Free Speech and Its Relation to Self-Government* 22–27 (1948).

18. *Id.* at 104.

19. Redish, *The First Amendment in the Marketplace: Commercial Speech and the Values of Free Expression*, 39 Geo. Wash. L. Rev. 429, 437 (1971).

20. *Id.* at 443.

21. *Id.* at 443–44. Burt Neuborne argues that, historically, free speech theory has been speaker-based. This is true, he asserts, for religion, politics, and art. However, he asserts that speech in the commercial arena, including SEC-regulated speech, usually lacks a speaker of "conscience" and, accordingly, is listener-based. Hence it should receive a lesser degree of constitutional protection, since the historical core meaning of the First Amendent is based on a speaker of "conscience" being protected. Neuborne, *The First Amendment and Government Regulation of Capital Markets*, 55 Brooklyn L. Rev. 5 (1989). He concedes that his argument is "intuitive." *Id.* at 14. Henry P. Monaghan, Harlan Fiske Stone Professor of Constitutional Law, Columbia University, disagrees convincingly with this history and with his theoretical construct. He points out that historical evidence indicates that increasing Court use of the First Amendment was based on a view that the government could not keep citizens from hearing diverse critical viewpoints of government policy. Monaghan, *Some Comments on Professor Neuborne's Paper*, 55 Brooklyn L. Rev. 65, 66 (1989). He points out that when the free-speech cases were considered by the Court in 1919, they involved the need for citizens to criticize government. But this at a fundamental level involved the right of citizens to hear the critics. *Id.* Holmes, he points out, in his famous dissent, asserted that the "best test of truth is the power of thought to get itself accepted in the competition of market. *Id.* at 67. Holmes, in other words, believed that truth is not "out there," but is "only what people will buy." *Id.* at 67. Finally, Monaghan asserts that members of the media operate in corporate form. Do they qualify as "speakers of conscience"? *Id.*

On a theoretical basis Monaghan criticizes the Neuborne thesis. He cannot draw a sharp distinction between speakers and listeners. *Id.* at 69. The distinction confuses the relation between them. *Id.*

Judge Ralph Winter, of the Second Circuit, has somewhat similar and effective criticisms of the distinction. Winter, A *First Amendment Overview*, 55 Brooklyn L. Rev. 71 (1989). He points out that if "you need an individual acting out of conscience to trigger first amendment protection, most political advertising in the United States would be excluded from the protection." *Id.* He points out that you can't separate the speaker from the listener. If you do, then the speaker can be limited to speaking in the woods. *Id.* He emphasizes that the Monaghan approach will make it difficult to grant First Amendment protection to the corporate media. *Id.* at 72.

Arthur Pinto argues that even the limited, hearer-based protection of Neuborne is questionable because securities are intangibles, difficult to understand, and prone to dealings by frauds. Pinto, *The Nature of the Capital Markets Allows a Greater Role for the Government*. 55 Brooklyn L. Rev. 77 (1989). Usually the Court argues that political speech is difficult to understand and complex, and hence should not be subject to government censorship by bureaucrats who may not understand the truth, or who may be biased. The Court argues that commercial speech is more easily verifiable, and hence the government has a role. If commercial SEC speech is tricky and complex, perhaps the government censor is the worst fellow to trust to verify it. On a more fundamental level, there is clearly a huge amount of political-economic artistic speech that is complex, difficult to understand, and subject to manipulation by self-interested politicians at the expense of easily gulled voters. If that is the test for limiting First Amendment protection, little so-called political speech of any significance would be left to fall within the scope of the First Amendment.

22. M. Redish, *Freedom of Expression, a Critical Analysis* 11 (1984).

23. *Id.* at 19–26.

24. *Id.* at 22.

25. *Id.* at 20.

26. *Id.* at 21.

27. *Id.* at 25.

28. *Id.*

29. *Id.* at 40.

30. *Id.* at 61, n. 197.

31. *Virginia State Board of Pharmacy v. Virginia Citizens Consumer Council*, 425 U.S. 748 (1976).

32. Redish, *Freedom of Expression* 62.

33. *Id.* at 63.

34. *Id.* at 64.

35. *Id.*

36. *Id.* at 65.

37. *Id.* at 13. Quoting Bork, *Neutral Principles and Some First Amendment Problems*, 47 Ind. L.J. 1, 22 (1971). Reference should be made to Levy, *Emergence of a Free Press* (1988) and Levy, *Legacy of Suppression* (1960). In the latter Levy argued that the framers intended the First Amendment as a limited defense against only prior restraint. In the former book he modified his earlier conclusion and argued for a broader historical meaning for the First Amendment.

38. Baker, *Commercial Speech: A Problem in the Theory of Freedom*, 62 Iowa L. Rev. 1 (1976).

39. *Id.* at 7 (emphasis omitted).

40. "As economic behavior becomes increasingly oriented toward the formally rational pursuit of profits, one should expect, and historically one finds, that the household or consumption-oriented arenas of life are increasingly, and more radically, separated from the profit-making enterprise." *Id.* at 12.

"Profits require a constant increase in our desires." *Id.* at 15.

"Moreover, increasing evidence suggests that neither happiness, nor a sense of freedom, nor any other important human goal closely correlates with a maximum satisfaction of market stimulated desires." *Id.* at 21. His sources for this last assertion are E. Fromm, *The Sane Society* (1955); H. Marcuse, *One Dimensional Man* (1964); and "[p]opular interpretations of the youth culture of the late sixties." For this last interpretation he cites C. Reich, *The Greening of America* (1970). *Id.* at 21, n. 79.

If he had cited and acknowledged the intellectual respectability of the literature on the correlation between market economies and the existence of political freedom,

such as Milton Friedman, *Capitalism and Freedom* (1962), and F. A. Hayek, *Law, Legislation and Liberty* (1979), he would have recognized that eminent thinkers believe that capitalism is essential for the existence of political and individual freedom. If he recognized the fact that there is emigration out of Eastern European socialist states into Western capitalist states, not the other way, he might then have reached a different conclusion. This points up the obviously heavily content larded element of his analysis. Put simply, he believes that corporate capitalism is evil, and hence corporate commercial speech should not receive First Amendment protection.

41. Baker at 34–41.

42. *Id.* at 25–34.

43. *Id.* at 29.

44. *Id.* at 30.

45. *Id.*

46. *Id.*

47. *Id.*

48. Jackson and Jeffries, *Commercial Speech: Economic Due Process and the First Amendment*, 65 Va. L. Rev. 1 (1979).

49. *Id.* at 9.

50. *Id.* at 11.

51. *Id.* at 12; footnote omitted. See T. Emerson, *The System of Freedom of Expression* (1970); T. Emerson, *Toward a General Theory of the First Amendment* (1966).

52. Emerson, *Toward a General Theory of the First Amendment*, 72 Yale L. J. 877, 879 (1963).

53. *Id.*

54. *Id.*

55. *Id.*

56. T. Emerson, *The System of Freedom of Expression* 6 (1970).

57. *Id.*

58. *Id.*

59. *Id.*

60. Emerson, *First Amendment Doctrine and the Burger Court*, 68 Calif. L. Rev. 422, 423 (1980).

61. Jackson and Jeffries, *Commercial Speech: Economic Due Process and the First Amendment*, 65 Va. L. Rev. 1, 13, n. 45 (1979).

62. *Id.* at 13, n. 46.

63. *Id.* at 14.

64. *Id.*

65. *Id.* at 14–15.

66. *Id.* at 15.

67. *Id.* at 16–17.

68. *Id.* at 17.

69. *Id.* at 30–31.

70. *Id.* at 34.

71. *Id.*

72. 478 U.S. 351 (1986).

73. 447 U.S. 557, 574–75 (1980).

74. F. Schauer, *Free Speech: A Philosophical Enquiry* 80–85 (1982).

75. *Id.* at 81.

76. *Id.* at 81–82.

77. Blasi, *The "Checking Value" in First Amendment Theory*, Am. B. Found. Research J. 521, 529–44 (1977).

78. Cass, *Commercial Speech, Constitutionalism, Collective Choice*, 56 U. Cin. L. Rev. 1317, 1355–58 (1988).

79. Schauer, *supra*, n. 74 at 83–85.

80. *Id.* at 161–62.

81. *Id.*

82. Blasi, *The "Checking Value" in First Amendment Theory*, Am. B. Found. Research J. 521, 529–44 (1977).

83. Blasi, *The Pathological Perspective and the First Amendment*, 85 Colum. L. Rev. 449, 455 (1985). *See also* Schauer, *Commercial Speech and the Architecture of the First Amendment*, 56 U. Cin. L. Rev. 1181 (1988).

84. *Id.* at 484–89.

85. *Id.* at 485.

86. *Id.* at 488.

87. *Id.*

88. *Id.*

89. Shiffrin, *The First Amendment and Economic Regulation: Away from a General Theory of the First Amendment*, 78 Nw. U. L. Rev. 1212 (1983).

90. *Id.* at 1252.

91. *Id.*

92. *Id.* at 1225–30.

93. *Id.* at 1230–31.

94. See discussion of case in chapter 2, *supra.*

95. Shiffrin at 1239–50.

96. *Id.* at 1256–57.

97. *Id.* at 1259.

98. *Id.*

99. *Id.*

100. *Id.*

101. *Id.* at 1261.

102. *Id.*

103. *Id.* at 1265.

104. *Id.* at 1266.

105. Manne, *Insider Trading and Property Rights in New Information*, 325. In *Economic Liberties and The Judiciary* (J. Dorn and H. Manne eds. 1987). Manne quoted G. Stigler, *The Theory of Economic Regulation*, Bell J. of Econ. and Management Science 2 (1971).

106. Shiffrin at 1266.

107. *Id.*

108. *Id.* at 1266–67.

109. *Id.* at 1268.

110. *See.* chapter 1.

111. L. Tribe, *American Constitutional Law* (2d ed. 1988).

112. *Id.* at 785.

113. *Id.* at 785, quoting Milton, *Areopagitica, a Speech for the Liberation of Unli-*

censed Printing, to the Parliament of England (1644), in *Prose Writings* 23–28 (Everyman ed. 1927).

114. *Id.* at 786.

115. *Id.*

116. *Id.*

117. *Id.*, referring to Meiklejohn, *The First Amendment Is an Absolute*, 1961 Sup. Ct. Rev. 245, 263 (1961).

118. *Id.* at 786–87 (footnotes omitted).

119. *Id.* at 787.

120. *Id.*

121. *Id.*, quoting Justice Harlan in *Cohen v. California*, 403 U.S. 15, 26 (1971).

122. *Id.* at 787.

123. *Id.* at 788, quoting Justice Brandeis' concurrence in *Whitney v. California*, 274 U.S. 357, (1927) (Brandeis, J., joined by Holmes, J., concurring).

124. *Id.* at 789.

125. *See, e.g.,* Canavan, *Freedom of Expression Purpose as Limit* (1984).

126. Tribe at 789.

127. *Id.* at 789–90.

128. *Id.* at 791.

129. *Id.* at 791–92.

130. *Id.* at 792.

131. *Id.*

132. *Id.* at 790.

133. *Id.* at 790, n. 11.

134. *Id.* at 795.

135. *Id.*

136. *Id.* at 833, quoting *Consolidated Edison Co. v. Public Service Commission*, 447 U.S. 530, 540 (1980).

137. *Id.* at 834.

138. *Id.* at 837.

139. *Id.* at 893.

140. *Id.* at 894.

141. *Id.*

142. *Id.* at 894–95.

143. *Id.* at 895–96.

144. *Id.* at 895.

145. *Id.* at 902–3.

146. *Id.* at 903.

147. *Id.* at 901–4.

148. *Id.* at 903.

149. *Id.* at 892 and n. 15.

150. *Id.* at 900.

4

Economic Theory, Free Speech, and the SEC

One of the major influences in modern law is the economic analysis of law. That body of scholarship has recently begun to analyze the free-speech doctrine. Although generalization is dangerous, it is fairly safe to assert that a predominant aspect of this analysis is the application of a cost-benefit analysis. Richard Posner, one of the most famous and influential of the law and economics scholars, has put it, "I shall not assume . . . that freedom of speech is a holy of holies which should be exempt from the normal tradeoffs that guide the formulation of legal policy."[1]

Posner took exception to the assertion of another scholar that "[o]ne of the things that separate our society from theirs [Nazis] is our absolute right to propagate opinions that the government finds wrong or even hateful."[2] Posner responded, "[V]aluable as the right of free speech is, I for one would be willing to trade off a modest curtailment of it in exchange for saving millions of lives."[3] He is not willing to permit the untrammeled propagation of vicious ideas that will lead to violence and totalitarian oppression. As he puts it, any other approach renders the "Constitution a suicide pact."[4]

In this chapter we consider the leading economic analyses of free speech. We begin with the essays of Ronald Coase and Aaron Director.

DIRECTOR AND COASE

In a piece first presented in 1953 (and published in 1964) Aaron Director argues that there is a marked identity between the market for ideas and the market for commercial goods and services.[5]

He asserts that the free market for ideas was supported long before free markets were advanced as a preferred modality of structuring economic affairs.[6] This, he suggests, was because the theory of the market for goods and services could arise only after the emergence of a considerable amount of competition.[7] He also points out that freedom of advocacy was defended well before the flowering of democracy.[8] This point implies that free speech is a method of achieving personal freedom and dignity apart from and before modern notions of representative democracy. Director then argues that Jeremy Bentham and James Mill successfully advanced the concept that speech is necessary for and associated with democracy.[9] Further, they asserted that free speech and democracy would decrease the power and sway of the sovereign power over the economic affairs of the people.[10]

Director then states that the intellectual climate changed in the direction of a "collectivist" orientation in economic affairs.[11] With it grew the split between the concept of liberty as participation in democracy and the rejection of liberty as a limit on governmental control of economic affairs."[12]

Director points out that he is aware of the special locus accorded to free speech in the Constitution[13]. But he believes that many scholars, because of their hostility to commerce, exaggerate the difference between the two markets.[14] He quotes in that regard Meiklejohn, who warns us that by confusing property and freedom of discussion, "we are in constant danger of giving to a man's possessions the same dignity, the same status, as we give to the man himself."[15]

Director then turns his attention to similarities between the markets in ideas and speech. First he offers a kind of public choice (i.e., interest) theory for the elevation of the market for ideas over goods: "Everyone tends to magnify the importance of his own occupation and to minimize that of his neighbor. Intellectuals are engaged in the pursuit of truth, while others are merely engaged in earning a livelihood."[16]

The preference for the free market of ideas, Director argues, also arises from the mistaken belief that democracy operates by discussion, and ignorance of the fact that democracy operates by majority rule that becomes more and more coercive as the "area of political decision is enlarged."[17] He might have added that limitation of free speech to political speech, narrowly construed, ignores the power of the modern democratic state to transform all of economic life to life controlled by the state and the politicians; hence that argument erroneously excludes economic speech from its proper constitutional protection.[18]

Director maintains that "[t]he priority accorded to the free market for ideas as against the free market for economic affairs is derived from an undue importance attached to discussion as a method of solving problems."[19] He quotes Knight, who emphasized that "[g]enuine, purely intellectual discussion is rare in modern society.... the immediate interest of the active parties centers chiefly in dominance, victory."[20]

Director asserts that the importance of the free market in economics is the freedom it gives us to choose between a wide variety of life-styles.[21] This freedom is broader than political discourse and involvement in government.[22] "It means responsibility, change, adventure, departure from accepted ways of doing things."[23]

He quotes John Stuart Mill: "[If the] industries, the university and the public charities were all of them branches of the government; ... if the employees of all these different enterprises were appointed and paid for by the government, and looked to the government for every rise in life; not all the freedom of the press and popular constitution of the legislature would make this or any other country free otherwise than in name."[24]

In legal literature many scholars have argued that self-expression is the fundamental value protected by the First Amendment.[25] One objection voiced to this approach is the difficulty of distinguishing between the values of self-expression inherent in freedom of action as contrasted to freedom of speech. Indeed, we shall observe later that Judge Posner excludes that value from his formula for free speech because of that difficulty.

Aaron Director eloquently emphasizes that a free market for ideas and a free market for goods are valuable because they expand the scope of human individual choice and expression. In fact he makes a powerful argument for the greater importance of the latter in that regard. He proves the unimportance of distinguishing the supposed unique character of free speech. Although the Constitution singles out free speech in the First Amendment, it does not follow that we are constrained to distinguish the values protected by free speech from the values protected by a free market for goods. Indeed, it is probably an impossible task. Even if we limit free speech to a fairly narrow definition of political speech, the problem is not solved. Modern public choice theory (discussed further below) underlines the point made above by Director, that we exaggerate the role intellectual discussion plays in the political process. Self-interest, maneuver, and deployment of power are the methods used in the democratic process. Democratic fulfillment comes from political conduct and action that results in victory. Political conduct, such as interest trade-offs, and occupation of buildings, plays a more important role than academic conversation. Thus we cannot argue that political speech serves a unique value; (i.e., the furtherance of the democratic political process). Political action does the same and more of it. Because not even the goals and values of political speech can be distinguished from the values and goals served by political action, it is difficult to "exclude nonpolitical speech that aids individual self-fulfillment on the ground that conduct may also aid such a goal."[26] Hence artistic speech, for example, must be protected even though the underlying value protected is self-expression, not something unique to speech.

R. H. Coase develops this argument in a later piece. He emphasizes that "as the range of activities to which the courts have extended the protection of the First Amendment grows, it becomes increasingly unplausible to tie First Amendment rights to the workings of the political system. Nude dancing is now covered by the First Amendment, and it would be difficult to argue that this activity... is vital to the working of a democratic system."[27]

Coase refers to Thomas I. Emerson's attempt to justify the special status of speech over goods in our society.[28] Emerson argued that the "fundamental purpose of the First Amendment [is] to guarantee the maintenance of an effective system of free expression."[29]

Emerson distinguished expression from action. Coase quotes Emerson as follows: "In order to achieve its desired goals, a society or state is entitled to exercise control over action.... But expression occupies a specially pro- tected position."[30]

Coase then summarizes Emerson's often-cited reasons for the primacy of verbal and written self-expression: (1) it guarantees personal autonomy, (2) it leads to the truth, (3) it facilitates democracy, and (4) it preserves peaceful change.[31]

Coase points out that Emerson "puts great stress on freedom of expression as leading to self-fulfillment."[32] Coase then argues, convincingly, "[b]ut free- dom to choose one's occupation, one's home, the school one (and one's children) attends, what is studied at school, the kind of medical attention one receives, how one's savings are to be invested, the equipment one uses, or the food one eats are surely equally necessary for self-fulfillment—and for most people are considerably more important than much of what is protected by the First Amendment."[33]

Coase also argues that the same holds true for the other merits of free expression that Emerson mentions. If freedom of speech facilitates truth- seeking, then freedom in the market for goods facilitates wise choice. If free speech aids in the democratic process (narrowly defined to be sure), then a free market in goods makes possible freedom in the all-important economic sphere of life. Finally, a free market is a sensitive device for adjusting to change in the market.[34]

Coase concludes that the market for goods and services and the market for ideas should be given parity of treatment.[35] It does not follow, therefore, that the market for ideas should be subject to regulation. Coase has great skepticism about the efficacy of government regulation. He recites the many studies that demonstrate the perverse effects of government regulation of goods and services.[36] Hence he applauds the assumption underlying the First Amendment that markets function best when government regulation is held to a minimum.[37] He does conclude, however, that the basic approaches to the justification for government regulation or the lack of it, are the same in both markets. They involve a balancing of the costs and benefits of the reg- ulation as compared with the benefits and costs of no regulation.

Coase next considers the place of advertising. He argues that advertising leads to more competition.[38] McChesney, in a more recent article, has stated that the empirical literature demonstrates that advertising makes for lower prices.[39] He also asserts that advertising facilitates entry of new sellers into markets.[40] He argues that with advertising, buyers know more about sellers, and hence force sellers to compete more strenuously.[41] In another article McChesney emphasizes that the distinction between informative and "persuasive" advertising is a myth.[42] As he puts it, "[e]very advertisement supplies some information, if only a reminder of the firm's existence and the product the firm sells. Moreover, even 'persuasive' advertising can improve consumer welfare by promoting the rapid entry of superior products into the market, by enhancing competition and thereby lowering prices, by stimulating product innovation and by reducing search costs for consumers."[43] All of these arguments, McChesney emphasizes, have been endorsed by the Supreme Court in its cases on commercial advertising.[44]

The value of some advertising and the uselessness, or worse, of other advertising ought not to dictate the application of the First Amendment, which, if anything, is supposedly content neutral. Coase does convincingly argue, however, that advertising is part of the market of ideas. It appears clearly that when it imparts information. Sometimes it changes consumers' tastes, but not always by the most intellectually rigorous means. As Coase point out, this, in the opinion of many, is bad because it is frequently corrupting.[45] Either vulgar tastes or new tastes no better than the old are created, thus wasting resources. Coase is more optimistic than this. It is clear, however, that the debate at this point is little different from the usual debate over ideas, aesthetic theories, and the like, all part of the market of ideas.

Before leaving Coase it is important to consider one further illuminating argument he makes. Coase persuasively argues that line drawing in the area of defining advertising is particularly difficult.[46] A commercial ad for a product or a service appears easy to conceptualize. But what of a talk by an attorney on a legal topic? This is a form of promotion. Will the Court analyze motive? The same question arises with an article written by a professor for gratis to advertise himself and obtain a better-paying position. Coase argues that the courts usually will refuse to get into motive. I think he is right. But it highlights the artificiality of restricting the definition of advertising to a conceptually satisfactory limit, since the speech and the article are both forms of advertisement.

A similar question can be raised about the corporate or individual attorney, physician, or business person speech about legislation designed to increase their, or its, sales. Indeed, the Court does define the latter as fully protected, non-commercial speech. But the artificiality of the distinction between ads for products or services and such speech about legislation is apparent.

Next question, is direct advertisement of a book or a religious emblem protected? Is it protected because the object sold is protected by the First Amendment? Suppose the product advertized and sold is sold by a non-profit group. Is the ad protected?

Perhaps we then define advertising only as advertising of businesses that directly impact sales of products not protected by the First Amendment.[47]

Coase then asks whether the motive of the buyer should be relevant. Suppose, in the case of the Chestensen submarine, the buyer wants to examine it to better understand defense policy. Suppose the buyers want to maximize their self-expression or their knowledge.

In these series of examples Coase raises questions that go beyond the usual line drawing problems in the law. He explores the fundamental ambiguity in the contours of advertising and illustrates the close connection of advertising and the market for ideas and the concept of self-expression.

THE POSNER FORMULA

Judge Richard Posner has presented an economic model of the costs and benefits of regulating free speech.[48] It is an audacious and provocative theory that challenges any who write in this field.

Because of its importance, I quote the formula at length.

I propose to build on the free-speech formula that [Judge] Hand used. . . . In symbols, regulate if but only if B < PL, where B is the cost of the regulation (including any loss from suppression of valuable information), P is the probability that the speech sought to be suppressed will do harm, and L is the magnitude (social cost) of the harm.

I shall expand the formula in a way that will facilitate discussion of its various components. I decompose B into its two principal components—V (for "value"), the social loss from suppressing valuable information, and E (for "error"), the legal-error costs incurred in trying to distinguish the information that society desires to suppress from valuable information. V is a function of the size of the actual and potential audience for the speech in question . . . and of the decrease in audience brought about by the challenged regulation. My other modification of Hand's formula is to discount L to present value. . . . With these adjustments, the Dennis formula becomes $V + E < P \times L/(1 + i)^n$, where n is the number of periods between the utterance of the speech and the resulting harm and i is an interest or discount rate which translates a future dollar of social cost into a present dollar.[49]

The left side of the equation measures the costs of suppression. Judge Posner points out that V, information loss, depends on the "nature and value" of the expression chilled and the quantity of speech suppressed.[50]

Posner rejects the argument that political speech can be placed at the top of a hierarchy of values. He finds it difficult to distinguish between political and economic speech. He finds it difficult to measure relative values. Hence he asserts that commercial speech, art and entertainment, scientific speech, and public relations cannot be given a lower value than political speech.[51]

He does find a significant difference in V between commercial speech and political speech in "market robustness (versus fragility) of the speech suppressed—more precisely, the degree to which the social benefits of the speech are "externalized."[52] This analysis corresponds to the many Supreme Court cases that based the less extensive protection of the First Amendment for commercial speech on the robustness of commercial speech.[53]

Posner argues that property rights in political speech are "difficult to obtain and maintain."[54] Except for materials protected by copyright, patent, or trade secret law, political speech will be appropriated by members of the public without payment to the producer. Therefore, less of it will be produced than would be the case if property rights were clear and extant. The speech is a public good. This externality effect makes the production of much of political speech fragile. Regulation will more easily chill it than would be the case if it were protected by property rights.[55]

Because less of it is being produced, a regulation that reduced output by n percent may produce a smaller loss in quantity than if the output were larger. There is the danger, however, that a tax, for example, might reduce output to zero because of the fragility of the output.[56]

Elsewhere Posner argues that it is extremely difficult to determine the value of political speech.[57] If that is true, then it is extremely difficult to determine whether the lack of robustness of political speech is good or bad. Perhaps Posner assumes that the increase in quantity of political speech, despite the impossibility of determining its value, is a good.

Commercial speech is different. There are less positive externalities. That is, the free-rider affect is small. Most of the benefits of advertising a particular product or service are captured by the advertiser, by sale of the product or service.[58] The advertisement may benefit producers of rival products by conveying information of value on other, competing products, but that problem of "external benefit" is small.[59] Hence commercial speech receives less judicial protection than political speech.[60]

Assume the regulation is in the form of an outright ban. Perhaps disseminators of commercial speech will have a greater incentive to violate the law, and hence some black-market commercial speech will persist in amounts greater than banned political speech. I'm not sure that difference is enough to support the four-prong *Central Hundson* test as distinguished from fully protected political speech. It seems to rest on the assumption that more regulation is okay since it won't be effective.

Assume now that the regulation is in the form of mandatory disclosure, a structure central to Securities and Exchange Commission (SEC) regulation. Commercial speech disseminators "carry the production of the information to the point where marginal social cost and marginal social benefit are equated."[61] It would appear that government mandatory disclosure will produce more information than is efficient. This cost will be peculiar to mandatory disclosure for commercial speech, not political speech. The latter is arguably underproduced, and therefore should be subject to mandatory disclosure regulation.

There are additional questions inherent in the "robustness" argument. All other factors being equal, commercial speech deserves less First Amendment protection because of the robustness factor, according to the argument of the Supreme Court and of Posner. However, the following problems are involved: (1) A crucial factor is the goodness or badness of the speech suppressed. If it is good, then robustness is a positive, since it stymies the regulation. If it is bad, then robustness thwarts valuable regulation. Presumably, the greater E, the error rate, the more uncertain is the impact of robustness, since we do not know if robustness is resisting good or evil regulation. (2) Because E is greatest in political speech,[62] we do not know if use of the First Amendment to increase fragile political speech is a good, unless we make certain fundamental assumptions about the inherent value of political speech (which Posner does not), despite the magnitude of E. (3) We can expect that government will always regulate more harshly the greater the robustness to overcome the resistance to the regulatory chill. To what extent this dynamic factor equalizes between more or less robust speech is difficult to say. (4) We can anticipate that businesses will alter their messages, to get them out to the public through the regulatory screen.

Political speech bears a "triple externality."[63] First, as stated, resources inure to the benefit of free riders who use it without payment. Second, Posner asserts, interest groups frequently work to get legislation passed that will hurt the public and benefit the vested interest.[64] A free press is necessary to protect the public.[65] As public choice theory teaches, the members of the interest group have an incentive to work together to achieve their end.[66] The negative impact on each member of the general public is not great enough to cause them to write, publish, and agitate against the interest group. The latter, therefore, has no incentive to publish the truth. Hence a free press is needed in the realm of political speech.

This argument may actually prove the lack of distinction between commercial and political speech. If indeed interest groups dominate political speech and political lobbying, this is a strong argument for the robustness of political speech. That is, because much of political speech is actually the propaganda of interest groups, that speech has less externality than Posner argues. The speech, when successful, achieves the desired regulation or statute; hence the speech captures economic benefit for the disseminator. Therefore, it is produced in quantity and is robust.

Further, consumers of products advertised by business, will, unlike consumers of political speech, have a great incentive to check out the advertisements, since it could harm them. Also, since political speech is produced in Posner's view by vested interest groups, it is likely to be harmful to the public, and, hence should be regulated. Posner relies on the press as a corrective. Given the power of self-interest and interest groups in Posner's argument, however, it is hardly clear why the press should be singularly clear of those influences.

The third externality of political speech is the alleged extreme elasticity of demand for it, as contrasted with commercial speech.[67] People get little private value from it because the individual vote counts for little.[68] Hence a tax on it, or other regulation will cause a great fall off of demand. From this results the argument that full protection of the First Amendment is needed to produce a little more of this fragile speech.

McChesney has made a different economic argument.[69] He asserts that public choice theory indicates that interest groups lobby for and get favorable constitutional First Amendment adjudication when it is in their interest and within their power. Under this theory First Amendment protection (or decreased protection) for commercial or political speech is the function of selfish interest group action. Posner theorizes, on the other hand, that judges and litigators develop First Amendment protection for political speech out of an apparently disinterested desire to increase fragile speech.

Posner points out that many people do vote, despite the lack of value in the individual vote, and despite the elasticity of demand.[70] He asserts, therefore, that economists do not understand why people exercise their vote.[71]

This lack of understanding may extend to the alleged robustness of commercial as opposed to political speech. It is commonplace to contrast the courage of the ideologue to the timidity of the businessman. The modern world is replete with stories of the fearless reformer who ultimately takes power. These men and women risk discomfort, if not life, in the pursuit of goals. They are ready to publish, let alone act, despite risk of suppression. Economists have yet to explain this kind of behavior. There may be psychological causes working here that are not fully encapsulated by the Posner assumptions.

The existence of copyright and trade secret law creates some difficulty in the Posner analysis. He points out that some political speech is protected by copyright.[72] Other political speech that simply repeats general, non copyrightable political ideas are not so protected.

Hence, for much of political, artistic, and others copyrightable or noncopyrightable speech, robustness appears equal to, if not greater than, the robustness of commercial speech. Therefore, much will depend on E (for error) on the left side of the equation.

Judge Posner argues that a lower E exists in the case of commercial speech than for political, artistic, or scientific speech.[73] Remember that this is one of the principal reasons given by the Supreme Court for giving commercial speech less protection than political speech.

This empirical proposition is not entirely free from doubt. Some commercial advertisements are easily verifiable. Thus "I will sell X good at Y price" is easily verifiable. Some political statements are obviously false: "The holocaust never occurred." Financial speech regulated by the SEC is complex and difficult to evaluate and verify. Judge Posner concedes that a lower E does not exist where the commercial representation "concerns an issue of contested scientific truth."[74] This is a vast area of commercial advertising. He argues that as a counterbalance to this, V is lower; but we have raised some question about that above.

He asserts that P (probability that the suppressed speech would do harm) will be higher than in the scientific marketplace.[75] Consumers are not scientists, and hence cannot verify the claim. Therefore, the magnitude of E is less important. But P in the area of harmful political speech that involves scientific claims should be as high (perhaps higher, since consumers may attempt to verify) as in the case of commercial speech.

Judge Posner also asserts that competing producers have "weak incentives" to expose a competitor's lies, unlike scientists.[76] For example, "smoking is good for your health."[77] Earlier Judge Posner highlights the importance of interest groups in political dialogue. He points out that the public has little interest or incentive to uncover lies, and indeed vested interest "proponents of the program would have no incentive to refrain from outrageous misrepresentations of its likely effects."[78] A free press may curb this, but Posner argues that externalities weaken the power of that press.

As stated above, it is not clear that commercial speech is readily verifiable. Nor is it clear that the government can identify deception, if it exists. McChesney has concluded as follows: "Does regulation of speech deter fraud and increase the amount of truthful information? There is no evidence that it does. . . . Posner's study found that the FTC 'brought little consumer protection' in exchange for millions of dollars spent policing allegedly fraudulent practices, but imposed millions of dollars more on the private sector in litigation and compliance costs."[79]

Also, Posner's formula appears to focus on the dissemination of information. Because much commercial speech involves opinion (e.g., "ABC shampoo will beautify your look and make you attractive to your partner"), the importance of E in distinguishing commercial speech from fully protected speech dwindles.

The Supreme Court has argued that the purpose of commercial speech is the dissemination of information. Hence the government has a legitimate interest in regulating it to assure truthfulness.[80] The Court asserts that political speech is frequently opinion or ideas that are not verifiable. Hence falsity is less important or more difficult to establish and the speech should be fully protected.[81]

The Posner formula appears to relate the First Amendment solely to protection of the communication of information. He asserts that "self-expression has no obvious connection with the first amendment."[82] This claim has been emphatically rejected by other scholars.[83]

His formula, based on information, makes it clear that verifiability and robustness are crucial. Absent differences in those two factors, there will be no difference between commercial speech and political speech. Indeed, the presence of these two factors amounts to his definition of commercial speech.

Therefore, he potentially opens the door to treating the two the same, unless his arguments on the two criteria are sound. Sometimes the Court appears to be making an effort at making a similar distinction (information versus opinion and ideas) between the two.[84] I doubt that the Court has succeeded, however, since information is often vital to political speech, and opinion is often a significant part of commercial speech.

Judge Posner argues that P in his formula is greater ("clearer" in the Holmes formula) where the risk is to a third party, not to the orator's audience.[85] He asserts that a member of the audience is equipped to fend off the speaker merely by closing his or her ears, unlike a third party.[86] This is a negative externality.

An example is a billboard displaying pornography. Noncustomers for the product are subject to the display. Another example cited by Posner is a speech by a racist. His hate speech to a white audience may result in harm to blacks not in the audience.[87] This is an argument for regulating that kind of speech.

Commercial speech may have negative externalities. For example, tobacco billboards may turn nonsmokers into users whose smoke harms nonsmokers. However, because commercial speech is usually an advertisement for a product or service, the amount of negative externalities is less than in the case of political speech, which is frequently designed to move an audience against political opponents.

POSITIVE REGULATORY THEORY

Fred S. McChesney has advanced a provocative public choice theory of First Amendment application.[88] He has argued that interest group agitation and litigation explain the legal treatment of commercial speech. He asserts that it is useless to analyze commercial speech in terms of the contribution of free speech to democracy, self-expression, justice, human dignity, free marketplace of ideas, or the like. Those are normative principles that fail to explain why and how First Amendment doctrine develops.[89]

As he coldly puts it: "The empirical evidence strongly favors the hypothesis that concern for public values like truth has less to do with government restrictions on speech than does bestowal of benefits on private interests."[90]

He asserts that "[i]n study after study, advertising has been shown to account for lower prices, a point noted by the Supreme Court. Ability to advertise also makes it easier for new sellers, or sellers of new products to enter a market, a point the Court has also recognized. "Not surprisingly then, many sellers have demonstrated keen interest in having advertising restricted or banned."[91]

This explains, McChesney argues, why professional associations enact codes of ethics that ban advertising.[92] It explains why economic interests will lobby and litigate to assure weakened constitutional protection for commercial speech.

There are industries, however, in which advertising will assist established businesses. These include industries in which new products of great complexity are marketed frequently. Sellers must then use advertising to massage demand."[93]

In such industries not all, but a majority of corporations will desire First Amendment protection. They will attempt to convince regulators to free up speech.[94]

He argues that the development of the commercial speech doctrine reflects this economic model. As new industry develops, the benefits of advertising grow and the political power within the industry moves toward those supporting free speech. He gives as further examples the growth of "cut-rate pharmacies, chain store optometrists and legal and medical clinics, all of which sell at lower profit margins and so require volume trade in order to survive."[95]

There is no doubt that economic interest motivates litigators and litigation, as well as interest group lobbying. Public choice theory has systematized this rather trivial insight. But the area of commercial speech doctrine creates, to date, an insuperable obstacle to the foregoing analysis. As is patently obvious, the changes in the commercial speech doctrine have occurred in the Supreme Court.[96] In every litigation before the Court there was a party requesting expansion of free speech and a party arguing for limitation of free speech doctrine in commercial expression. Interest group pressure, as described by McChesney, simply does not explain why the Court broke with the *Valentine* case and applied First Amendment protection to commercial speech.[97] The Court has life tenure. The justices do not depend on contributions from interest groups for reelection. There is no evidence that the economic power of a particular litigant affected Court doctrine, as distinguished from intellectual analysis of the briefs. If McChesney were correct, no brief need be written. The more powerful litigant should simply inform the Court of its clout, rather than waste time with intelligent argument in the brief. He admits to this gap. "The interest-group model of the first amendment outlined in this section admittedly does not explain these episodes."[98]

McChesney asserts that

[t]he fact that different industries have different demands, sometimes at different periods in their history, for regulation of commercial speech explains why such regulation has never been prohibited constitutionally.... It is likely that the advantages of increasing demand relative to the lure of higher prices will lessen over time in a given industry....

In summary, exclusion of commercial speech from full constitutional protection can be explained in terms of an interest group model.... Nor would one expect a uniform constitutional rule to be applied to all industries.[99]

I submit that the development of commercial speech doctrine cannot be explained in terms of this version of the interest group model. The Court has, over time, developed a uniform constitutional rule limiting regulation of commercial speech; it is the famous four prong test of the *Central Hudson* case.[100] That rule will apply to industries that now demand freedom from regulation for the first time, and to those same industries when they demand regulation of commercial speech. Because the long-term commercial interest, according to McChesney, is eventually to restrict or ban commercial speech, it appears that, in terms of McChesney's model, short-term interest in free speech leads to a constitutional uniform doctrine that will work against the long-term interests of industry.

Also, the exclusion of commercial speech from full protection argument is premised on the unsupported empirical guess that pro-protection groups are less powerful than anti-protection groups. This question begs assumption.

Further, the development of the four-prong test applies to all industries. Therefore, given McChesney's assumptions, it immediately hurt mature industries, since they wanted regulations that restrict commercial speech. Either these industries were too weak to achieve legal doctrine that helps them, or commercial speech doctrine has a sort of fortuitous impact. One victory in constitutional litigation by one party impacts all industry across the board indefinitely.

There is another difficulty in the McChesney analysis. He constantly asserts that *majority* interests in a particular industry will, when it suits their interest, obtain freedom from regulation of their commercial speech. He gives legal clinics and chain-store optometrists as examples. But conceding for the moment that his assumption about who is in the majority is accurate, interest group analysis might conclude that the wealthier or better connected economic interests would prevail. Put crudely, money may influence regulation more than simple nose counts. This is a fairly reasonable proposition when complex, expensive litigation is involved. Powerful establishment law firms should have a fair chance, given McChesney's interest group assumptions, to say the least, to prevail in litigation over the application of this or that commercial speech doctrine.

McChesney next analyzes political speech. He asserts that "[p]olitical speech, defined initially as communications from a politician or candidate to the electorate to secure its vote, is akin to commercial speech, which is also made to secure listeners' patronage."[101]

If McChesney is correct, then the Posner argument for the greater robustness of commercial speech over political is, to some extent, rebutted. Politicians have a direct monetary interest in supplying speech in order to be elected.

McChesney, however, argues that incumbents will be interested in chilling the political speech of challengers. "Like better-established sellers in commercial markets, incumbent politicians have established reputations."[102]

He argues, however, that challengers are in the majority. They seek freedom of speech. Therefore, this majority is fully protected constitutionally. The protection is complete, not limited as in the case of commercial speech. Although the incumbents have the power to change legislation, they cannot easily alter a constitutional protection.[103]

It is not clear whether McChesney is making a kind of original-intent argument. That is, the founding fathers, sympathetic to the future legions of challengers (of which they might be a part), passed the First Amendment to buttress their campaigns. Perhaps he is also making an argument that current constitutional interpretation is influenced by the majority power of challengers. These are difficult positions to take. Ninety-nine percent of House incumbents are currently reelected.[104] Challengers are effectively eliminated from the process. Yet the Constitution has not prevented this development. Recent constitutional adjudication has not remedied the situation. Where is the supposed majoritarian power of the majority challengers? They have not been able to develop the obvious constitutional answer: a doctrine that would create a level playing field in respect to the ability of challengers and incumbents to publicize their respective campaigns.

McChesney pursues this theme with reference to books and articles and all other forms of noncommercial speech: "the majority favoring free speech will always outnumber the proregulation minority."[105] Hence they seek and get the full protection of artistic or political speech, not the limited protection of commercial speech. (Note that because they are so powerful, they have little to fear even if the Constitution does not protect them.)

It is surely a debatable proposition that the majority needs, hence seeks, First Amendment protection. He cites no evidence one way or the other. Perhaps a majority of intellectuals (defined to include only those who write for a living) might, although this is a debatable proposition. There is a shabby tradition among some left-wing or right-wing thinkers for limits on free speech. In any event, significant intellectual and non-intellectual elements (perhaps a majority) in society seek limits at various times on free speech. Religious fundamentalists are one obvious example. It is a truism, since true, that the First Amendment and other constitutional rights are designed to protect the minority from the majority. It is not at all clear, based on McChesney's group interest model, why such powerful antispeech groups cannot get constitutional adjudication favoring their interests.

This discussion of the gaps in McChesney's chain of cause and effect illustrates that we run the risk of identifying a particular current Supreme Court constitutional result (e.g., full protection of X speech) with a particular economic interest (something we can always find), and then assume that it was the power of that interest group (not the content of their ideas or their legal briefs or psychological or cultural factors) and the weakness of all other interest groups on the other side (not the content of their ideas or psychological or cultural factors, or their briefs) that caused the particular constitutional result. It may very well be that vested interest groups determine the outcome of First Amendment constitutional development in the courts. However, something very particular in the way of individual and societal causation is called for to make the case.

COST-BENEFIT ANALYSIS

Another significant economic analysis of the commercial speech doctrine has been presented by a distinguished economist, George J. Benston.[106] He begins his analysis on the assumption of no externalities.[107] He then asserts that the "basic" reason for the First Amendment is the inability to know truth with certainty,[108] and "that the expected damage from disseminated falsehoods is less than the benefits from the truth that would be expressed."[109] The statement that the truth cannot be known is debateable. Many political statements are verifiable. Moreover the cost benefit assertion is an empirically empty statement. If benefits exceed costs, then support the First Amendment. But how to measure them is the question. Further, less than absolute certainty as to truth does not necessarily imply anything about the First Amendment. The question could then be phrased in terms of measuring the *probability* of this or that X amount of cost or benefit occurring. If X amount of harm of Z amount of censorship discounted by n degree of uncertainty as to the harm will be less than the Y amount of value of truth sometimes suppressed, discounted by b degree of uncertainty as to the truth, then coercion is supported. The difficulty of measuring and weighing all of those imponderables is obvious. But the difficulty of measurement does not prove that free speech is beneficial or harmful unless some additional underlying assumption, is being made. If Benston cannot give us anything more precise than this, he has not advanced the argument.

In simply assuming the primary importance of this "reason" he makes an important error. It is clear from the previous materials in this book that two other reasons for the support of free speech have gained wide acceptance. Indeed, many scholars believe them to be more important than the "truth cannot be known with certainty" argument. The first is the close association of free speech with democratic values. The second justification is the personal values inherent in free expression. He mentions the other reasons,[110] recites some criticisms of them, but then merely asserts that "the 'uncertainty about truth and falsehood' theory alone sufficiently supports freedom for all types of speech, assuming no externalities."[111] This is the basic free market of ideas concept that was evaluated and found to some extent wanting in the previous chapter.

Benston does not give any scientific meaning to his cost-benefit analysis. That is, he talks cost and benefit, but his arguments often are identical to the so-called soft arguments of the attorney, the newspaper editorial writer, or the preacher. For example, when the physicist presents the formula for movement of the planets a physicist can measure it. All reasonable men and women will agree to accept the measurements. Benston's arguments on the relative amounts of cost and benefit are not measurable by any such objective gauge. Therefore, the use of the words cost and benefit does not add an element of scientific certainty any different than the arguments of noneconomists. A discussion that uses said words without any commonly accepted measure is as normative, or nonpositive, as any discussion that eschews such words and talks of the values of democracy and free speech.

Let me give an example of his argument in the political area of speech. Benston argues that individuals tend to "be the best judges of their own interests."[112] Also, government officials "tend to make choices that further their own self-interests."[113] Therefore, he supports free speech in the political realm. This is a good beginning presentation. But it is hardly new to non-economists. He has made a number of plausible empirical assertions that may or may not be true, or if true, true in strength and degree that are empirical hypotheses, not easily testable or measurable. For example, the German people in large numbers voted for Hitler in the 1930s. Did they know their own interest? How often will the Hitler phenomenon occur? Are there kinds of candidates so poisonous that they should be barred from running for office? Benston offers no approach on this that is different from the usual "soft" noneeconomic arguments of political writers of the past.

Many Americans believe in creationism. They believe that dissemination of that belief is in their self-interest. Shall it be taught in the public schools even though it is false? Although individuals frequently are the best judge of their own interest, are there occasionally? usually? information inequalities and other market failures that call for government intervention in speech? Benston's arguments do not add a new dimension to the resolution of these and numerous other issues on free speech. To encapsulate these familiar arguments with the terms cost and benefit does not advance the debate.

Next, Benston brings in the concept of externalities. This is an example of the fruitful use of established economic theory. The Supreme Court has not been unaware of this. Recall its emphasis on the alleged robustness of commercial speech. This is a recognition that, unlike political speech, arguably, the benefits of commercial speech can be captured commercially. Political speech, the Court pointed out, is allegedly fragile; that is, the speech can be used by free riders, and hence the political speaker captures only a small portion of its commercial value and has less incentive to produce more of it. We have discussed these ideas at length previously.

He emphasizes negative externalites, rather than the positive, or free rider effects, discussed by Posner. For example, he points out that "an unconstrained right could inflict damage on third, noncontracting parties."[114] For example, a speaker criticizes communism. People in the immediate audience can listen to or ignore the speaker, and can disagree with the speaker. The speech, however, can have impact on communists everywhere. Members of the audience may turn against communists wherever they meet them in the future. Since it is difficult to know which speech is correct, Benston argues that negative externalities should not chill political speech. After all, he argues, the possibility exists that communists may be in error. Hence limits on speech may harm society.[115]

He argues that externalities are less in the case of commercial speech. Commercial speech concentrates on reaching consumers of the service or product, who can sue if the product is defective.[116] Hence, he believes the case for restricting commercial speech is weaker, in this respect, than in the case of political speech.

The SEC, as we know, imposes, under appropriate statutes, a structure of mandatory disclosure. In chapter 5 I argue that this is a method of imposing government orthodoxy on financial disclosure. In Benston's piece on the First Amendment he asserts that the "question . . . often is one of costs and benefit rather than the prescription of a government orthodoxy."[117] He asserts that fear of an "imposed orthodoxy" is acceptable only "where there is significant limitation on the expression of alternative or supplementary speech"[118] Absent that, "required disclosure of political, artistic, and commercial speech can be justified."[119]

This is a startling conclusion. It would emasculate most of the restraints that the First Amendment imposes on government. For example, the government could require congressional candidates to "balance out" their speeches. It could require congressional candidates to avoid material omissions. Because the congressional candidate could comment on his required disclosure, or other public figures and newspapers could speak out, the Benston condition of alternative speech is satisfied. This sounds like legitimating proxy-style regulation of political speech. Benston does say that mandatory disclosure could be applied to facts as to which there is little dispute.[120] It is not clear that this is a limit on the alternative speech qualification above. Politicians and businesses never agree as to what important information is beyond dispute. The government would have to make that judgment.

NOTES

1. Posner, *Free Speech in an Economic Perspective*, 20 Suffolk U.L. Rev. 1 (Spring 1986).

2. *Id* at 6, quoting Judge Frank Easterbrook in *American Booksellers Association, Inc. v. Hudnut*, 771 F.2d 323, 328 (7th Cir. 1985), *aff'd without opinion*, 106 S. Ct. 1172 (1986). Judge Easterbrook is another famous scholar of law and economics.

3. Posner at 6.

4. *Id.* at 7.

5. Director, *The Parity of the Economic Market Place*, 7 J. Law & Econ. 1, 3 (1964).

6. *Id.*

7. *Id.*

8. *Id.*

9. *Id.* at 4 See J. Mill, 1 *Dissertations and Discussions*, 377 (1859) and J. Bentham, *Manual of Political Economy*, in 1 J. *Bentham's Economic Writings* 229 (1953).

10. *Id.*

11. *Id.* at 5.

12. *Id.*

13. *Id.*

14. *Id.*

15. *Id.* at 6, quoting Meiklejohn, *Free Speech and Its Relation to Self-Government* 2 (1948).

16. *Id.* at 6.

17. *Id.* at 7.

18. M. Redish, *Freedom of Expression: A Critical Analysis* 19–25 (1984).

19. Director at 7.

20. *Id.* at 8, quoting Knight, *The Planful Act*, in *Freedom and Reform* 349 (1947).

21. *Id.* at 8.

22. *Id.*

23. *Id.* at 8–9.

24. *Id.* at 9, quoting Mill, *On Liberty*, in *Utilitarianism, Liberty and Respresentative Government* 223 (1951).

25. F. Schauer, *Free Speech: A Philosophical Enquiry* 47–72

26. Redish, *supra* note 18 at 17.

27. Coase, *Advertising and Free Speech*, in *Advertising and Free Speech* 12 (A. Hyman and M. Johnson eds. 1977).

28. *Id* at 12.

29. T. Emerson, *Toward a General Theory of the First Amendment* viii (1966).

30. Emerson, *supra* at 6.

31. Coase at 13.

32. *Id.*

33. *Id.*

34. *Id.*

35. *Id.* at 6.

36. *Id.* at 6–7, 11.

37. *Id.* at 4.

38. *Id.* at 10.

39. McChesney, *A Positive Regulatory Theory of the First Amendment* 20 Conn. L. Rev. 355, 360 (1988).

40. *Id.* at 360–61.

41. *Id.* at 360.

42. McChesney, *Commercial Speech in the Professions: The Supreme Court's Unanswered Questions and Questionable Answers*, 134 U. Pa. L. Rev. 45, n. 124 at 69 (1985).

43. *Id.*

44. *Id.* at 45–57.

45. Coase at 8–9.

46. Coase at 18–19.

47. *Id.* at 19.

48. Posner, *Free Speech in an Economic Perspective*, 20 Suffolk U.L. Rev. 1 (1986).

49. *Id.* at 8. Footnotes omitted. The reference to Dennis is *United States v. Dennis*, 183 F.2d 201, 212 (2d Cir. 1950), *aff'd*, 341 U.S. 494 (1951).

50. *See* Posner, *supra* note 1 at 9.

51. *Id.* at 9–12.

52. *Id.* at 19–24, 39–40.

53. See chapter 1.

54. Posner, *supra* note 1 at 19.

55. *Id.* at 19–20.

56. *Id.* at 20.

57. *Id.* at 9–12, 24–29.

58. *Id.* at 40.

59. *Id.* at 22.

60. *Id.*

61. *Id.* at 20.

62. *Id.* at 24–29.

63. *Id.* at 23.

64. *Id.* at 22–23.

65. *Id.* at 22.

66. *See* n. 39, *supra*.

67. *See* Posner, *supra* note 1 at 23.

68. *Id.* at 23.

69. McChesney, *A Postive Regulatory Theory of the First Amendment*, 20 Conn. L. Rev. 355 (1988).

70. Posner, *supra* note 1 at 23.

71. *Id.*

72. Posner, *supra* note 1 at 19–20.

73. Posner, *supra* note 1 at 39–40.

74. *Id.* at 40.

75. *Id.*

76. *Id.*

77. *Id.*

78. *Id.* at 22.

79. *See* McChensney, *supra* note 39 at 377 (footnotes omitted).

80. See chapter 1 at n. 168.

81. *Id.* at n. 171.

82. Posner, *supra* note 1 at 49.

83. F. Schauer, *Free Speech: A Philosophical Enquiry* 47–72 (1982).

84. *See* n. 83, *supra*.

85. Posner, *supra* note 1 at 29.

86. *Id.*

87. *Id.* at 30.

88. McChesney, *supra* note 39.

89. *Id.* at 355–59.

90. *Id.* at 358.

91. *Id.* at 360–61.

92. McChesney has pointed out in an earlier article that an

important source of consumer information about a professional's quality is the reputation the professional has built up through prior services to other clients. Newer attorneys have had less time.... For newcomers, therefore, advertising and other promotion offer more valuable means of communicating their location and availability....

One important result of the promotional bans traditionally imposed by the state bars, then, has been a competitive tilt in favor of larger firms as well as more experienced, higher income lawyers generally.

McChesney, *Commercial Speech in the Professions: The Supreme Court's Unanswered Questions and Questionable Answers*, 134 U. Pa. L. Rev. 45, 90–91 (1985) (footnote omitted).

93. McChesney, *supra* note 39 at 362.

94. *Id.*

95. *Id.* at 363–64.

96. *See* chapter 1.

97. *Id.*

98. McChesney, *supra* note 39 at 373 (footnote omitted).

99. *Id.* at 364–65.

100. See chapter 1.

101. McChesney, *supra* note 39 at 365.

102. *Id.* at 366.

103. *Id.* at 366–67.

104. Crovitz, *The Least Responsive Branch*, 87 Commentary 38 (March 1989).

105. *Id.* at 369.

106. Benston, *Government Constraints on Political, Artistic and Commercial Speech*, 20 Conn. L. Rev. 303 (1988).

107. *Id.* at 306.

108. *Id.*

109. *Id.*

110. *Id.* at 310.

111. *Id.* at 311.

112. *Id.* at 307.

113. *Id.*

114. *Id.* at 311.

115. *Id.* at 313.

116. *Id.* at 308 and 313.

117. *Id.* at 315.

118. *Id.* at 316.

119. *Id.* at 317.

120. *Id.* at 315.

5

The First Amendment and the SEC

DIFFERENCES BETWEEN COMMERCIAL SPEECH AND POLITICAL, ARTISTIC SPEECH

Recap of the Traditional Legal Doctrine

Until fairly recently, in constitutional jurisprudence, what has come to be known as commercial speech had been excluded from the coverage of the First Amendment. Commercial speech, most narrowly construed, is any speech or publication that advertises a product or service for profit or business purposes.[1] Some authorities, however, assert a considerably broader definition of the concept. Commercial speech has been extensively regulated at the state and federal levels. For example, food and drug ads are subject to extensive regulation. The states and the federal government extensively regulate the speech and publications of corporations and other business entities.

The modern commercial speech doctrine began in 1942 with the *Valentine v. Chrestensen* case.[2] In that litigation a businessman in New York City disseminated a leaflet that on one side advertised a business exhibition of a former navy submarine and on the other side contained a purportively po-

Portions of this chapter appeared in an earlier version in an article by the author entitled *The First Amendment and the SEC*, in 20 Conn. L. Rev. 265 (1988). The earlier materials have been extensively revised, reorganized, and rewritten for this book. The article was originally written for a Liberty Fund, Inc. conference on October 30–November 2, 1986. I thank the Law Review and the Liberty Fund for permission to use the materials in this book. The Liberty Fund conference was creatively administered by the Law and Economics Center of George Mason University.

litical critique of the municipality's refusal to grant wharfage facilities for the show. The defendant was convicted of violating a statute banning the dissemination of advertisements in the streets. In upholding the conviction the Supreme Court stated:

This court has unequivocally held that the streets are proper places for the exercise of the freedom of communicating information and disseminating opinion and that though the states and municipalities may appropriately regulate the privilege in the public interest, they may not unduly burden or proscribe its employment in these public thoroughfares. *We are equally clear that the Constitution imposes no such restraint on government as respects purely commercial advertising.*[3]

This decision was always read to exclude commercial speech (even where incidently enriched by a political message) from the protections of the First Amendment. In a series of decisions beginning in the midseventies, the Court reversed itself and introduced limited First Amendment protection to commercial speech. For example, in *Virginia State Board of Pharmacy v. Virginia Citizens Consumer Council, Inc.*[4] the Court protected from prior restraint the advertisement of prescription drug prices. In *Linmark Associates, Inc. v. Town of Willingboro*[5] the Court held that a city may not prohibit by ordinance the posting of "For Sale" or "Sold" signs despite the municipality's purpose to chill white flight of homeowners from a racially integrated area. The Court always emphasized that because of the supposed robustness of commercial speech, and the assumed relative ease of verification, the First Amendment protection would be far more limited than political or artistic speech. For example, courts have always held that potentially misleading commercial speech could be restrained by governmental regulation.

In *Central Hudson Gas & Electric Corporation v. Public Service Commission*[6] the Court struck down a public utility regulation banning public utility advertising promoting the use of electricity. The state utility commission had maintained that the ads violated the national goal of preserving energy. The Court applied the following four-part test for commercial speech:

At the outset, we must determine whether the expression is protected by the First Amendment. For commercial speech to come within that provision, it at least must concern lawful activity and not be misleading. Next, we ask whether the asserted government interest is substantial. If both inquiries yield positive answers, we must determine whether the regulation directly advances the governmental interest asserted, and whether it is not more extensive than is necesssary to serve that interest.[7]

The Court concluded that the complete ban on the ads was more pervasive regulation than necessary to satisfy the public policy of preserving energy.

In 1989 the Court directly construed the meaning of the fourth prong of that test. It rejected the "least restrictive means" interpretation. As the Court put it:

"In sum while we have insisted that "the free flow of commercial information is valuable enough to justify imposing on would-be regulators the costs of distinguishing . . . the harmless from the harmful," *Shapero*, 486 U.S., at—, quoting *Zauderer*, 471 U.S., at 646, we have not gone so far as to impose upon them the burden of demonstrating that the distinguishment is 100% complete, or that the manner of restriction is absolutely the least severe that will achieve the desired end. What our decisions require is a " 'fit' between the legislature's ends and the means chosen to accomplish those ends," *Posadas*, 478 U.S. at 341—a fit that is not necessarily perfect, but reasonable; that represents not necessarily the single best disposition but one whose scope is in "proportion to the interest served," *In re R.M.J.*, *supra* at 203; that employs not necessarily the least restrictive means, but, as we have put it in the other contexts discussed above, a means narrowly tailored to achieve the desired objective.[8]

The courts and commentators are far from unanimous in defining the contours of commercial speech.[9] There are some who assert that such speech includes any publication or speech that is primarily, or perhaps solely, related to the economic self-interest of the speaker or his audience and the implementation of a commercial action. They would emphatically not limit the definition to product or service advertisements. Obviously much turns on the exact definition of the doctrine.

Although a completely satisfactory definition of commercial speech may be elusive, everyone agrees that it certainly includes advertising of a product or service for purposes of profit. For example, the salesperson who hypes shaving cream is engaged in commercial speech. However, the political philosopher who hypes socialism in a book for large royalties is uttering protected First Amendment noncommercial speech. The government, under certain circumstances, can lawfully restrain even truthful shaving cream advertisements before they are published or spoken.[10] With respect to truthful speech, the regulatory agency must follow the *Central Hudson* test set forth above.[11] The government can civilly or criminally punish the huckster after the fact if the ad is fraudulent.[12] The political philosopher is in a different league. The government cannot engage in prior restraint of the political message. Further, the government cannot successfully prosecute the political philosopher on the grounds that his statements are false.

The Purposes Served by the First Amendment: Commercial Speech Compared with Fully Protected Speech

One popular rationale for the difference between the limited protections of commercial speech and the greater protection of political speech, or for that matter for a position that would deny any First Amendment protection to commercial speech, is the crucial role political speech, as distinguished from commercial speech, plays in the free democratic society.[13] Political speech is essential for the workings of a free democratic society. Almost by definition democracy entails the conflict and contest among competing political parties and ideas. For that to work, unfettered political expression is necessary.

Some have argued that the only purpose intended to be served by the First Amendment is to aid the democratic political process, sometimes defined as a kind of New England town meeeting.[14] Professor Robert Bork, in a famous article, argued that no speech, including artistic, not advancing a political goal, is constitutionally protected.[15] These positions, at least under a narrow construction, that would exclude artistic and scientific speech have been rejected by many commentators and all the courts. They unacceptably deprive us of protection for most speech, except campaign utterances. They certainly appear to rest on dubious and narrow assumptions about the nature of the political process. They disregard the learning, on the right, of interest group theory and, on the left, of Marxist analysis, and in the center the commonsense of journalists and the rest of us, about the inextricable interplay of the economic, artistic, financial, and political.

A second reason, often suggested, is that unfettered competition among differing political ideals will ultimately lead to the truth. The free market in ideas will finally winnow out falsehood.[16] Truth in politics or art, unlike in the commercial realm, is not easy to achieve. Truth will emerge only after a sometimes lengthy process of debate and intellectual confrontation. The government bureaucrat, by fiat or command, cannot, or out of bias will not, determine the relative truthfulness of contrasting political or artistic ideas. She is able, it is asserted, to perform that function with respect to commercial speech. Therefore, the free competition among ideas, in Justice Holmes' famous marketplace of ideas, is a better process for arriving at political truth than is government dictation.

A third reason often advanced is that free speech in the political and artistic worlds (but not the commercial arena) is important for the growth and flowering of the human personality.[17] This argument from the values of self-expression extends to the listener or the disseminator of the speech. In this sense, free speech is related to the ideal of privacy or autonomy. Each person should be free to express himself or herself in speech or writing, or to receive without restriction information and opinions and artistic messages.

Commercial speech, particularly in its clearest mode (i.e., the advertisement of services or products), does not, in the opinion of many scholarly commentators, fall within the intendment of one or more of these reasons.

Let us initially take up the third goal, that of self-expression of listener or transmitter. The Supreme Court has emphasized that advertisements impart information and opinion to the consumer. Only if we engage in a kind of invidious content discrimination, and denigrate the content value of advertisements, as compared with the content value of campaign speeches and trivial novels, can we escape the conclusion that ads contribute to the personal edification of the listener.

Take the mundane sale of shampoo and the shampoo advertisement. A shampoo ad is unqualifiedly commercial speech. The shampoo advertisement, however, is an idea or concept as well as a description of a collection of chemicals. It embodies a particular culture's idea of personal hygiene and beauty and the expression (albeit non-profound—there goes my personal bias) of the human personality. The countercultural hippie of the 1960s no doubt would scoff at the idea of beautifying hair shampoo as a bourgeoisie conceit. Conceits of the middleclass, however, need protection of the First Amendment, just as do notions of the (self-described) elite.

Manufacturers of shampoo and hair conditioners sell not just an aggregate of chemicals. They sell a particular concept of beauty and cleanliness. Some may ridicule the intellectual weight of the hair shampoo idea, but that very ridicule represents an artistic and cultural judgment. For example, in another realm of discourse, music, some may advocate rock music and some may deem it garbage, but most would grant the music full First Amendment protection.

Certainly we cannot base a distinction between the advertisement of shampoo and the dissemination of a political or artistic idea on the absence or presence of the profit motive. In that regard, consider the following series of thought experiments. Harold Kasofsky authors a book extolling the merits of ABC shampoo. The Macmillan Publishing Company publishes the book. Harold and the publisher both have a clear and direct economic interest in the success of the book. It appears clear, however, that the government cannot engage in prior restraint or censorship of the book, or in criminal prosecution after the publication. (I assume in this example that Harold has no financial interest in the shampoo company.) I would think that if the government could restrain publication of the book on the grounds that the book is false, we would have opened a vast breach in First Amendment protection of political and artistic speech. For example, take a novel in which a much admired hero uses and extols the virtues of ABC shampoo. Should the government be able to restrain, in advance, the publication on the grounds that the shampoo leaves the hair a mess? As we like to say, to ask the question is to answer it.

But consider Macmillan ads promoting sales of the book. That appears to fit the definition of commercial speech. Yet if we permit prior restraint of the ad, we have in effect almost succeeded in prior restraint of the book in the sense that it will be difficult to sell it by word of mouth.

Remember that the strongest (i.e., least controversial) definition of commercial speech is the advertisement of a product or a service for sale. In modern society, however, it is virtually impossible to promote ideas unless the promoter of the idea can in some way commercially merchandise the concept. Traditional political speech is always an ad for an idea.

For example, consider a political science professor who, based on his serious research, wants to extol the virtues of tougher antimerger laws. He can chat about it at a party given at his house. Obviously that is an absurdly ineffectual method. He can write a widely read book. That is an effective method, but it entails the sale *by him* of a product (i.e., a book for profit) and the sale of that book by a *commercial publisher*. He can hit the lecture circuit if he is well known. There he can give speeches for a fee to promote his idea. In all those cases he is selling an idea for a fee. Unless we agree that we can distinguish between advertising ideas and products, his material is nothing more than commercial speech.

Now let us consider the argument that political speech is necessary for the success of the democratic system. Commercial speech, it is asserted, does not meet that noble purpose. Debate on socialism versus capitalism, conservatism versus liberalism, and the like, it is argued, is the warp and woof of democratic discourse and struggle. The selling of shampoo is ignoble trade. Government can ban the advertising of shampoo, where such advertising has the tendency to be fraudulent, without impairing the quality of democracy.

The argument based on democracy succeeds only by a tortured definition of the term. If we define the democratic process as campaign speeches by politicians running for office, and limit unfettered First Amendment protection only to that speech, we reach an unnaturally constrained result. Obviously we have to open up the definition to reach everyone in society who wants to comment on the political debate. Moreover, the debate frequently centers on economic interests of business or labor. Further, we cannot limit comment to the issues raised by the elected politicians. Every member of society must have the freedom to attempt to express his definition of the issues in the political process.

Assume that the ABC Shampoo Company desires a sharp tax break for its shampoo business. Further, it wants a decrease in food and drug regulation of its product. Also, it wants to eliminate government regulation of its product ads. There is no doubt under the current state of the law that the government cannot prevent spokespersons for the company from writing articles and giving speeches (so long as they are not in reality advertisements for a product) promoting the changes.[18] They are self-interested in the proposals, but surely self-interest cannot be a bar. That would limit debate to saints, and in a world of saints we do not need a democracy, only the rule of God. We cannot bar or censor their speeches and ads because they involve an economic or commercial subject. That would limit free debate to theological issues only.

The courts, however, assert that the shampoo ad itself is commercial speech. How does the ad differ from the corporate campaign to cut shampoo business taxes and eliminate regulation of the product, including the elimination of regulation of the ads? The difference is scarcely obvious. Some have argued that the ad is an element of the contract of sale.[19] A misrepresentation of fact would involve a violation of the contract, and basic contract law is somehow immune from usual First Amendment principle. Of course, that argument assumes the answer. The issue is whether ads (i.e., a kind of speech), even if deemed part of a contract, can be censored or otherwise regulated. At that point we are back to the issue of the policy difference, if any, between ads and so-called political speech.

Justice Brennan has forcefully pointed out that economic or commercial speech is an essential part of the political process:

Speech about commercial or economic matters, even if not directly implicating "the central meaning of the First Amendment," ... is an important part of our public discourse. ... As *Thornhill* suggests, the choices we make when we step into the voting booth may well be the products of what we have learned from the myriad of daily economic and social phenomenon that surround us.[20]

A major rationale for the First Amendment (in the realm of politics and science, albeit fiercely criticized in the scholarly literature)[21] is the free marketplace-of-ideas concept. The free clash of ideas will lead to the truth. Related to that is the rationale that truth in ideas is elusive and not easily ascertainable by the government bureaucrat. Indeed, he may not want the truth if it will harm his selfish bureaucratic interests. In this sense of the First Amendment there is an obvious similarity between the free market of the economist and the Oliver Wendell Holmes sense of the free market in ideas.[22] Both involve a laissez-faire attitude to the world. Indeed, Ronald Coase has pointed out the identity between the two concepts and argued, therefore, for a similarity in treatment between product ads and political ideas.[23] He has asserted that the realm of political and artistic ideas is the business of the intellectual. The latter promotes the First Amendment to protect his business. The intellectual, however, denigrates the usefulness of the world of the businessman, and hence argues for a lesser protection under the First Amendment for product ads and whatever might be deemed merely commercial speech.

Let us evaluate the argument that free speech produces the truth. In certain senses this appears valid. The free pursuit of the scientific method, untrammeled by government censorship, will produce truth in the fields of physics, biology, chemistry, and the like. Even there the process is long, painful, and sometimes quite messy. The process is less obvious in certain artistic and political realms. Popular results may be achieved, but that is merely a definitional statement if we presume the majority vote democratic process. For example, many thinkers believe that the welfare system in modern liberal capitalist societies is a disaster, but the system persists.[24] This does not prove that their view is correct or incorrect. Indeed, each opposition party passionately believes that their election defeat is a grievous blow against the truth as well as other values. Thus Democratic party activists (who admire the welfare system) argue that the Republican party victories at the national level are catastrophes for the causes of truth, equality, and justice. But I need not belabor the point. Some may argue that in the long run the truth will emerge. There is no empirical evidence for that Pollyannish point of view. In any event, in the short run, which may last for decades, considerable harm may ensue. A famous example is the electoral victory of the Nazis in Germany in the early 1930s.

It is often argued that the falsity or truth of a product ad is far more easily ascertainable than artistic or political speech. If the shampoo ad asserts that Whiz Shampoo preserves a bouncy look for the entire day, then government chemists can verify the claim or disprove it. (Even there, much may depend on the subjective notion of "bouncy.") Hence, it is argued, censorship of the ad, or punishment for its publication, should be permissible in certain cases. In certain instances this claim has some limited validity. There may be various product claims that can be easily verified or disproved by government bureaucrats. There are many claims, however, that are not easily verifiable. The artificial heart (when introduced into the market) is an example. Scientific dispute about the state of the art is acute and vigorous. The argument approaches, and frequently passes beyond, the border of so-called fact into the realm of delicate judgment and value-balancing. The same is true in the so-called realm of the political.

Some political claims are clearly false. For example, the political argument by some that the Nazi holocaust against the Jews is a fiction is indisputably false. Yet few would argue that the First Amendment does not protect the right of Americans in the United States to advertise or publicize the loathsome lie. The rationale is the slippery slope thesis. If the government is permitted to censor in one area, albeit obvious, it will soon act to censor the truth when it harms the government.

There are other political positions that many experts take to be false. For example, most professional economists would agree about the general evils of protectionism.[25] Nonetheless, they would agree (at least on advice of counsel) that the First Amendment permits fools, as they see it, to make fallacious arguments in favor of protectionism. It is not clear why apparently false product ads, however, should be censored. In many instances false political ideas (e.g., racism) can cause immeasurably greater harm than a false product ad; yet the former are protected by the full strength of the First Amendment. For example, the appeasement doctrines in Great Britain in the 1930s led to disaster for the country in World War II. Yet most would assert the need for First Amendment protection of such nonsense. Indeed, the argument is frequently made that it is only false or grotesque speech that needs protection, since other kinds of speech will not need it.

During the past few decades a voluminous literature has developed about the harmful effects of government economic regulation.[26] Such studies demonstrate that it is not enough to measure a free-market approach against some ideal of government regulation. It is important, rather, to compare the free market, imperfect as it may be, with the costs of imperfect government regulation. In that comparison, government regulation is often found seriously wanting. Further, in many cases it is hardly clear that government regulation actually does improve things. One thing is constant, however; regulation almost always restrains free choice of groups and individuals. Therefore, it is doubtful that product ad regulation will invariably or even usually benefit the consumer or the public. Because there is a growing body of evidence that product ad regulation may be more harmful than previously imagined, the balance in favor of affording such speech full First Amendment protection shifts.[27]

The direct and indirect costs of political censorship are frequently cited. That is, censorship, even though it occasionally will stop a blatantly false and dangerous idea, will cost too much in lost human autonomy and the disasters that might result from mistaken governmental action. Government restraint chills individual freedoms and is fallible. Hence the fundamental decision is made in favor of laissez-faire in political and, likewise, in artistic speech. The same argument would seem to be indicated for commercial speech. For example, federal restraint of drug advertising and sales has, according to some convincing research, actually caused more harm than good.[28] It has chilled the development and sale of valuable drugs that would have saved many lives.

The argument is often made that commercial speech (i.e., product ads) is difficult to chill by government censorship. This is the robustness argument of economists.[29] Put simply, the contention is that the commercial interest is great enough to withstand the costs of government restraint. It is further asserted that proponents of political speech are comparatively easy to intimidate by government action. This is an empirical proposition that is debatable. We have considered this issue at length in chapter 4. The timidity of businessmen is often noted. The tenacity of committed political activists, on the other hand, is a common phenomenon. It is most plausible indeed to assert the exact opposite. That is, regulation of political speech will tend to chill less than restraint of commercial speech.

Some Concluding Remarks on Commercial Speech

I have mentioned that the definition of commercial speech, narrowly construed, includes only product or service advertisements. Some have argued for a broader definition that encompasses speech closely connected to economic self-interest. The latter definition is, as much of the preceding discussion indicates, too broad. Much of political or artistic speech directly or indirectly involves economic interest. Political issues such as protection versus free trade, tax policy, and agricultural programs are debated by groups with a vested interest in the issue. If we barred economic greed, we would exclude much of so-called political speech from the full protection of the First Amendment.

In conclusion, the distinction between commercial and noncommercial speech doesn't have much of a foundation in policy or logic. We have established, at the very least, that whatever commercial speech may be, it cannot turn on economic self-interest, robustness, ease of verification, or commercial greed. However, even if there is a significant distinction, which I do not concede, between the most naked of advertisements for a product or a service and political speech, the federal securities laws (which we discuss in the balance of this chapter) restrain corporate speech that more closely approaches fully protected speech than traditionally defined commercial speech. *The federal securities laws regulate speech that is impossible to meaningfully distinguish from speech that all of us would concede should receive the full protection of the First Amendment.*

SEC SPEECH: PRELIMINARY CONSIDERATIONS

SEC Speech—Mandatory Disclosure versus Outright Prohibition

We must, at this point, consider the differences between mandatory disclosure requirements and outright prohibitions on speech. For example, the Investment Advisers Act of 1940, as interpreted by the Securities and Exchange Commission (SEC) for the past few decades (until the Supreme Court disagreed), forbade the dissemination of investment letters unless the investment adviser was first registered with the SEC.[30] The SEC contended that if the investment adviser's registration is rejected or revoked, as is permitted under the Act, because of specified prior misconduct, then no market letter, however truthful, may be disseminated. (We discuss the recent Supreme Court new treatment of this act below.) On the other hand, corporate proxy statements and prospectuses may be published and disseminated (without licensing of the corporation), provided they satisfy certain SEC disclosure mandates.[31] In both instances the government engages in a form of prior restraint.[32] The question is whether the two cases entail the same legal inquiry under the First Amendment. The Supreme Court, to date, has indicated that there are significant differences between disclosure requirements and outright prohibitions on speech. In the *Zauderer vs. Office of Disciplinary Council* case the Court asserted that although it "has not attempted to prescribe what shall be orthodox in politics, nationalism, religion, or other matters of opinion . . . [it has permitted prescription of] what shall be orthodox in commercial advertising."[33] The Supreme Court reasoned that "the extension of First Amendment protection to commercial speech is justified principally by the value to consumers of the information such speech provides."[34] In this regard, the Court asserted that it would not subject mandatory disclosure requirements to the *Central Hudson* strict, "least restrictive means" test pursuant to "which they must be struck down if there are other means by which the States' purposes may be served."[35] Hence SEC mandatory disclosure would, under this analysis, be subject to a less rigorous test than the four part *Central Hudson* test.

The attempted distinction between mandatory disclosure and outright prohibition cannot survive analysis. The giveaway is the Court's statement that although the government cannot proscribe orthodoxy in politics, it can do so in commercial advertising. It is indeed true that a regime of mandatory disclosures will create government *orthodoxy* in whatever field, including commercial advertising, the government invades.

The evils of mandatory disclosure in the political and artistic domains are clear enough. The mischief inherent in the government's power to "correct" disclosures before publication is identical to the mischief inherent in its power to issue a blanket prior bar. Government censors, by the use of disclosure requirements, can gut arguments with which they disagree and tip the dialectical balance irretrievably in the direction they favor. Consider the debate in the summer of 1985 on the White House flat tax proposals.[36] Career bureaucratic government censors, who are hostile to the White House position, could, under an SEC-type disclosure statute, require "disclosure" that the proposal unduly favors the wealthy, gives little comfort to the poor, and harms the middle class. Different government censors, favorable to the proposal, might require their Democratic opponents to "disclose" that the White House tax bill will maximize incentive, assist the poor, and benefit the middle class. These examples can be multiplied endlessly. They simply illustrate that in political or artistic debate, truth is often in the eye of the partisan beholder.

The same obnoxious result can occur in SEC financial disclosures. For decades the SEC required disclosure of historical "hard" data. It forbade the disclosure of so-called soft projection data about predictions of future earnings and budgets.[37] Yet the futuristic "soft" data were crucial to an informed evaluation of investments. This mandatory disclosure structure led to a defective system of disclosure that frustrated investors and distorted the financial truth.[38] The moral here, as in the political area, is clear; in technical-financial disclosures, as in political speech, the government's power to require specific disclosure is the power to mandate the government's version of proper *orthodoxy*. That power interferes with all of the various values the First Amendment is presumed to advance. It interferes with the free market's pursuit of truth because governments have no monopoly on that precious commodity, and indeed frequently have an interest in suppressing it. Government-mandated disclosure stifles the receipt by investors of information, and hence interferes with personal development and freedom. Government-mandated disclosure also harms the political-democratic process, since it imposes government orthodoxy in important economic and financial areas of a supposedly free society. In short, the government's power to mandate specified disclosure possesses to an identical degree and kind the evils that all of us recognize in outright prohibition.

SEC Speech: Distinguished from Commercial Speech

We have established in the previous chapters that commercial speech, as used in the courts, usually is defined as an advertisement of a product or service for business purposes. It may include a wider variety of economically centered speech. But the wider and more inclusive the definition, the greater is the difficulty in distinguishing commercial speech, so liberally defined, from fully protected speech, however the latter is defined.

As we have noted, some economists distinguish commercial speech from political speech by the presence or absence of externalities. Speech in the form of an advertisement for a product or a service seems not to be affected by complexities of external benefits.[39] Most of the "benefits" of advertising particular goods or services are captured by the seller of the products.[40] Hence commercial speech is robust and not easily chilled by regulation. The amount of such speech is not underproduced, as a result of the absence of free riders capturing the benefit of the speech. Political speech, however, it is argued, is underproduced.[41] Property rights in such speech are diffuse and undeveloped. Therefore, disseminators are less than amply rewarded, and free riders can reproduce the speech without penalty. Accordingly, some argue that the First Amendment is necessary to facilitate some production of that fragile product. But the government cannot require it or censor it or regulate its content, since that would create a government orthodoxy of thought that is repugnant to First Amendment philosophy. Moreover, some argue that the government can more easily distinguish truth from falsity in the area of commercial speech than in the area of political speech.[42] These arguments of economists have been endorsed by the Supreme Court in many opinions. Consequently, all other matters kept equal, there are, it is asserted, good reasons for applying the protections of the First Amendment to political speech in more ample form than to commercial speech.

We have analyzed these arguments in detail in chapter 4. We shall review these arguments in the SEC context below. These distinctions of economists do not serve to distinguish SEC-regulated speech from political speech, or to conflate it with commercial speech, as traditionally defined in the courts.

In the *SEC v. Wall Street Publishing Institute, Inc.* case (see chapter 2) the court declined to apply the definition of commercial speech to speech involving the purchase and sale of securities. Nevertheless, it developed a theory that speech relating to economic transactions, such as sale of securities and taxation, was subject to governmental power on a scale at least as great as is the case with commercial speech. We have had occasion to criticize this extension of government power in chapter 2. The court, however, recognized that the speech regulated by the commission is obviously different in a significant sense from the advertisement of a product or a service. A toothpaste corporation advertises toothpaste. That is traditional commercial speech. A publicly held toothpaste corporation is the scene of a vigorous battle between contending shareholder groups for power in the organization. The groups disseminate messages to shareholders. That is proxy speech. But as we shall demonstrate soon, that is speech about the governance of a corporation, not the advertisement of a product or a service. It is speech that is political in a traditional sense (i.e., speech about who shall govern). It is about complex financial and economic issues that government cannot easily verify as to truth or falsity. It is also speech that in one form or another corporations will voluntarily supply because of the economic advantages to the corporation in doing so.

The toothpaste corporation may be the subject of a hostile takeover. The commission regulates the disclosure statements of bidder and target corporations. This, like the proxy campaign, is a conflict over control. In that sense it is like proxy battles, similar to traditional political campaigns. The difference is that the subject of the struggle for power is a corporation, not a political agency or department.

The toothpaste corporation may sell securities to the public to raise capital. The purchasers become "owners" of the organization. Even the purchasers of debt securities become important stakeholders in the organization with rights, frequently, as to direction of the business or financial structure. Corporate speech about the transaction in the form of prospectuses and registration statements is entirely different from the traditional advertisement of toothpaste. It is more akin to the enrollment of members in an organization.

Corporations issue periodic statements about financial and business news. The SEC regulates the content and periodicity of such information. For example, corporations are circumscribed with respect to their ability to time the announcements of ending merger negotiations. This speech, again, is not an advertisement for a product or a service. It is information about an organization that is of use to its members (i.e., shareholders and noteholders) and of use to prospective shareholders.

All of the speech regulated by the SEC is potentially complex, subject to different interpretations by experts, and essentially difficult to verify because of the financial subtleties involved. All of it is directly or indirectly related to the governance of publicly held corporations. It is speech vastly different from commercial speech as traditionally defined.

ANALYSIS OF VARIETIES OF SEC-REGULATED SPEECH

Proxy Speech

Judge Tamm, in a famous opinion on proxy regulation stated that "it is obvious to the point of banality to restate the proposition that Congress intended by its enactment of section 14 of the Securities Exchange Act of 1934 to give true vitality to the concept of shareholder democracy."[43]

The judge then referred to the legislative history:

Even those who in former days managed great corporations were by reason of their personal contacts with their shareholders constantly aware of their responsibilities. But as management became divorced from ownership and came under the control of banking groups, men forgot that they were dealing with the savings of men and the making of profits became an impersonal thing. When men do not know the victims of their aggression they are not always conscious of their wrongs. . . .

Fair corporate suffrage is an important right that should attach to every equity security brought on a public exchange. Managements of properties owned by the investing public should not be permitted to perpetuate themselves by the misuse of corporate proxies.[44]

The commission has attempted to implement this mandate by developing proxy rules that require detailed disclosure of the matters proposed for action at shareholder meetings. It has also promulgated Rule 14a–8 requiring corporations at corporate expense to include certain shareholder proposals in the corporate proxy statement.[45] The commission has, to date, excluded shareholder proposals to nominate candidates for the board of directors from this cost-free privilege.[46] Shareholders, of course, are free to solicit at their own expense proxies for any valid corporate purpose, subject to the proxy regulations on required disclosure.[47]

Proxy Regulation as Control of Corporate Governance

Proxy regulation, then, rests on the notion of maximizing democracy for shareholders in the corporation. Commission regulation covers shareholder policy proposals as well as contested elections of directorial slates. In both instances the basic pattern of regulation is fairly constant. Corporate management, or the insurgent shareholder group, in the case of elections, is required to file detailed disclosure documents with the commission. Many of such filings must be made before transmission to the public shareholders. The staff reviews the materials for purposes of evaluating the truth or falsehood of the materials. If the staff believes the material to be misleading, it will go to a federal district court to enjoin the proxy disclosure. Under a recent statutory amendment it may proceed administratively against the offending material and the person who wrote it.

Naturally the process would not withstand the usual First Amendment scrutiny in the case of political contests. In fact, no statute that required congressional candidates to clear the content of their speeches in advance (or subsequent to delivery) with the SEC would withstand constitutional attack. Yet the purpose of the commission proxy regulation is to promote democracy in the governance of corporations. Let us consider if, on proper analysis, this is permissible regulation, even within the orthodox legal concept, and not forbidden restraint of fully protected speech.

Assume that Virtue Inc. is a publicly held publishing corporation. The management and board of directors are currently dominated by Harold Victorian, the chief executive officer, who believes in the moral necessity of publishing ethically uplifting romances. Under his direction the corporation publishes only novels that eschew sexually explicit content and promotes only happy endings for the good guys and gals and bad endings for the evil characters. To date, this concept of morality has resulted in smashing economic success for the shareholders. Recently, however, earnings have begun to trend downward. An insurgent group of shareholders wants to elect a new group of directors who will reverse the aesthetic judgments of Harold and select sexually salacious novels. Both groups file proxy materials with the SEC, as they are required to do. The SEC staff evaluates their contrasting aesthetic and economic claims. Perhaps the Harold group writes that ethically "pure" books are better literature. The SEC staff will, no doubt, request additional proxy material, admitting that many critics deplore the literary values of latter-day Victorian prudery. The reader can imagine other SEC censorious edicts that might ensue. The point is that federal proxy rules permit an intrusuion into what appears to be a political and artistic process.

Assume now that Virtue, Inc. publishes a book by Professor So-and-So devoted to the theme that a return to some Victorian modesty in the novel will be a literary improvement to be devoutly prayed for. Assuredly, no government censor could lawfully require the book to be prefiled (or postfiled) with the SEC for review and comment. Yet, if distributed as proxy material, it is deemed to be of different constitutional texture.

The usual rationale for SEC regulation (except for the *SEC v. Wall Street Publishing Institute* case) of the proxy materials is that they deal with commercial speech (see chapter 2). Shareholders invest in the corporation. They make intelligent governance decisions to hold or sell only if, *inter alia*, proxy regulation provides them with truthful information. Although governance decisions usually may be made for economic investment reasons, there is a difference between ordinary purchase decisions and the process of corporate governance. The latter requires shareholder choices that affect employees, communities, and fellow shareholders. This is governance, not merely a share or product purchase decision.

Shareholder democracy is supposed to facilitate the shareholder control and management of a business in which each shareholder has invested. This is clearly a different process than a product advertisement. The latter is traditionally defined as commercial speech. Yet even such ads are not easily differentiated from fully protected speech. But, governance of a corporation is surely different from an advertisement. It is true that the shareholders' interest in the corporation is primarily economic. However, the citizens' interest in the polity also is, to a considerable extent, economic. Yet the First

Amendment protects the citizens' speech. Because much of American life
revolves around and is affected by the modern corporation, it would seem
that shareholders and management should enjoy the strong version of First
Amendment protection in their speech dealing with the governance of that
significant element in Amercian life.

The First Amendment also recognizes the freedom of individuals to associate, to govern their own organizations, and to control their membership,
free of interference by the government. This freedom is based on the First
Amendment right of free expression. Any governmental interference must
prove a compelling state interest for the restriction. The Court has distinguished between organizations that are primarily expressive in nature, and
those that are commercial. Hence it maintains the right of the government,
for example, to interfere in the internal governance of the business corporation. By now, however, it must be apparent that it is inherently impossible
to distinguish between the political and the economic, at least in speech that
is not merely an advertisement for a specific product or service. Most political
organizations have economic interests that they pursue on behalf of the
membership. It appears unduly artificial to distinguish business corporations
from bar associations, or real estate trade groups, or chiropodist associations,
all of whom, directly or indirectly, lobby legislators for their economic advantage.

The Bellotti and Austin Cases—Corporate External Political Speech

In our further analysis we are going to do the following. First, we explore
the Supreme Court doctrine on corporate external political free speech, as
distinguished from internal or proxy speech. We demonstrate that the two
kinds of speech cannot be meaningfully distinguished. We explore in that
regard the rights of minority shareholders to express their opinions. Next,
we analyze the complexity of proxy disclosure. In that context we demonstrate
the inability of government to easily differentiate truth from falsehood. We
explore the government tendency to establish a prevailing orthodoxy on
disclosure that is not neccssarily married to truth or lack of bias. We discuss
the fragility or robustness of proxy speech. We close with an analysis of the
role of the free market in gathering and disseminating information.

In *First National Bank of Boston v. Bellotti*[48] a Massachusetts statute prohibited certain corporations from making expenditures "for the purpose of
. . . influencing or affecting the vote on any question submitted to the voters,
other than one materially affecting any of the property, business or assets of
the corporation."[49] The statute specified that "[n]o question submitted to the
voters solely concerning the taxation of the income, property or transactions
of individuals shall be deemed materially to affect the property, business or
assets of the corporation."[50]

The corporate appellants wanted to spend money to state their opinions opposing a proposed constitutional amendment to impose a graduated income tax on individuals. The attorney general of Massachusetts stated that he would enforce the statute against them. The corporations brought the action to have the statute declared unconstitutional.

Justice Powell, speaking for the Court, stated that press corporations do "not have a monopoly on either the First Amendment or the ability to enlighten."[51] Further, the prior cases granting First Amendment rights to press corporations (which appellants were not) are based not only on the speakers' rights to self-expression, but also on the public's right to "discussion, debate and the dissemination of information and ideas.' "[52] This approach differs from the argument of Baker that emphasizes the allegedly coercive profit-seeking imperatives of the corporate speaker.[53]

The Court emphasized that its commercial speech cases also are based on the "societal" interest in the "free flow of commercial information,"[54] not the interest of the seller in his business.[55] Ironically, the statute would free up corporate speech directly pertaining to business, but restrict speech of a political nature. Yet the commercial speech doctrine gives lesser protection to commercial speech than to political speech.

Next, the Court points out that the legislature is prevented from "dictating the subjects about which persons may speak and the speakers who may address a public issue."[56] Hence the government cannot restrict corporations to discuss only their business.[57] This traditional explication of First Amendment doctrine indicates that the Court might take a dim view of Massachusetts efforts in the future to impose disclosure requirements on the speech in question, as distinguished from the flat ban in question in the case.

The Court considered two possible justifications for the ban on corporate speech. One was the alleged overwhelming influence and power of the corporations. The Court distinguished referenda on issues from campaigns for candidates. Hence it was able to distinguish statutes such as the Federal Corrupt Practices Act that banned certain corporate contributions to political candidates.[58] The Court argued that contributions to corporate-sponsored candidates created the possibility of corruption of elected officials through the "creation of political debts."[59]

Further, the Court asserted that there had been no proof that the speech of corporations in Massachusetts had been "overwhelming" in its influence.[60] Moreover, the Court emphasized that the Constitution "protects expression which is eloquent no less than that which is unconvincing."[61] The Court cited at this point *Miami Herald Publishing Co. v. Tornillo*, where it held that the First Amendment "prohibits a State from requiring a newspaper to make space available at no cost for a reply from a candidate whom the newspaper has criticized."[62]

Appellee argued that the state had an interest in protecting the rights of corporate shareholders who might disagree with the positions of the corporate management.[63] The Court questioned this supposed purpose because of the overinclusiveness and underinclusiveness of the statute.[64] That is, it permitted corporations, for example, to spend funds on speaking out against legislation as distinguished from referendum. This suggested that the state was interested in chilling speech on certain topics, not in protecting share- holders. Also, it prohibited corporate action on the latter even if all of the shareholders supported it. But in the final analysis, the Court argued that "shareholders may decide, through the procedures of corporate democracy, whether their corporation should engage in debate on public issues."[65] Fur- ther, shareholders have the judicial remedy of a derivative action to challenge improper corporate expenditures. The Court responded to Justice White, dissenting, who argued that union members in closed or agency shops may not be compelled to make union dues payments for political purposes with which they disagreed. Justice Powell emphasized that "no shareholder has been 'compelled' to contribute anything. ... [T]he shareholder invests in a corporation of his own volition and is free to withdraw his investment at any time and for any reason."[66] Therefore, even assuming that protection of shareholders is a "compelling" interest,[67] the Court found no "substantially relevant correlation between the government interest asserted and the State's effort" to ban the speech.[68]

Although Justice Powell doesn't discuss the difference between definitions of commercial and political, the difficulty of the distinction in the corporate setting is evident in this case. It is inherently incoherent to distinguish protec- tion of external corporate political speech from internal proxy commercial speech. The corporations argued for the inadvisability of a graduated income for individuals. They believed that the adoption of the tax would "materially affect their business in a variety of ways,"[69] such as "discouraging highly qual- ified executives ... from settling ... in Massachusetts ... and tending to shrink the disposable income of individuals available for the purchase of the consumer products manufactured by at least one of the plaintif corporations."[70]

Now assume an internal corporate struggle over the inadvisability or ad- visability of opposing the tax legislation. The SEC proxy regulations would apply if the corporations' securities involved met the definitions in the proxy statute and the regulations thereunder. The commission would take the po- sition that proxy speech is commercial speech, and hence subject only to the limited protection of the four-prong *Central Hudson* case. That protection is diluted by the *Zauderer* doctrine that liberally permits mandatory disclo- sure regulation of commercial speech by the government.[71] In this example the speech, when external, is political, but is transmogrified to commercial when internal proxy speech.

Naturally government power over internal proxy speech means govern- ment influence over ultimate external corporate speech. If the latter, as in the *Bellotti* case, is fully protected, it appears fairly obvious that the SEC must be appropriately limited when attempting to interfere with that speech in the proxy realm.

The role of minority shareholders must be considered. Perhaps SEC censorship and regulation of proxy speech is justified as a method of protecting their interests. As a distinguished economist has argued, "[a]s owners, dissident shareholders possess the right to present these views together with management's views."[72]

Justice Powell answered that contention. He pointed out that shareholders govern the corporation and are the ultimate arbiters of corporate speech and conduct. The majority controls. In addition, minority shareholders have resource to derivative suits. Also, minority shareholders have greater freedom to move in and out of the corporation than does the citizen who dissents from political policy of a given state and wants to move out. The lazy or imperfect management are subject to the disciplining threat of hostile takeovers.

Consider a member of a congressional district who votes against the incumbent congresswoman. Should she have the right to compel the member of Congress to insert the views of the minority who voted against her, in all of her important speeches? Should an impartial government arbiter be established to allocate scarce space in her speeches to minority views or views of the weak and uninfluential? This would involve a drastic reordering of constitutional policy. Some elements of that concern, it is true, are evident in the various corrupt practices acts that attempt to lessen the power of rich and powerful constituents. But a constitutional doctrine that went much further along the lines suggested by proxy regulation would constitute an entirely different structure. In the realm of the publicly held corporation the dangers of majority coercion are less than in the political world. Shareholders can sell out, can diversify their portfolios, and can pick and choose their investments. It does appear that the free market in securities is a stronger buffer for minorities than for their equivalents in the world of politics.

On March 27, 1990, the Court handed down an opinion that seemed to undermine the principles of the *Bellotti* opinion.[73] The Court by a 6-to-3 opinion upheld a Michigan statute that prohibited corporations, excluding media corporations, from using general treasury funds for supporting, by way of newspaper advertisement or otherwise, candidates for state elections. PAC contributions were permitted by the statute.

Appellee Michigan State Chamber of Commerce, a nonprofit corporation, desired to place a newspaper advertisement in support of a particular candidate for state office. It brought suit for relief against the statute on First Amendment grounds.[74]

The Court (Justice Marshall writing the opinion) concluded that the statute was supported by a compelling state interest. That interest was the prevention of corruption or the appearance of corruption by the use of vast corporate wealth. That evil is compounded by the fact that corporations receive the benefit of special state law, such as limited liability, and have "little or no correlation to the public's support for the corporation's political ideas."[75]

The Court felt that the statute was "sufficiently narrowly tailored to achieve its goal" because it is exactly drafted to achieve its object while at the same time allowing for corporate political activity through the use of PACs. The latter structure permits individual contributors to give to a group whose ideas they share. On the other hand a corporation that makes political expenditures coerces minority shareholders who do not share the political viewpoint of management.[76]

The decision against the Chamber's advertisement would not penalize politically oriented not-for-profit corporations. The Chamber was a business entity. Its members would be like shareholders of a profit corporation: even if they dissent from the political message they will be reluctant to leave because of the economic incentives inducing them to join in the first place[77]

The Michigan statute is not "underinclusive" because it does not apply to the expenditures for political speech of unincorporated labor unions. Business corporations have a special ability to amass great wealth. Also, union members can forgo contribution to union political activities; stockholders cannot do this in corporations.[78]

Finally, the Court concluded that the statute did not violate the Equal Protection Clause of the Fourteenth Amendment, despite its exclusion of media corporations. The media's crucial role in distributing news and opinions would thereby be preserved.[79]

Justice Scalia delivered a stinging dissent.[80] He called it an "Orwellian announcement."[81] He pointed out that other groups and individuals are given state advantages ranging from tax breaks to cash subsidies. He argued that it is basic that the state cannot condition such favors on loss of the First Amendment protection.

The other reason for restricting corporate speech on candidates was that corporations are wealthy. Scalia pointed out that this will also bar wealthy individuals from speech, something the Court did not concede it was doing.[82]

He recognized that prior cases conceded that corporate political contributions to candidates could be corrupting.[83] He argued that campaign expenditures were a different matter. He quoted *Buckley v. Valeo* to the effect that independent advocacy "may well provide little assistance to the candidates' campaign and indeed may prove couterproductive."[84] That is, candidates may suffer public disfavor from corporate endorsements. He argued that corporate speech on candidates will be effective only if the public finds it true.[85]

The Court argued that corporate wealth has no bearing on the public support for the ideas it espouses. This is a concept similar to the argument advanced by Professor Baker described in chapter 3. Justice Scalia countered that this constitutes government interference in the relative power of different advocates. This, he submitted, is foreign to First Amendment doctrine, which leaves it to the marketplace of ideas rather than using government to chill more powerful voices.[86] Scalia further argued that it is impossible to find any so-called neutral principle that distinguishes too much power from just enough power.[87]

Justice Brennan in his concurrence argued that the statute protects minority shareholders. Scalia pointed out that the statute permitted corporate expenditures for political positions not directed at a particular candidate. This distinguished it, in the Court's opinion, from the *Bellotti* statute, which banned corporate general political speech.[88] Shareholders were not uniformly protected, therefore, by the Michigan statute. The Michigan statute seemed to be designed solely to protect political candidates.[89]

Justice Scalia argued that shareholders, when they become members, know that the majority of shareholders or management may make new or different business decisions. This may include investment in South Africa or operation of an abortion clinic. That, as he put it, is the "deal."[90] He can always sell out if he disagrees.[91] Further, the Brennan concern should extend to dissenting members of groups like the American Civil Liberties Union, not just corporations that are run for profit.[92]

Next, Scalia pointed out that government restrictions on political speech must be "narrowly tailored to serve a compelling governmental interest."[93] He pointed out that all corporations, not just wealthy entities, were covered.[94]

Scalia then addressed the exemption for media corporations. They are exempted because of their crucial role in educating the public. Justice Scalia maintained that giant wealthy media corporations, given the Court concern with the power of corporate wealth, would be more likely to corrupt the political dialogue than business corporations who usually concentrate on economic transactions.[93] Scalia also argued that the majority decision might permit statutes that banned media corporations, on the theory that they too were potentially corrupting due to their amassed wealth.[96]

Finally, Scalia eloquently argued that the First Amendment was premised on the philosophy that the government cannot be trusted to set the parameters of fair debate.[97] He emphasized that the First Amendment was not designed to chill the dissemination of ideas with little initial public support because of the origin of the ideas. Further, he argued that to eliminate the opinion of powerful corporations with great economic interest in Michigan would impoverish the debate.[98] Also, he asserted that the decision gave unincorporated unions an advantage over large employers.[99]

Justice Kennedy also wrote a dissenting opinion in which Scalia joined. He argued that the Court decision reduces the amount and diversity of expression and the size of the audience. This follows because in modern society all effective communication requires the payment of money.[100]

This Court opinion undermines the *Bellotti* rationale. By emphasizing the corrupting nature of corporate expenditures for candidates, and legitimating governmental leveling of the political playing field, the court may be moving toward greater and greater restriction on corporate speech. Ironically, Justice Scalia, who wrote the opinion in the *Board of Trustees of the State University of New York* case (see chapter 2), narrowing protection of commercial speech, defends corporate political speech in this opinion. Since the Court is restricting corporate political speech, it will be logically easier, in the future, for the Court to further lessen the protection afforded to commercial speech and speech regulated by the SEC. Also ironically, Justice Brennan, who has written stirring defenses of First Amendment protection of commercial speech, concurred in the Austin decision.

Rule 14a–8: Brigading of Commercial and Political

Rule 14a–8 of the commission requires the corporation to carry at its cost certain messages of dissident shareholders that it opposes. These proposals are not necessarily limited to commercial issues, but may include political and social messages such as proposals to limit investment in South Africa and resolutions to cease the sale of napalm because of use in the Vietnam war.[101]

In the *Pacific Gas & Electric Co. v. Public Utility Commission* case[102] the Court held that California could not compel the utility to transmit messages of a consumer group with which it disagreed. The plurality opinion of Justice Powell argued that this would burden the utility's expression by chilling its views in order to avoid disseminating hostile views, and would interfere with editorial judgment.[103]

Justice Stevens, dissenting, cautioned the plurality that the California rule was similar to SEC Rule 14a–8, which "[p]resumably the plurality does not doubt the constitutionality of.[104] The Justice also stated that "[t]his regulation [14a–8] cannot be justified on the basis of the commercial character of the communication, because the Rule can and has been used to propagate purely political proposals."[105] In this passage the justice, while supporting the regulation, inadvertently raises the kind of questions I have raised above about the inherent inability to distinguish the commercial in proxy regulation from the noncommercial.

The plurality opinion, in response, argued that the SEC Rule 14a–8 "allocates shareholder property between management and certain groups of shareholders. Management has no interest in corporate property except such interest as derives from the shareholders; therefore, regulations that limit management's ability to exclude some shareholders' views from corporate communications do not infringe corporate First Amendment rights".[106]

This approach directly conflicts with Justice Powell's earlier views in *Bellotti* on management power to disseminate views despite the objections of a minority shareholder group. It is consistent with the *Austin* opinion. It adopts the impartial arbiter-SEC view. It grants to the SEC power to allocate corporate property, that is, space on proxy statements, as between disparate groups within the corporate organization. It permits the government to impose costs on the majority to benefit a minority view. Thus, in dicta, it moves in the direction of government as impartial speech allocator, despite Court doctrine in the traditional political area (now diluted by *Austin*) that the government cannot equalize speech between contesting groups of uneuqal power because of the First Amendment. Such governmental power would create the substantial risk that government bureaucrats would distort the internal debate because of their bias, or ignorance, or self-interest, or inability to distinguish truth from falsehood, or from their desire to perpetuate their power. The plurality opinion further distinguishes corporate speech to the external world (the *Bellotti* case) from speech by the corporation "*to itself*."[107] The plurality, rather superficially in my opinion, asserts that such rules on internal governance do not "limit the range of information that the corporation may contribute to the public debate."[108] I have addressed this issue above.

The evolution of Rule 14a–8 demonstrates dramatically the difficulty of distinguishing the commercial from the political. In the late 1960s the rule permitted management to exclude a proposal if "it clearly appears that the proposal is submitted by the security holder ... primarily for the purpose of promoting general economic, political, racial, religious, social or similar causes...."[109] In 1968 an organization called the Medical Committee for Human Rights requested Dow Chemical Corporation to include a resolution calling on the board of directors to cease the sale of napalm for use in the Vietnam war. The court, emphasizing the purpose of the proxy rules to facilitate shareholder democracy, doubted that exclusion of proposals motivated by general political concerns would be consistent with congressional intent.[110] The resolution was within the corporate power to implement, since the product was produced and sold by the corporation. Clearly, business and political motives or effects were involved. In the instant case napalm production was a small part of the company's business, but in that era able young executives might not work for a company that produced napalm for the war.

The rule was amended several times subsequent to the litigation.[111] In relevant part it now permits omission of a proposal that relates to operations accounting for less than 5 percent of assets and sales, "and which is not otherwise significantly related to the issuer's business."[112] The reference to social or political motivation as a disqualifier has been dropped. The "significantly related" escape clause may permit proposals of social or political concern that are within the corporate power to accomplish (e.g., cease investment in South Africa) to be included where moral or political issues are deemed material to shareholders under the securities laws, despite being immaterial on a purely financial basis.[113] Thus the rule now recognizes the frequent conflation of the moral, political, and economic in corporate governance.

Truth and Falsehood

We are by now familiar with the argument that government cannot easily distinguish truth from falsehood in the sphere of political speech.[114] A related, but still distinct concept is that government may be biased and may, nay often, impose an orthodoxy when it can censor, based on the biases, conflicts of interest and stupidities of the government bureaucrat.

Commercial speech is arguably different in these respects. But surely this cannot be so in the area of proxy speech (or SEC speech in general). Corporate financial and business disclosure is a complex and controversial area. Experts continually debate the meaning and accuracy of modes of disclosure. A distinguished testament to such debate and complexity is the book by Homer Kripke in which he discusses a myriad of complex accounting disclosures and financial disputes among SEC experts.[115] One example he discusses was the decades-long disastrous fixation of the commission on so-called hard, or historical, data versus so-called soft, or futuristic, data. Outside experts long argued, in vain, that the SEC chilling of corporate budget and earnings forecasts deprived investors of the most significant information they would need. Kripke remarks, "SEC thinking does change, but slowly."[116] Ultimately the commission liberalized its rules on projections, but not until decades had elspsed under the dominion of the old doctrine.

A prior SEC chairman, the late William J. Casey, once said while chairman: "I am even more unhappy with the content of the contemporary prospectus. ... The disclosure system exists to help investors. Yet as now administered it does so in a strange way by blocking out as obscene—utterly devoid of any redeeming social value—any reference to the matters in which investors are most keenly interested. Projections of future earnings are one example."[117]

The official commission note to SEC antifraud proxy Rule 14a–9 formerly included as samples of potentially misleading statements "predictions as to specific future ... earnings, or dividends." The prohibition was dropped in July 1979, after the commission was finally convinced of the value of future projections.[118] Up to then someone could go to jail for violating that note, which encompassed the commission's belief in the value of hard historical data, as against predictions.

Violations of proxy and other disclosure rules are governed by commission and court notions of "materiality."[119] Every fledgling corporate attorney already understands the slippery and indefinable nature of the term. It is fact intensive, and reasonable women and men can and often do disagree about its meaning in a given case or in the abstract. As the Court once put it, the determination of materiality "requires delicate assessments of the inferences a 'reasonable shareholder' would draw from a given set of facts and the significance of those inferences to him."[120] As a distinguished federal district court judge once said, "since no one knows what moves the mythical 'average prudent investor,' it comes down to a question of judgment."[121]

SEC Bias

The commission is hardly free of bias. The interest theory of regulation suggests that interest groups, such as attorneys or investment bankers, may have a powerful influence on the agency. As Dean Henry Manne has stated, since the development of this theory of regulation, scholars "have been well advised . . . to ask who would be benefitted most by the rule."[122]

The SEC is run by attorneys. The influence of attorneys may be an institutional bias toward more, rather than less, regulation. An attorney staffer who continually resists new regulations (or new enforcement actions) may lose influence within the agency and with the media. An activist attorney, ironically, by securing a great reputation as a regulator, increases his or her market worth when leaving the agency for private practice. This is not based on personal sinister motive, but is the result of impersonal institutional structure and sincere belief in the rightness of regulation and enforcement.

Also, government agencies, as George Benston has argued, "prefer to minimize risk" and "tend to require conservative, uniform procedures that are likely to result in the publication of misleading financial statements." They will tend to demand accounting principles that understate income, future growth and overemphasize contingent liberties.[123] The SEC emphasis on hard historic data, mentioned above, is an example of such bias.

I mention these rather obvious potential distortions of truth, high possibilities of error, biases, conflicts of interest, and drive for power simply to demonstrate that the commission is not some impartial arbiter that can avoid one of the root dangers of government censorship and regulation of speech, to wit, bureaucratically biased and self-interested imposition of orthodoxy.

Fragility or Robustness of Proxy Speech

The next issue turns on the fragility or robustness of the supply of proxy speech in the absence of regulation. The Supreme Court, and scholars in law and economics, such as Richard Posner, have used the notion of robustness to justify greater regulation of commercial speech.[124] I suppose if proxy speech is indeed fragile (i.e., underproduced absent regulation), it is ironicallly in the same category as political speech, if we follow the Posner thinking on fragility and robustness. That is, it should be fully protected by the First Amendment to get out more of it.[125] I am not sure that proxy speech is indeed fragile. There is good evidence that corporations published ample financial disclosure before passage of the securities legislation in 1933 and 1934.[126] I suspect such corporate voluntary disclosure of financial information in the 1920s provided ample alternative or substitute disclosure in lieu of proxy disclosure of matters taken up at meetings of shareholders.

Benston has provided a theoretical argument for why corporations would voluntarily provide an adequate supply of financial information.[127] He points out that first, such disclosure assists prospective shareholders and lenders of funds. This will tend to make them pay more for their investment because it is cheaper for the corporation to provide the information than for them to get it on their own. Second, voluntary supplying of independent CPA-audited reports will reassure such investors, who will then pay more for their investments. Third, provision of the information on a continuous basis signals to investors that the corporation has nothing to hide. This makes potential investors more likely to invest. Benston also provides data for voluntary corporate disclosure of financial information preceding the federal securities acts that is quite impressive in its demonstration of the extent of such voluntary disclosure.

The Benston argument demonstrates that proxy information (as well as all corporate information) may possess a certain real robustness of supply. But, contrary to the Supreme Court argument and the Posner theory, this is an argument against the need for government mandatory disclosure. Because robustness (as Benston demonstrates) leads to an efficient supply of valid information without SEC regulation, and SEC regulation may produce more information than investors need, the argument for mandatory disclosure for robust corporate proxy speech, based on its robustness, is weak.

Many scholars dispute the Benston mode of analysis. They assert that corporations will not voluntarily produce adequate disclosure.[128] If they are correct, that is an argument for the fragility of SEC speech. In the political realm supposed fragility of speech is an argument for the full protection of the First Amendment. That same argument applies to supposedly fragile SEC speech, unless we can agree that, unlike political speech, the government can operate as a safe, unbiased, accurate arbiter of truthful speech.

But that in part turns on the comparative advantage of government to distinguish truth from falsity as compared with the free market. On that issue, as we have already seen, the case for the SEC is hardly free from substantial doubt.

The fragility argument is made to support the need for a First Amendment in the case of political speech. But if we concede that, because of externalities and free-rider effects, not enough political speech is produced, that is an argument for mandatory disclosure of political speech, not merely a passive First Amendment approach. The First Amendment ban against government censorship will not produce nearly as much political speech as a system of mandatory disclosure for fragile political speech. I don't think mandatory disclosure in the case of traditional political speech would be anything but a disaster. But the case for it is ironically stronger than for robust proxy speech (or any speech regulated by the SEC), so long as we make the traditional assumption that the supply of political speech is fragile because of lack of sufficient definition of property rights in it.

Concluding Remarks on Proxy Speech

It is argued that corporate management is too strong in relation to shareholders. Hence proxy restraint of management speech is necessary for the protection of small investors. Until the *Austin* case, this kind of argument had been rejected in the political realms.[129] Surely an incumbent U.S. Senator is more powerful than the ordinary citizen. His or her access to the media is far greater. Both enjoy the same formal freedom, however, under the First Amendment. Shall we limit her speech? Certainly the *New York Times* corporation is more powerful than the ordinary citizen. Both, however, enjoy the same First Amendment rights to publish on matters of public concern.[130] Shall we limit her speech? The costs of limiting free speech by some means test related to power and wealth are, in my opinion, for the reasons expressed in the dissents of Justices Scalia and Kennedy, in the *Austin* Case, too great.

There are considerable arguments against this approach in the realms of art and politics. The dangers of government bias and self-interest outweigh the arguments from disparity of power and influence. Certainly the courts (even after *Austin*) cannot force newspapers and publishers of books to carry the views of individuals, although they often do so by way of letters to the editor and op ed pages. There is no reason to establish a different policy for proxy material. Indeed, the escape hatches and alternatives for the small shareholder are far greater than in the world of politics. The shareholder can always sell out when the stock price declines. The shareholder can diversify his portfolio and, hence, avoid catastrophic loss. The shareholder can profit from hostile takeovers in which lazy or inefficient incumbent managements are knocked off in transactions in which target-company shareholders usually make enormous gains.[131] The free market in the corporate area thus provides safeguards to the small shareholder not present in politics; therefore, the arguments for limiting the free speech attributes of the powerful are less forceful in the corporate realm than the political.

The Supreme Court, in a series of opinions, has ruled that the First Amendment prohibits Congress from limiting political expenditures by candidates or independent groups.[132] That position was qualified by the recent *Austin* case. Contributions to political candidates can be limited because of the Court's conclusion that there is a potential for corruption in that area.[133] Until the *Austin* case, discussed above, the Supreme Court had recognized that money and speech in modern society are inextricably related. Hence speech that is self-interested or that is disseminated by the use of financial power is not, therefore, stripped of First Amendment protection.

The Court has ruled that newspapers cannot constitutionally be forced to publish the views of individuals or groups that disagree with its editorials.[134] Television networks, on the other hand, were subject to a fairness doctrine because the Court had concluded that they enjoy a special monopoly because of the peculiarities of television broadcast technology.[135] Publicly held corporations are not usually monopolies. Proxy regulation is designed to improve the corporate-political leverage of the shareholder. Yet First Amendment doctrine should not permit a kind of government-controlled egalitarian treatment of speech, including proxy speech. Furthermore, the shareholder has greater ability and opportunity to opt out of the corporation than the ordinary citizen has to opt out of the polity.

Even after *Austin* the Court agrees that corporations have full First Amendment protection to discuss political issues (as distinguished from expending funds to support specific candidates).[136] The First Amendment is not limited to natural persons. Yet proxy regulation can interfere with corporate political speech. Assume that a corporation speaks out for a tax decrease on products. Full First Amendment protection would appear to be granted. However, an internal dispute over the advisability of such a program, if brought to the point of a proxy contest for differing slates of directors, would be subject to the full range of proxy regulation. That is a policy difference without a good reason.

The modern publicly held corporation is a significant intermediating structure in American life. Like the family, church, and other private groups, it stands between state and individual, preserves the individual from state domination, and enriches the life and diversity of individuals. It is an anomaly that First Amendment principles that apply to so-called political governance should not extend to the governance of the corporation.

Some, including me have argued that the modern corporation should not be analogized to a minipolity for purposes of justifying increased government regulation.[137] I have maintained that the modern publicly held corporation is a dynamic economic aggregate of interests that is subject to effective discipline from market forces. Hostile takeovers, and the threat of same, may frequently operate to weed out inefficient managements. Such forces operate more effectively than increased government surveillance and interference. This position, however, is not inconsistent with a call for full First Amendment protection of corporate and shareholder proxy speech. To the contrary, it is perfectly consistent with such a philosophy. There is no good reason why economic organizations should enjoy less free-speech protection than other groups.

The economic picture of the corporation emphasizes the powerful competitive forces that serve, even in the absence of free speech, to protect the shareholder. The free markets for control (i.e., hostile takeovers) serve to protect the shareholder from lazy or incompetent managers.[138] Furthermore, shareholders can always sell out and leave a stupid or incompetent management. Shareholders, using modern portfolio theory, can diversify their holdings and avoid catastrophically large investment in one corporation. None of these escape valves are present in state or federal governmental politics. Since shareholders have the escape valves of the free market in shares, the dangers that corporate managements, in proxy communications, may engage in false speech are less threatening than the danger that politicians may lie to their constituents. Yet we protect the politician's speech and regulate the corporate manager's speech.

The free market works by way of free individuals seeking out new information and reacting to new demands of consumers and competitors. The free market is basically a process of information-gathering and disseminating. As new events occur, entrepreneurs respond. They seek out new demands and wants of the consumer. They attempt to perceive demands and wants that the consumer is, as yet, only himself dimly aware of. It is for this reason that the free market is so superior to command economies.[139] The government bureaucrat in the socialist state cannot effectively grasp the complexities of society. Thousands of individual businessmen, however, each responding to needs and wants in various communities, can more effectively seek out and transmit information than the government bureaucrat. Price is the key mechanism by which the free-market entrepreneur detects changes in demand and supply. Essential to this, as in the case of the polity, is a free market in speech. Free speech, in business and within the corporation, is essential for the effective functioning of the free market. Proxy speech is part of that process. Shareholders can communicate their demands and wants to management and fellow shareholders. Corporate management is involved in the process. The government censor (i.e., the SEC) is ill-equipped to fulfill that role for much the same reasons as a ministry of culture should not censor novels, and a ministry of politics should not censor politicians.

The constitutional scope of the First Amendment includes a protection of the right of free association.[140] The government cannot prevent a free people from joining private organizations.[141] Neither can the government enjoin the speech people use in connection with their right of free association.[142] It is obvious that the government could not censor the in-house communications of the Democratic or Republican parties. The only distinction, in the case of the corporation, is that it is a commercial organization. However, speech cannot be distinguished based on the presence or lack of economic motive. That would eliminate most speech from First Amendment coverage. Likewise, if one eliminates the right of association from economically interested groups, one would eliminate most groups, with the possible exception of the purest of religious groups.

Hostile Takeover Speech

The Williams Act amendments to the Securities Exchange Act of 1934 require specified disclosure by hostile bidders for the stock of target corporations.[143] The targets' responses are similarly controlled by rules of mandatory disclosure.[144] As in the case of proxy disclosure and the balance of SEC- regulated speech, the government regulation is controlled by the four-prong *Central Hundson* test, and the modification thereof contained in the *Zauderer* and *State University of New York* cases. But as in the case of proxy speech and, again, all SEC-regulated speech, the similarity between traditionally defined commercial speech, and takeover speech is strained. The SEC-regulated takeover speech cannot be rationally distinguished from so-called political speech.

The hostile takeover phenomenon is an alternative method to proxy contests for the acquisition of control over the target corporation.[145] It replaced the proxy contest route in the 1980s because it proved a much more potent weapon in the hands of the rivals for control. The development of this technique has aroused a national debate.[146] Proponents argue that hostile takeovers discipline indifferent or incompetent incumbent managements, or create synergy benefits in which costs drop as a result of the felicitous combination of different businesses. Opponents of the merger movement argue that it creates unhealthy preoccupation with the short run, makes for a noncompetitive economy, displaces competent managements, harms the local communities, and creates unemployment. These are but some of the arguments advanced.[147]

Concern for the target shareholder and for adequate disclosure to them led originally to the Williams Act amendments to the 1934 Act. That Act, as we have indicated, created mandatory disclosure authority for the commission. It also created some substantive interference with the processes of bidders, to protect target shareholders. For example, bidders were prohibited from paying more to selected target shareholders than to others. States have entered the picture. They have created various forms of barriers to hostile takeovers. For example, one form forbids mergers for several years after the bid between target and bidder.[148] Some forms deprive the bidder of voting rights in the target stock acquired unless a disinterested majority of target shareholders approve of the transaction.[149] Some forms forbid the clean-up merger after the bid unless the cash-out merger is made at a specified fair price.[150]

Let us consider the mandatory speech regulation. The arguments made in the proxy section above apply in the case of takeover speech regulation. First, the speech pertains directly to a battle for control. As such, it is speech about corporate governance. Therefore, it is far removed from the traditional advertisement of a product or a service. Second, as in the case of proxy speech, it is impossible to successfully distinguish this speech from all of the kinds of political cum economic speech (e.g., speech about taxes, price supports, and savings and loan policy) that are traditionally fully protected by the First Amendment. Indeed, the takover movement has been described as one of the major political-economic issues confronting the nation. Moreover, each individual takeover battle creates a potentially significant economic impact on the local community, labor, and suppliers, as well as possible artistic and musical effects on the local culture, depending on the charitable contributions policies of the target and bidder corporations. Bidder and target speech frequently invoke these artistic cum economic, cum social issues. Frequently target managements, in the midst of the battle, will run to Congress or the state legislature and engage in lobbying campaigns to seek legislative support for their battle. The *Bellotti* case (even after the *Austin* case) protects lobbying speech; it should certainly protect takeover speech. Indeed, on traditional grounds, the *Bellotti* case is persuasive. The *Bellotti* case applies to external speech of the corporation. Certainly the takeover speech of the bidder is external; it is directed at the shareholders of the target corporation. Third, the disclosure issues are incredibly complex, elusive, subjective, and partisan, in the sense that competing bidders and target management differ as to the proper disclosure and interpretation. Therefore, it is difficult for government to adequately distinguish truth from falsehood. Fourth, bidders certainly have economic incentives to quickly and adequately disclose their bidding terms, to prevail against competing bidders.

Not only formal takeover speech should be subject to the full protection of the First Amendment, rather than limited commercial speech protection. The state and federal interference with internal corporate governance procedures, to "protect" the target shareholder, should be subject to First Amendment freedom of association scrutiny. For example, some states have prohibited clean-up, or second-stage, mergers for n period of years after the bidder acquires a specified amount of the target corporation stock.[151] Target shareholders may or may not be able to opt out of such restrictions, depending on the nature of the state statute. That restriction constitutes an interference with the internal governance of the target corporation. The regulation, as noted above in the proxy setting, can escape First Amendment scrutiny only if the court concludes that the corporation serves a nonexpressive purpose, and hence is not protected by the First Amendment. I have analyzed the infirmities, as I see them, in such a legal approach.

Laurence Tribe, in his treatise "American Constitutional Law," has observed that "[c]ritics of the American Constitution as an unacceptably individualistic document . . . will find at least a limited answer in the 'freedom of association' that the Supreme Court has repeatedly described as among the preferred rights derived by implication from the first amendment's guarantees of speech, press, petition, and assembly."[152] As Tribe points out,[153] Alexis de Tocqueville asserted that the "most natural privilege of man, next to the right of acting for himself, is that of combining his exertions with those of his fellow creatures and of acting in common with them."[154]

Tribe asserts that the cases demonstrate that the government may not interfere in the internal structure of an association, under the First and Fourteenth Amendments, for relatively non-significant reasons.[155] Even when the government interference is supported by an important goal,[156] the government must still demonstrate that a significant *set back* to the goal would result absent the contested interference,[157] and lesser interference would suffice.[158] Further, the right of association includes the right not to associate with others.[159]

These principles should have a direct bearing on government interference in corporate governance provisions designed to chill, or facilitate, changes in control. Again, the only argument against application of these principles is the proposition (discussed above) that organizations formed for purposes of economic gain fall outside their scope.

In the case of *TW Services, Inc. v. SWT Acquisition Corporation*[160] the Delaware court interfered in the internal governance of a corporation against the wishes of a majority of shareholders. SWT sought a preliminary injunction requiring TW to cancel out (redeem) its "poison pill" defense against the hostile takeover effort of SWT. SWT had made a tender offer at 29 dollars a share for all of the shares of TW. Some 88 percent of TW's common stock had accepted the tender. SWT could not close the purchase unless the target management redeemed the "poison pill." The "poison pill" included a flip-in feature that permitted TW shareholders other than SWT to buy additional TW common stock at half price. It also contained a flip-over provision allowing TW shareholders to acquire shares of the bidder at half price in the event the bidder entered into a merger with the target. These provisions would result in a chilling punitive dilution of the target equity at the expense of the bidder.

The issue involved a conflict between the desires of a great majority of the shareholders of the target corporation and the judgment of the management. The latter argued that the long-term interests of the corporation mandated their refusal to permit the takeover to go forward. The 88 percent majority had voted with their pocket-book to go for immediate gain. The management had, in a sense, taken up the cause of future shareholders of the target (similar to the generational issues of political government, the living versus the yet unborn) as well as current shareholders who held for future years. Management also had perhaps taken up the cause, as it saw it, of the future interests of community and labor and suppliers of the corporation.

As this is written, the chancery court refused to enter an injunction against the target management. The chancellor asserted that

[q]uestions of this type call upon one to ask, what is our model of corporate governance? "Shareholder democracy" is an appealing phrase, and the notion of shareholders as the ultimate voting constituency of the board has obvious pertinence, but that phrase would not constitute the only element in a well articulated model. While corporate democracy is a pertinent concept, a corporation is not a New England town meeting; directors, not shareholders have responsibilities to manage. . . . In all events, resolution of these questions . . . seem inescapably to involve normative questions.[161]

However, the judge admitted that directors should "affirmatively respond" when a "predominating proportion of shares sought a fundamental structural change."[162] He did not in this case, at this juncture, agree that the directors must rescind the poison pill because the bidder also had requested a merger agreement that, under state law, as he saw it, required, even in the case where more than 80 percent of the shareholders wanted to accept the tender offer, directorial initiative and approval.[163]

The Court, as a corollary to the right to associate for lawful ends, has recognized the negative or flipside of the issue. It has endorsed the right not to associate with others in the association. This right must, perforce, include the power of members to end the association. The Delaware court thwarted that right.

State law everywhere grants, over a wide array of circumstances, shareholders the power to veto and sometimes the power to initiate major structural changes. Moreover, state law is largely a kind of enabling clause, pursuant to which shareholders may freely contract among themselves as to the configuration of the corporate governance procedures they desire.[164] The Delaware court appeared to move in a spirit contrary to this structure.

Perhaps the most appropriate method to analyze the Delaware case is in terms of the First Amendment right of free association. Under this philosophical approach the Delaware court appears to have permitted management to interfere with the First Amendment right of the shareholders to determine when and under what circumstances they may terminate the association. The court accomplished that end by denying the right of a majority of shareholders to end the association by selling their stock to the bidder.

Prospectus Speech

In the preceding section we considered proxy and hostile takeover speech. The arguments pertaining to externalities, or fragility of speech, robustness, and ability to distinguish truth from falsity, and bias of the agency apply with equal measure to all SEC regulated speech and need not be repeated. In this section I want to focus on the mandatory disclosure system applied to the sale of securities.

The Securities Act of 1933 regulates the corporate offer and sale of securities.[165] In that Act, Congress established a mandatory system of disclosure. The so-called Truth in Securities Disclosure Act, and regulations passed under authority of the Act, requires corporations to provide specified "news" to potential purchasers of securities. The material must be pre-filed with the SEC before sales may be made.[166] The commission can, by administrative action or with the "assistance" of court injunctive action, engage in prior restraint of prohibited corporate disclosure.[167] The U.S. government can criminally prosecute violators of the disclosure law and regulations.

Section 5(c) of the Act prohibits any offer of a security by mails or in interstate commerce unless a registration statement containing prescribed information has been filed with the commission. Section 5(b)(1) prohibits the use of general written literature for offerings of securities unless in the form of a specified document called a prospectus. There are limited exceptions for written documents called tombstone advertisements and posteffective documents preceded by a statutory prospectus.[168] The contents of the registration statements are specified in complex regulations of the commission, which have evolved over the years.

The justification for this regulation of speech is the commercial speech doctrine. Modern constitutional doctrine, although it gives some protection to that speech, still permits prior restraint of corporate prospectuses and registration statements that offer securities for sale. It also permits criminal prosecution for false or misleading statements. As we have seen, commercial speech has been defined by the Court as advertisements for the sale of services or products.

Corporations sell products or services. The sale of shares of common stock, however, is not the sale of a corporate service or product, since a share of common stock is an ownership interest in an organization. It carries with it certain rights to vote for the election of directors. It represents an interest in a future flow of corporate earnings. The latter carries a present value that is reflected in trading data on the exchanges or the organized over-the-counter markets. The purchase of stock reflects the buyer's judgment that the economic organization, called a corporation, will earn a return that is better than that derived from alternative uses of his cash. The stock purchaser, in the ordinary course of life, also becomes a member of other kinds of organizations. He may join the Democratic party, a trade union, an environmental group, a trade asociation, or the American Bar Association, if a lawyer. The government may not censor the published speech of these non-stock corporate entities. It may, however, censor the speech of corporations when that speech promotes the sale of stock.

A share of common stock is an interest in an organization. The organization is called a corporation and is operated for profit purposes. The stock corporation may manufacture steel, sell books or newspapers, or distribute information in the form of computer software. Membership in a publicly held corporation should rest on the same constitutional plateau as membership in other organizations. Consider the American Bar Association. That organization is established and run for the betterment of attorneys. The government could not constitutionally censor the public statements of that group (atleast so long as membership is voluntary and not compelled by statute) about, let us say, the need to eliminate tax legislation that harms the membership. More particularly, the government could not censor for content promotional information that it presents to prospective new members. I see no difference between the latter transaction and the sale of common stock in the corporation. Likewise, the government could not censor promotional public information disseminated by the B'nai B'rith Anti-Defamation League to prospective new members. Ditto for the Catholic Church, the Democratic party, and a local free-trade association.

It will be argued that a stock corporation is primarily an economic entity. Indeed, by law, it must be run with the goal of making, if at all possible, a profit for its shareholders. Hence some will assert that constitutional doctrine can distinguish between that entity and most other associations in the United States.[169] By now it must be clear that the argument will not sustain rigorous analysis. It is difficult enough to make a credible argument for the distinction between the barebones advertisement of a good or service and fully protected speech. The Court, in the case of an advertisement describing the price of prescription drugs, stated that commercial speech is protected to facilitate intelligent private economic decisions and "[t]o this end, the free flow of commercial information is indispensible."[170] That function of commercial speech is more important to most people than most political campaign rhetoric. It is impossible to distinguish in a principled manner between corporations run for economic purposes and all other groups. Indeed, even political parties, such as the Republican and Democratic parties, are organized to further the economic interests of members. The same is true for labor unions. It is true that a stock corporation is operated with the aim of making a cash profit for shareholders in the form of dividends and capital gains. Yet that is a difference from, let us say, the local free-trade association without much meaning. A remarkably huge number of organizations, associations, and groupings in the United States are created and operated to further the narrow economic interests of their members. Their goal is the ultimate cash (i.e., economic benefit of their members). They attempt to attract membership by publication in the print and television media. If government may censor their books and speeches and other publications, the free-speech process would be severely impaired.

Ironically, modern corporate law reformers seek to emphasize the social and ethical nature of the corporation. For example, the drafts of the American Law Institute Code of Corporate Governance emphasize the ethical, as well as the economic, goals of the publicly held corporation.[171] Even many business leaders, as well as political leaders, are fond of demanding socially responsible action from the large corporation.[172] Modern state statutes all legitimate corporate charitable contributions. Modern courts are more willing than courts in prior years to permit corporate expenditures that do not necessarily maximize the bottom line, as long as ethical and moral purposes are accomplished. In a case often cited in law school casebooks, *Shlensky v. Wrigley*, plaintiff charged the board of directors of the Chicago Cubs with failure to install night lights; hence the shareholders were damaged.[173] The court upheld the director's decision, which was based in part on the desire to preserve the neighborhood, a socially laudable purpose. This is one of many cases in which directors make decisions that are, to some extent, affected by social, as distinct from profit, purposes. This is not the place to debate the wisdom of such judicial doctrine. It is, as I mentioned at the beginning of this section, ironic that corporations are urged to moderate their passion for profits on the ground that they are properly more than economic entities, yet constitutional doctrine punishes them because they are deemed to be economic entities. I am not here arguing a sort of estoppel assertion against such thinking. I'm not suggesting that we should grant First Amendment protection to corporations because they assert the ethical and political function of such organizations. But their concern reflects the inextricable ties, intermingling, and close association of economic organizations with political purposes and the reverse.

It is mistakenly asserted that the arguments made here apply to shares of common stock but not to debt instruments. The former are apparently ownership interests in an organization; the latter are merely indicia of a creditor-debtor relationship. But that is to emphasize a difference that is not relevant to economic theory or appropriate constitutional doctrine. The public holder of a debt security acquires a series of rights in the corporate organization in the same sense as the holder of common stock. Obviously there are differences. Holders of debt securities receive fixed interest, not a residual share in profits. They usually have no vote for directors. They frequently have rights and powers expressed in the trust indenture, however, that, under certain circumstances (for example, when the debt is not timely paid), in effect give them more power than the common shareholders. Debt holders have simply struck a different bargain in the organization than have the common shareholders. Some might describe them as more pessimistic investors than the common shareholders. They are, nevertheless, both investors (i.e., participants or members of the corporate organization). They are in a dramatically different relation to the organization than a purchaser of its products or services.

Investment Advice Speech: Licensing Professionals

As the reader will recall from chapter 2, in June 1985 the Supreme Court struck down a court injunction against Mr. Lowe and his investment newsletters under the Investment Advisers Act of 1940.[174] The SEC had obtained the injunction on the grounds that his publications were illegal because he was neither registered nor exempt from registration as an adviser under the Act. I consider the case in this chapter in order to focus on its impact on licensing of professionals.

Lowe was the president and principal shareholder of the Lowe Management Corporation. While registered as an investment adviser, he was convicted of misappropriating funds of clients, of failing to register with New York's Department of Law, of tampering with evidence to hide a fraud of a client, and of converting funds from a bank. The commission, under authority in the Advisers Act and after an appropriate hearing, revoked the license of the Lowe Management Corporation. About a year later the commission sought an injunction in the U.S. District Court for the Eastern District of New York restraining the further distribution of Lowe's investment advisory publications.

As the Supreme Court pointed out, a typical publication "contained general commentary about the securities and bullion markets, reviews of market indicators and investment strategies, and specific recommendations for buying, selling, or holding stock and bullion.[175] The subscribers numbered from 3,000 to 19,000. The Court stated that "it was advertised as a semi-monthly publication, but only eight issues were published in the 15 months after the entry of the 1981 order [revoking registration]."[176] The Court further stated that there was "no adverse evidence concerning the quality of the publications ... no evidence that Lowe's criminal convictions were related to the publications; no evidence that Lowe had engaged in any trading activity in any securities that were the subject of advice ... and no contention that any of the information published in the advisory services had been false or materially misleading."[177]

The Supreme Court had consented to hear the case in order to determine the constitutional issue of whether the injunction against publication and distribution of the market letters was forbidden by the First Amendment. However, Justice Stevens, joined by four of his colleagues, employed a statutory construction to avoid the constitutional issue.[178] He argued that the publications fit within the statutory exemption for *bona fide publications*, and hence were not covered by the Act.[179] Therefore, the commission had no authority to enjoin their publication. The statutory construction knocked out of the regulatory registration requirement box the entire industry of market letters. The Court argued that the legislative history showed that Congress, "sensitive to First Amendment concerns, wanted to make clear that it did not seek to regulate the press through the licensing of nonpersonalized publishing activities."[180]

Justice White, joined by Chief Justice Burger and Justice Rehnquist, directly bit the constitutional bullet. They concluded that the publications were covered by the Act, but that banning their publication and distribution violated the First Amendment.[181] Justice White stated that the issue "involves a collision between the power of government to license and regulate those who would pursue a profession or vocation and the rights of freedom of speech."[182] He concluded that a person

who takes the affairs of a client personally in hand and purports to exercise judgment on behalf of the client in the light of the client's individual needs and circumstances is properly viewed as engaging in the practice of a profession ... the professional's speech is *incidental* to the conduct of the profession. If the government enacts generally applicable licensing provisions limiting the class of persons who may practice the profession, it cannot be said to have enacted a limitation on freedom of speech or the press subject to First Amendment scrutiny. Where the personal nexus between professional and client does not exist ... government regulation ceases to function as legitimate regulation of professional practice with only incidental impact on speech; it becomes regulation of speaking or publishing as such.[183]

Hence the justice concluded that the blanket prohibition of Lowe's investment advisory publications violated the First Amendment. Those publications were addressed to a general audience and no element of personal one-on-one communication or individualized advice was involved. To the extent the Act applied to individualized advice, it was constitutionally sound.

Justice White further asserted that it was not necessary for him to determine whether the newsletters contained fully protected speech or so-called commercial speech. Because the lower-court ban extended to "legitimate, disinterested advice"[184] as well as to "advice that is fraudulent, deceptive or manipulative,"[185] it went too far even if mere commercial speech was involved, since the First Amendment "permits restraints on commercial speech only when they are narrowly tailored to advance a legitimate governmental interest."[186] Although the goal was legitimate—prevention of fraud—less drastic means could have legitimately been used, such as application of anti-fraud concepts and use of reporting provisions. However, in this case, the government would prohibit any newsletter, no matter how accurate. Naturally, if the publications were not mere commercial speech, the ban must fall also. For those reasons Justice White and his colleagues joined in the result but not the opinion of the court majority.

The refusal to enjoin seems eminently correct. The opinion of the Court majority, however, is a fairly strained attempt to avoid a constitutional issue.[187]

Regarding an issue avoided by the concurring opinion, it cannot be cogently argued that the Lowe newsletters constitute commercial speech. Commercial speech, in its most commonly accepted meaning, is a product or service advertisement. The Lowe investment letters were not advertisements of Lowe's market services; they were analyses of securities issued by corporations that had absolutely no connection to Lowe or his publications. If Lowe advertised his market letters, those ads would be commercial speech. The court majority emphasized, in the course of its statutory analysis, that "because we have squarely held that the expression of opinion about a commercial product such as a loudspeaker is protected by the First Amendment, *Bose Corp. v. Consumers Union of U.S., Inc.* . . . , it is difficult to see why the expression of an opinion about a marketable security should not also be protected."[188] Unless we expand the notion of commercial speech to encompass self-interested speech, we do not have commercial speech in Lowe's investment newsletters. The broader interpretation would delegitimate most of what usually is characterized as political speech.

The concurring opinion, and no doubt all of the other justices, would permit commission regulation of personalized advice. They would permit a complete ban against the rendering of personalized advice by an unregistered investment adviser. They would permit the commission to revoke the registration of an adviser, and thereupon obtain an injunction against his practice of personalized advice. They would permit a statute that required certain standards of education, prior record of honesty, as well as absence of a criminal record as a condition to practice of that profession. Absent such a posture, all state regulation of businesses and professions in the nature of licensing requirements would collapse.

The distinction hangs on dubious assumptions. An investment newsletter that is bought by 300,000 subscribers can do enormous financial harm. For example, if it adheres to a technical or chartist theory, much academic research proves that the advice is worthless.[189] Yet the government could not enjoin its publication. An adviser who personally counsels eighteen persons may be enjoined by a court from rendering such advice (no matter how truthful) if his registration has been denied or revoked.

The justices' definition of harm requires some clarification. Even if we grant that a newsletter may do less harm to one reader than personalized advice to one client, the lesser harm to a reader, multiplied by the total readership, may be greater than the total harm to the limited personal clientele of the adviser.

The justices and the lower courts defended the power of the government to regulate the professions. The states can prevent disbarred attorneys from giving personal advice to an individual. The states can prevent a licensed attorney from soliciting a client in a hospital ward, no matter how truthful his advice. Yet they cannot enjoin in advance the publishing efforts of disbarred attorneys and nonregistered investment advisers.[190] This position is maintained despite the power of the published work to injure its readers, or, indirectly, non-readers who are affected by the dissemination of such opinions.

The courts defend this anomaly on the grounds that professionals engage in a unique and confidential relationship with their clients or patients.[191] Hence they can do great damage to those who depend on them. Further, professionals qua professionals hold themselves out as rather special, knowledgeable, and faithful to clients. All of this is no doubt true. It also is true that popular books and newspapers have a powerful influence for good or evil that far transcends the personalized influence of a professional on his relatively few clients.

The distinction, to the extent that it is altruistic in motive, depends on a cynical view of the First Amendment. It appears to assert that where speech can have great influence, as in the case of professional advice, it is subject to greater government control than where it supposedly has less influence, for example, in the form of impersonal newsletters. In a sense, it also is a product of the same mentality that yawns at 50,000 traffic deaths each year, but focuses on the news of an individual murder or death where the victim can be identified and comprehended. I mentioned the word altruism although it is hardly clear that the movements for licensing requirements for professionals are designed to protect the consumer. There is a considerable and compelling literature that demonstrates that licensing is designed to restrict the supply of more professionals, and thus increase the compensation of the groups already within the tent.[192]

The regulatory function in the investment adviser area cannot be considered without some mention being made of the dubious assumptions on which it rests. Modern discoveries of the efficient market and random-walk theories of stock prices have demonstrated that it is impossible, or at least difficult, for any single, gifted analyst to successfully select an individual stock. No one has the ability or power to predict the future earnings of an individual issuer, absent the illegal use of inside information.[193] Therefore, licensing restrictions that condition registration on educational requirements, or past criminal record, or experience have no provable connection with ability to select good investments. The process is largely an exercise in magic and faith. Hence the regulatory effort floats in midair, loose from any rational moorings.

Insider Trading, Scalping, and the Press

The Supreme Court, in its various commercial speech cases, has always endorsed the constitutional ability of the government to prosecute fraudulent statements after the fact of publication. A recent criminal insider trading case involving a former reporter of the *Wall Street Journal* has aroused some doubts about this as it impacts on the media. R. Foster Winans wrote the influential journal column titled "Heard on the Street." He allegedly engaged in a scalping scheme in which he tipped confederates about future stories. The articles themselves were routine analyses based on publicly available data. They would then buy; the price of the stock would rise on publication of the column. Thereupon his confederates would sell out to the great profit of all of them. His stories were apparently factual and correct. It was the reputation of the column that drove the price of the subject stock up. This practice is commonly called "scalping." The government, in its criminal case, alleged that he had violated his fiduciary duty to his employer not to scalp; hence he had engaged in a federal fraud under Rule 10b–5 in connection with the buying and selling of stock.[194] The government argued that the defendants had unlawfully misappropriated information of the employer in connection with the purchase and sale of securities. The government also alleged violation of the wire and mail fraud statutes.[195] A conviction was obtained in June 1985.[196] The Supreme Court split 4–4 on the SEC Rule 10b–5 insider-trading misappropriation of information theory of the government.[197] It unanimously affirmed the conviction based on the wire and mail fraud counts.[198] In 1988 Congress passed a statute that approved future misappropriation actions under Rule 10b–5.[199]

The media groups bitterly complained that this prosecution would open the doors to government power to mandate the content of news stories.[200] Under the government's theory of action it is in effect instructing the newspaper that advance disclosure of Winan's financial interest (i.e., the scalping scheme) or, alternatively, a decision not to publish the column would cure the offense. That is, the government is mandating news disclosure, or its suppression. The implication is that the government has the power to specify the kinds of financial conflict of interest that a reporter must disclose when discussing the securities markets. The precedent would extend to political matters with a suitable drafted statute. Perhaps Dan Rather could be required to disclose his political biases before reporting on a sensitive news story or risk a government fraud suit.[201]

The issue can be broadened beyond the scalping problem. Assume that Senator X, in running for office, adopts a notoriously and nasty racist position. He advocates the view that blacks and Jews are inferior creatures who should be barred from the political process. I doubt that a statute that permitted a government fraud or criminal suit against him could withstand constitutional attack unless he defamed a particular person. If he supports a flat tax and omits qualifiers that would be material in an SEC fraud sense, no government criminal litigation against him could withstand First Amendment protection. When we consider SEC fraud or criminal litigation, however, their validity, or distinction from the senator's example above, must be sustained on some argument that commercial speech is different from political speech. At that point we are back to familiar ground.

Consider the *Wall Street Journal* reporter case.[202] He was commenting on the security of a corporation with respect to which he had no connection. In that respect he is similar to Lowe. The news and comment column he authored was part of a bona fide newspaper of general circulation. He was not offering individualized advice in a professional setting.

It should be eminently clear by now that, particularly in the SEC domain, the differences between so-called political speech and commercial speech are hardly self-evident. The *Wall Street Journal* case is a good reminder that there are many instances in which fraud prosecution will seriously impinge on traditional press media and their control over news content. A tremendous component of legitimate newspaper coverage pertains to economic news and the interests of special interest groups. Extension of SEC fraud and criminal doctrine to the *Wall Street Journal* reporter is dangerous, since it serves as the camel's nose under the tent for legislation regulating considerable areas of newspaper coverage.

Duty to Disclose; Duty to Update

Another disclosure issue of great importance arising under SEC Rule 10b–5 doctrine is the timing of preliminary merger announcements. In the Supreme Court case of *Basic v. Levinson* the Court held that a corporation may not, on pain of violating Rule 10b–5, issue press releases falsely denying materially significant merger talks.[203] The Court did not hold that a corporation (absent insider trading) has an absolute duty to disclose preliminary negotiation talks. The Court asserted that management could safely say "no comment" (i.e., be silent) in response to curious reporters atleast so long as the corporation had followed a consistent policy in that regard in the past. That is, a corporation that in the past truthfully denied false rumors of merger talks where there were none, and said "no comment" when the rumors were true, is in an obvious box. The "no comment" is, in that context, a signal of preliminary talks. The signal might be so indistinct as to raise questions of adequacy under antifraud Rule 10b–5. To be safe, a corporation perhaps must say "no comment" in the face of rumors true or false or alternatively, always publicly disclose the exact nature of preliminary negotiations when asked.

The corporate management is in a tight spot. The Court's "no comment" escape hatch is narrow and perilous. Lack of consistency in the past may torpedo the "no comment" response. Management may be required to assert "no comment" in the face of false rumors in order to preserve the ability to keep silent in the face of accurate rumors. But problems under SEC Rule 10b–5 are not solved by an initial, truthful response to a truthful preliminary merger rumor. Assume that the management confirms that XYZ corporation is talking stock for stock merger in the 40-to-45-dollar-per-share range. Negotiations change, proposed terms quickly vary. Must the target corporation in our scenario update the previous confirmation of merger talks? The law on this duty to update is hardly clear. Rule 10b–5 prosecution threatens the management that fails to update when required.[204]

Management is faced with danger if it discloses early stages of the negotiations, but is confronted with grave risk if it keeps silent. In both cases there is the threat of antifraud prosecution. On the purely financial-business front, as distinguished from legal consequences, management may fear that early disclosure of ongoing merger talks will chill the prospects of efficacious mergers. Disclosure may trigger bidding competition. Newspaper publicity may freeze or distort the negotiation posture of the participants around the bargaining table. The disclosure is tricky. Shareholders may not understand the odds against successful completion of the deal.

Whether early disclosure helps or hurts investors is not obvious, or of uniform impact across all deals. Perhaps early disclosure will, by attracting possible bidding competitors, improve the deal for shareholders of one of the two corporations (i.e., the ultimate target corporation). Perhaps early disclosure will chill the prospect of the deal, and hence hurt shareholders. Also, concern about shareholder understanding of disclosure may be totally unfounded.

Corporate law scholarship usually will approach this problem in the following manner. Free-market advocates of the view of the corporation as a set of contracts between and among shareholders, management, and other constituencies will argue for a voluntary solution. They will argue that the corporation should be free to voluntarily provide by charter, or charter amendment, for the treatment of the corporate information. This set of scholars will assert that if by charter, shareholders have delegated to senior management the power to determine timing of the preliminary talks, that settles the matter as far as the courts are involved.

Another body of scholars will argue that market failures of various kinds argue against this freedom to contract approach. They will attempt to demonstrate that information and power disparities between shareholders and management require governmental intervention in the process of timing and nature of disclosure. They will point to the asserted ability of management to cheat in the short run without disclosure. They will argue that small shareholders have no rational incentive to take the time neccessary to process complex information or to monitor management.

If, however, corporate speech is fully protected by the First Amendment, the nature of the analysis changes. The First Amendment prevents the government from interfering with the right of free association. Therefore, management, given appropriate charter provisions permitting it, should be free to control timing and nature of disclosure about preliminary merger negotiations.

In this regard, a First Amendment distinction can perhaps be made between the case of corporate management flatly lying about the existence of preliminary merger talks (or anything elese), and the case where management decides to be silent (i.e., the "no comment" position) about the rumor of talks. In the former the situation is similar to an actionable defamation case in the following respect. There is no information value to the lie. Further, the falsity of the denial is clearly and easily known by management. The First Amendment would clearly protect, however, the right of senior management to determine the timing of the announcement where practice or corporate charter grants that power to the management. The relative cost and benefit of early or later disclosure is difficult to ascertain. Government has no clear advantage over private parties in determining the proper time for disclosure.

A First Amendment analysis should also limit the duty of the management to correct earlier disclosure, particularly where management reserves the right publicly not to correct. Preliminary merger negotiation are complex, move rapidly, and change in a multiplicity of facets. Negotiation positions change so rapidly that there is little information value in repeated efforts to disclose the latest nuance in the bargaining position.

I recognize that political lies are, absent clear exceptions such as defamation, protected from government regulation by the First Amendment. Hence a pure absolutist might argue that the corporate lie in the first scenario above should be absolutely protected. In any event, a First Amendment type of analysis in the *Basic* case would certainly give greater deference to management's determination whether a given stage of negotiation is material. It is obvious that a First Amendment analysis of *Basic* case kind of issues radically improves the argument in favor of corporate control over the timing and nature of its disclosure.

Remember that a principal argument for the inferior treatment of commercial speech, including SEC speech, is the supposed hardiness of commercial speech. I cannot imagine a more fragile kind of speech than announcements about preliminary merger talks. First Amendment protection

154 Corporate Rights and the SEC

of this category of speech would permit management to disclose ongoing talks with less fear of prosecution for failure to update thereafter, while at the same time permitting management to be intelligently silent, when that also is important.

Issues of materiality, timing, and accuracy are incredibly complex and difficult in this area. The argument is frequently made that commercial speech is easily verifiable by the disseminator, and hence should receive less First Amendment protection. Clearly, ease of verifiability, or the E, for error, factor, to recall Judge Richard Posner's formula, in preliminary merger cases is similar in difficulty to political speech.

MANDATORY DISCLOSURE, PRIOR RESTRAINT, AND THE STRUCTURE OF SEC REGULATION

Tribe, in his monumental treatise on constitutional law, emphasizes that a major aspect of prior restraint doctrine is what he terms First Amendment due process.[205] This is a shorthand reference, so to speak, to judicial reluctance to permit administrative power, "directly or indirectly to determine *finally* the scope of application of first amendment privileges."[206] Therefore, the Court will frequently strike down overbroad delegation to censors or licensors of the power to restrain publication.[207] Open-ended delegation will be striken even where there is immediate judicial review because of the ability of censors to create "retrospective rationalization" and "contradictory testimony" in the record.[208] In the *Posadas* commercial speech case the administrators were granted the power to censor before publication offending, as they saw it, casino advertisements. The Court majority did not pass on it because it had not been raised by the challengers to the statute.[209] But Justice Stevens, dissenting, stated, "A more obvious form of prior restraint is difficult to imagine."[110]

First Amendment due process also involves the requirement to subject even adequately precise delegation to sufficient judicial review. Tribe summarizes this doctrine of restraint on censorship as follows: (1). The government has the burden of proof to justify the censorship decision; (2) the licensor or censor must act within a specified brief time; (3) the censor must go to court to restrain the unlicensed speech; (4) *ex parte* orders are frowned on; (5) restraints before final judicial determination must be for the shortest possible time; (6) the censorship scheme must assure a rapid final judicial decision; and (7) lower-court orders must be subject to immediate appellate review.[211]

Another aspect to the doctrine of prior restraint (not designated First Amendment due process) implicates the following kinds of issues. For example, certain news is significant only if timely released. Hence prior restraint, let us say, exercised through a lower-court injunction, as distinguished from criminal prosecution after the timely publication, may operate to unduly chill expression. In addition, in certain cases it may be difficult to measure the harm of publication before publication.[212] For example, the argument that publication will harm security may be impossible to measure before the publication. Hence the government has a forbidding burden to justify prior restraint. A publisher cannot disregard a court injunction against publication (as it can with a criminal statute) and then test its constitutionality. The publisher is required to appeal the injunction, and refrain from publication until after the appeal is decided.[213]

Prior restraint is a procedural doctrine. If the speech is protected by the First Amendment, it is protecteted before or after the fact of publication. If the speech is not covered by the First Amendment it may be prior restrained. The Court has indicated that because of the lower constitutional status of commercial speech, prior restraint doctrine may not apply to it.[214] For all of the reasons I have given for distinguishing SEC speech from traditional commercial speech, I would question that approach in the SEC area, insofar as First Amendment due process is concerned.

Let us consider the policy implications of First Amendment due process and SEC regulation of corporate speech. The SEC regulates through two modes of governance. The first is the system of mandatory disclosure described above. The second is criminal prosecution by the US Justice Department after the fact of publication. I am going to argue that the former structure involves the same dangers at which First Amendment due process is directed. I will not assert that the SEC system necessarily violates technical prior restraint doctrine, a doctrine which is in great need of precise definition. I am attempting to draw certain broad policy parallels or analogies in analyzing prior restraint doctrine. However, the policy points have validity independent of whatever the courts and commentators define as technical prior restraint doctrine.

Let us start with a consideration of mandatory disclosure in the context of corporate stock and security offerings. The commission has established an elaborate system of disclosure under Regulation SK and a mass of administrative determinations. The corporation must adhere to this system. As we have observed above, this system amounts to government orthodoxy in corporate disclosure. But there is another aspect to this structure. The proposed registration document is filed in preliminary form with the commission staff. Although there are exceptions in certain cases, the staff reviews the filings and makes comments. As the leading commentator on securities law, in his definitive treatise observes:

Although in theory the Commission's staff merely "suggests" amendments, the practicalities of financing do not allow any real alternative to complying. The privilege of testing the staff's views by defending a stop-order proceeding is an expensive one in terms of the success of the financing. And although the Commission's final order is subject to judicial review, a court proceeding that may take a year or more is hardly a realistic way to determine whether a company in need of financing is right in insisting that a particular item of information may properly go in the footnote rather than the text of the financial statements."[215]

This analysis captures the process of corporate securities offerings. With modification of detail, it captures the essence of the entire mandatory disclosure structure of the SEC. The corporation is faced with an elaborate structure of pre-publication mandated form and content of expression. The corporation faces enormous cost and time delay in challenging the commission in court, if it wants to vary from the government-imposed orthodoxy. The structure creates evils, all of which are not dissimilar from the evils "due process" prior restraint doctrine, as defined by Tribe, endeavors to prevent.

The essence of SEC mandatory disclosure is administrative (i.e., SEC) primacy in the resolution of First Amendment issues.[216] There is no doubt that the corporation, or corporate employee, will get ultimate judicial resolution of his assertion that a particular SEC disclosure structure violates the commercial speech doctrine, or in general the First Amendment. But the playing field is drastically tilted in favor of the commission. The agency employees, over the years, establish the matrix of appropriate disclosure. Almost every sentence, every paragraph, every financial datum and table is required, or implicated, or implied by the complex detailed nature of the commission's disclosure system. The corporation, as Loss suggests, avoids this at its peril.

Entirely different would be a system devoid of mandatory disclosure requirements and specifications, and limited to after-the-fact criminal prosecution for a fraudulent statement. I am not making the empirically debatable statement that prior restraint of a *particular* alleged fraudulent statement is always more chilling than fear of a long prison term for publication of the *same*. I am asserting that there is a significant difference between a structure, devoid of mandatory disclosure, in which the Justice Department can initiate criminal prosecution for a lying statement, and the current system of mandatory disclosure.

The latter structure is surely more oppressive, in a First Amendment "due process" sense. The corporation is faced with mandatory administrative requirements as to what it shall publish on descriptions of business, descriptions of property, descriptions of securities, management discussion of financial condition, executive compensation, disagreements with accountants, and much more. The regulation chiefly concerned with this runs for fifty plus printed pages. There are numerous other regulations of the same variety. This creates a disclosure straightjacket, which is, after all, what the commission desires.

As a result, the commission, not the courts, makes all of the initial and decisive decisions in the First Amendment area. It decides what is material disclosure. It decides what is valid or misleading disclosure. It makes the initial, and often final, decisions as to whether the speech is fully protected speech or commercial speech. The corporation can appeal to the courts, but the process is slow and expensive, and, where speed is of the essence, the appeal may not be taken.

On a public policy level, limiting government involvement to the power to criminally prosecute deliberatively lying corporate speech after the fact of publication would present less of an opportunity for the imposition of government orthodoxy in corporate speech. The corporation would have the choice of alternative methods of disclosure untrammeled by the imposed form of mandatory disclosure.

CONCLUSION

SEC mandatory disclosure regulation of financial statements and business descriptions amounts to a major constraint on corporate and shareholder freedom of expression. The rationale for the supposed constitutionality of such government restraint turns on notions of the difference between commercial speech and political or artistic speech or on some notions of regulation of professionals in the securities industry. On analysis, the distinctions between commercial speech and other forms of expression, and notions of professional regulation do not stand up. Moreover, we have demonstrated that whatever commercial speech is, or stands for, speech regulated by the SEC is not commercial speech as traditionally defined, and is indistinguishable from fully protected speech.

Because the Supreme Court first recognized that commercial speech is constitutionally protected to some extent, it has become more and more difficult to rationally distinguish between commercial speech and other forms of expression. Virtually all of political speech is a dialogue involving economic self-interest. Farmers demand relief against supposedly oppressive bank credit. Their speech is political and protected. Their economic self-interest is obviously not to be denied. Bankers demand more or less regulation, depending on which kinds of banks they represent. Their speech is political. Their interest is selfish and economic. Ministers demand tax breaks for their dwellings. Their vocation is divine; their speech is political; their interest in this regard is economic.

I need not add other examples to belabor what is obvious. When investment advisers opine on the stocks of corporate issuers (something the financial section of the *New York Times* does every day), their interest is commercial; their speech, I submit, is as political as other varieties of free expression. The Supreme Court majority in the *Lowe v. SEC* case ducked the constitutional issue for reasons that by now should be obvious. Perhaps they were concerned with the possibility that the speech of investment advisers is constitutionally protected, beyond the level now accorded to commercial speech. The same can be said for corporate prospectuses, corporate proxy statements, and perhaps even certain areas of allegedly fraudulent statements involving the media that were invoked in the Winans case.

Everybody does agree that product or service advertisements, if nothing else, are commercial speech. As such, the Supreme Court currently affords them limited First Amendment protection. We have demonstrated, I hope, in this book that even such examples of "pure" commercial speech are difficult to distinguish from political speech.

Even if we accept such distinctions, however, we have demonstrated that corporate proxy and financial statements do not easily fit in with the orthodox definition of commercial speech. Part of the problem is that corporations are organizations. They are owned and managed or involved with various shareholder and management groups. Shares of stock, and even debt instruments, constitute various bundles of rights within such organizations. Therefore, messages by corporate managers, for example, to shareholders, or messages from one shareholder group to another, invoke rights to freedom of expression and freedom of association, all of which should be fully protected by the First Amendment. In addition, corporate speech frequently involves economic and social issues that are indistinguishable from the usual issues that are in the traditional political arena.

Further, such speech is incredibly complex and subjective, and therefore, just as in the case of political speech, difficult for government to verify. Also, the SEC, like any other government agency, is subject to institutional bias, self-interest, and interest group influence, in the fashioning of its disclosure and enforcement policies.

The Court has asserted that commercial speech, unlike political speech, is robust, and hence resistant to regulation. We have demonstrated that there is little, if any, empirical basis for that sweeping conclusion. We have pointed out that commercial speakers will, under threat of regulation and penalty, change their message, if necessary, to get it out to the public. To the extent the argument assumes that commercial speakers will defy regulation and risk punishment, the thesis seems to be that the First Amendment is not needed, since the speakers will get their message out regardless of its absence. This optimistic prediction of commercial bravado is hardly an eloquent argument for removal of First Amendment protection. If the government is an effective verifier of the true and the false in matters commercial, robustness is, therefore, a vice, and more strenuous regulation will make up for the robustness. If, as the evidence indicates, the government is not, then First Amendment protection is called for, rather than speculation about bravado, defined as robustness

The Supreme Court case in *Lowe v. SEC* not only threatens the foundations of SEC financial disclosure regulation, but it and related cases cast a pall on the validity of government regulation of the professions. The judicial distinction rests on personal communication versus publications. The attorney or investment advisers, when dealing one on one with a client, may be constitutionally regulated. When they issue publications to thousands or millions, the First Amendment protection emerges. This great distinction turns on a dubious empirical hypothesis. That hypothesis is that the individual client is more easily gulled by the advisers or lawyer than is a reader of a book or article. Therefore, the harm in the former case is greater than the aggregate harm in the latter. However, it appears far more plausible that a successful, manipulative, and scheming attorney or advisers can do far more harm to society by virtue of successful books and articles than the same individual could when advising a few score clients face to face. At best, therefore, the vast edifice of government regulation of the professions now rests on a dubious empirical assumption. ´

NOTES

1. *See* J. Nowak, R. Rotunda, and J. Young, *Constitutional Law* 904 (3d ed. 1986).
2. 316 U.S. 52 (1942).
3. 316 U.S. at 54 (emphasis added).
4. 425 U.S. 748 (1976).
5. 431 U.S. 85 (1977).
6. 447 U.S. 557 (1980).
7. 447 U.S. at 566. *See* Schoeman, *The First Amendment and Restrictions on Advertising of Securities Under the Securities Act of 1933*, 41 Bus. Law. 377 (1966).
8. Board of Trustees of State University of *New York v. Todd Fox* 109 S. Ct. 3028 (1989.
9. *See* Contrasting Discussion and Authorities cited in Brief for the SEC, 34–49 and Brief of Petitioners, 29–37 in *Lowe v. SEC* 472 U.S. 181 (1985).
10. *Central Hudson Gas, supra* note 6.
11. *Id.* at 556. The Supreme Court in 1986, using the *Central Hudson* test in a remarkably permissive manner, sustained a ban on advertisements that spoke the truth about a legal product. It ruled 5–4 that Puerto Rico could prevent licensed casinos from soliciting gamblers on the island. Justice Rehnquist, writing for bare majority, argued that whenever a government is permitted to ban a product, it has the consequential power to chill speech about that product. *Posadas de Puerto Rico Association v. Tourism Co.*, 106 S. Ct. 2968, 2979.
12. *Id.*
13. As Justices Black and Douglas asserted in their concurring opinion in *New York Times v. Sullivan*, 376 U.S. 254, 296–97 (1964): "[F]reedom to discuss public affairs and public officials is unquestionably, as the Court today holds, the kind of speech the First Amendment was primarily designed to keep within the area of free discussion."
14. *See* Meklejohn, *Political Freedom* (1965).
15. Bork, *Neutral Principles and Some First Amendment Problems*, 47 Ind. L.J. 1 (1971). Judge Bork has since renounced his former stance on what speech falls under

the protection of the First Amendment. *See*, e.g., *N.Y. Times*, Sept. 17, 1987, at Al, col. 6.

16. *Abrams v. United States*, 250 U.S. 616, 630 (1919) (Holmes, J., dissenting).

17. *Whitney v. California*, 274 U.S. 357, 375 (1927). (Brandeis, J., concurring).

18. *See First National Bank of Boston v. Bellotti*, 435 U.S. 765 (1978). Some troublesome questions can arise as to whether a particular document is an editorial advertisement or an advertisement for a product line. Thus the Federal Trade Commission (FTC) has recently filed a complaint against the R. J. Reynolds Tobacco Company resulting from its publication in the *New York Times* and elsewhere of an editorial advertisement making certain points about a scientific study of risk factor and cigarette smoking. The Reynolds' advertisement did not promote the purchase of any cigarettes and contained no mention of the brand of any of its cigarettes. Abrams, *A Chilling Effect on Corporate Speech*, *New York Times*, July 6, 1986, §3, at 2. The administrative law judge ruled against the FTC on First Amendment grounds. R. J. Reynolds Tobacco Company, Inc. 108 F.T.C. No. 9206 (Aug. 4, 1986). The FTC and the tobacco company agreed to settle the case in October 1989. Reynolds pledged not to misrepresent scientific studies, but did not acknowledge any wrongdoing or that its materials were advertisements. *New York Times*, Oct. 21, 1989, 50.

19. *See* Farber, *Commercial Speech and First Amendment Theory*, 74 Nw. U.L. Rev. 372, 407–8 (1979).

20. *Dun & Bradstreet, Inc. v. Greenmoss Builders, Inc.*, 472 U.S. 749, 787–88 (1985) (Brennan, J., dissenting, citing *New Yorks Times v. Sullivan*, 376 U.S. 254, 273 (1964); Thornhill v. Alabama, 310 U.S. 88, 102 (1940).

21. *See arguments pro and con in* Greenwalt, *Free Speech Justifications*, 89 Columbia L. Rev. 119 (1989).

22. *Abrams v. United States*, 250 U.S. 616, 630 (1919) (Holmes, J., dissenting).

23. R. Coase, *Advertising and Free Speech in Advertising and Freee Speech* (A. Hyman & H. Johnson eds. 1973). *See generally*, B. Siegan, *Economic Liberties and the Constitution* (1980).

24. C. Murray, *Losing Ground* (1984).

25. M. Friedman and R. Friedman, *Free to Choose* 39 (1979) [hereinafter Friedman].

26. *See, e.g.*, G. Stigler, *The Citizen and the State: Essays on Regulation (1975)*; Friedman at 190–94, 222–27.

27. *See, e.g.*, R. Posner, *Regulation of Advertising by the FTC* 21 (1973).

28. *See, e.g.*, S. Peltzman, *Regulation of Pharmaceutical Innovation: The 1962 Amendments* (1974).

29. *See discussion of* R. Posner in chapter 4.

30. *Lowe v. SEC*, 472 U.S. 181 (1985); the Act permits revocation of the advisers's registration because of specified prior misconduct. 15 U.S.C. §80b–3(e) (1982).

31. *See* T. Hazen, *The Law of Securities Regulation* 7–8, 297–310 (1985).

32. See Chapter 5, *infra*.

33. 471 U.S. 626, 651 (1985).

34. *Id*. at 652.

35. *Id*. at 651, n. 14. In *Zauderer* the court held that the state may not discipline an attorney who seeks clients by using newspaper advertisements that contain truthful illustrations and legal advice. *Id*. at 655–56. The attorney had offered in his advertisements to represent women who had been injured by the Dalkan Shield intrauterine device. *Id*. at 630. The court, however, premitted the state to discipline the attorney

for failure to make required disclosure. He had represented that he would work on a contingent fee basis and, without recovery, would impose no legal fee. *Id.* at 652. He failed to disclose that the clients might have to pay litigation costs. The court thus distinguished between mandatory disclosure requirements and outright bans of experssion. *Id.*

36. *See. e.g.,* Schucker, *Reagan's Tax Plan Is unfair, New York Times,* June 12, 1985, at A. 27 col. 1 (asserting that Reagans's flat tax proposal is unfair and ignorant of social realities).

37. *See* L. Loss, *Fundamentals of Securities Regulation 542, n. 81* (1983); R. Hamilton, *Cases and Materials on Corporations* 543 (2d ed. 1981).

38. *Id.*

39. Posner, *Free Speech in an Economic Perspective,* 20 Suffolk L. Rev. 1, 22 (1986).

40. *Id.*

41. *Id.*

42. *Id.* at 39–40.

43. *Medical Committee for Human Rights v. SEC,* 432 F.2d 659 (D.C. Cir. 1970), *vacated as moot,* 404 U.S. 403 (1972).

44. *Id.*

45. Proxy Rule 14a–8. *See, generally,* Ryan, *Rule 14a–8, Institutional Shareholder Proposals, and Corporate Democracy,* 23 Ga. L Rev. 97 (1988); Liebler, *A Proposal to Rescind the Shareholder Proposal Rule,* 18 Ga. L. Rev. 425 (1984).

46. Rule 14a–8 (c) (8).

47. See Hamilton, *Corporations, Cases and Materials* 571–578 (3d ed. 1986).

48. 435 U.S. 765 (1978).

49. *Id.* at 768 (quoting Mass. Gen. Laws. Ann. ch 55, §8 [West Supp.1977].

50. *Id.*

51. *Id.* at 782 (footnote omitted).

52. *Id.* at 783 (footnote omitted).

53. *See* chapter 3.

54. 435 U.S. at 783.

55. *Id.* at 783 (citing *Virginia State Board of Pharmacy v. Virginia Citizens Consumer Council,* 425 U.S. 748, 764 (1976).

56. *Id.* at 785.

57. *Id.*

58. *Id.* at 787–88 and n. 26.

59. *Id.* at 788 and n. 26.

60. *Id.* at 789.

61. *Id.* at 790 (quoting *Kingsley Int'l Pictures v. Regents,* 360 U.S. at 689).

62. *Id.* at 791, n. 30.

63. *Id.* at 792.

64. *Id.* at 793–94.

65. *Id.* at 794 (footnote omitted).

66. *Id.* at 794, n. 34.

67. *Id.* at 795.

68. *Id.* (quoting *Shelton v. Tucker,* 364 U.S. at 485).

69. *Id.* at 770, n. 4.

70. *Id.* (quoting court below, 371 Mass. at 77, 359 N.E.2d at 1266).

71. *See* chapter 2.

72. Benston, *Government Constraints on Political, Artistic, and Commercial Speech*, 20 Conn. L. Rev. 303, 318 (1988).

73. *Austin v. Michigan Chamber of Commerce*, 1990 U.S. Lexus 1665 (March 27, 1990).

74. *Id.* at 1.

75. *Id.* at 12–14.

76. *Id.* at 14–15.

77. *Id.* at 17–21.

78. *Id.* at 22.

79. *Id.* at 24–29.

80. *Id.* at 45.

81. *Id.* at 46.

82. *Id.* at 47.

83. *Id.* at 52.

84. *Id.* at 52 quoting 424 U.S. at 45.

85. *Id.* at 53.

86. *Id.* at 54.

87. *Id.* at 53.

88. *Id.* at 56.

89. *Id.* at 56.

90. *Id.*

91. *Id.*

92. *Id.* at 58.

93. *Id.* at 59.

94. *Id.*

95. *Id.* at 64.

96. *Id.*

97. *Id.* at 67–68

98. *Id.*

99. *Id.* at 68

100. *Id.* at 85.

101. Hamilton, *Cases and Materials on Corporations* 610–22 (3d Ed. 1986).

102. 475 U.S. 1 (1986).

103. *Id.* at 10 (citing *Miami Herald Publishing Co. v. Tornillo*, 418 U.S. 241 (1974)

104. *Id.* at 39

105. *Id.* at 39,n. 8.

106. *Id.* at 14, n. 10.

107. *Id.*

108. *Id.*

109. *Medical Committee for Human Rights v. SEC*, 432 F2d 659 (D.C. Cir 1979), *vacated as moot*, 404 U.S. 403 (1972).

110. *Id.*

111. Hamilton, note 73 *supra* at 610–22.

112. Proxy Rule 14a–8 (c) (5).

113. *See* Ryan, *supra* note 45; Hamilton, *supra* note 47 at 620.

114. *See* chapter 2.

115. Kripke, *The SEC and Corporate Disclosure: Regulation in Search of a Purpose* (1979).

First Amendment and the SEC

163

116. *Id.* at 5. *See* Schneider, *Nits, Grits and Soft Information in SEC Filings*, 121 U. Pa. L. Rev. 254 (1972).

117. *Id.* at 6.

118. R. Hamilton, *Cases and Materials on Corporations* 589 (3d ed. 1986).

119. N. Wolfson, *The Modern Corporation, Free Markets v. Regulation* 122–24 (1984).

120. *TSC Industries Inc. v. Northway, Inc.*, 426 U.S. 438 (1976).

121. *Escott v. Barchris Construction Co.*, 283 F.Supp. 643, 682 (1968).

122. H. Manne, *Insider Trading and Property Rights in New Information in Economic Liberties and the Judiciary* 317, 325 (J. Dorn and H. Manne eds., 1987).

123. Benston, *The Costs and Benefits of Government Required Disclosures: SEC and FTC Requirements, An Appraisal, in Corporations at the Crossroads: Governanace and Reform* 55–57 (D. Demott ed. 1980).

124. *See* chapter 4.

125. *Id.*

126. Benston, *Required Periodic Disclosure Under The Securities Acts And the Proposed Federal Securities Code*, 33 Univ. Miami L. Rev. 1471, (1979).

127. *Id.* at 1471–84.

128. Sommer, Jr., *Book Review*, 93 Harv. L. Rev. 1595 (1980).

129. The First Amendment forbids the favoring of one group over another. " '[T]he concept that government may restrict the speech of some elements of our society in order to enhance the relative voice of others is wholly foreign to the First Amendment. . . . ' " *First Nat'l Bank v. Bellotti*, at 765, 790–91 (1978) (quoting Buckely v. Valeo, 424 U.S. 1, 48–49 (1976). This argument, however, has been questioned by the *Austin* case.

130. *Id.*

131. N. Wolfson, *The Modern Corporation, Free Markets v. Regulation* 46–50, 106–7 (1984).

132. *See* Buckley, 424 U.S. at 19–23.

133. *Id.* at 23–38.

134. *Miami Herald Publishing Co. v. Tornillo*, 418 U.S. 241 258 (1974). In *Pacific Gas & Elec. Co. v. Public Utilities Commission of California*, 106 S. Ct. 903, 910–12 (1981) the Court held that a utility commission order requiring a privately owned utility to include in its billing envelopes speech of a third party with which the corporation does not agree unlawfully impairs its First Amendment rights. This opinion puts into doubt SEC Regulation 14a–8, which requires the board of directors to send out proposals of shareholders that it opposes. *See* 17 C.F.R. § 240. 14a–8 (1985).

135. *See* Nowak, Rotunda, and Young, *supra* not 1 at 874–85. The FCC has announced that it will no longer enforce the fairness doctrine, finding that it is a violation of the First Amendment rights of broadcasters. S. Freeman, *The Fairness Doctrine: The Electronic Media and Free Speech*, 1, 5 (Anti-Defamation League of B'nai-Brith, Civil Rights Division Policy Background Report, September 1987).

136. Bellotti, *supra* note 18 at 77.

137. N. Wolfson, *supra* note 131 at 41, 54–55.

138. Easterbrook, *Manager's Discretion and Investors' Welfare: Theories and Evidence*, 9 Del. J. Corp. L. 540, 564–68 (1984); Manne, *Mergers and the Market for Corporate Control*, 73 J. Pol. Econ. 110 (1965).

139. *See* T. Sowell, *Knowledge and Decisions* 200 (1980).

140. *See* Nowak, *supra* note 1 at 947–52.

141. *NAACP v. Alabama*, 357 U.S. 449, 460 (1958).

142. *See* n. 169, *infra*.

143. Securities Exchange Act of 1934, Sections 13(d) and 14(d), 15 U.S.C. A. Sections 78m(d) and 78n(d).

144. Securities Exchange Act of 1934, Section 14(d) (4), 15 U.S.C. A. Section 78n(d) (4).

145. For a sampling of significant articles on the market for control, *see* Manne, *Mergers and the Market for Corporate Control*, 73 J. Pol. Econ. 110 (1965); Easterbrook and Fischel, *The Proper Role of a Target's Management in Responding to a Tender Offer*, 94 Harv. L. Rev. 1161 (1981); Jensen, *Takeovers: Their Causes and Consequences*, 2 J. Econ. Perspectives 21 (1988); Black, *Bidder Overpayment in Takeovers*, 41 Stan. L. Rev. 597(1989).

146. *See, e.g.*, Ribstein, *Takeover Defenses and the Corporate Contract*, 78 Georgetown L. Rev. 71 (1989); Coffee, *The Uncertain Case for Takeover Reform: An Essay on Stockholders, Stakeholders and Bustups*, 1988 Wis. L. Rev. 435; Coffee, *Regulating the Market for Corporate Control: A Critical Assessment of the Tender Offer's Role in Corporate Governance*, 84 Colum. L. Rev. 1145 (1984).

147. *Id*.

148. See Connecticut Public Act 88–350.

149. Butler and Ribstein, *The Contract Clause and The Corporation*, 55 Brooklyn L. Rev. 767, 795 (1989).

150. See Connecticut Public Act 84–431.

151. See note 148, *supra*.

152. L. Tribe, *American Constitutional Law* 1010 (2d ed. 1988).

153. *Id*. at 1011.

154. A. de Tocqueville, 1 *Democracy in America* 196 (P. Bradley ed. 1945).

155. Tribe at 1016.

156. *Id*.

157. *Id*.

158. *Id*. at 1017.

159. *Id*. at 1014.

160. CCH Fed. Sec. L. Rep. ¶94, 334 (1989).

161. *Id*. at 92, 180 n. 14.

162. *Id*.

163. Id. at 92, 181.

164. Butler and Ribstein, *The Contract Clause and the Corporation*, 55 Brooklyn L. Rev. 767 (1989).

165. Section 5 of the Securities Act of 1933, 15 U.S.C. 77e (1982).

166. *See generally* Schneider, Manko, and Kant, *Going Public: Practice, Procedure and Consequences*, 27 Villanova L. Rev. 1 (1981).

167. *See* M. Budd and N. Wolfson, *Securities Regulation* 7, 125 (1984).

168. *Id*. at 37–50.

169. Justice O'Connor emphasizes this distinction in her concurrence in the *Roberts* decision. *Roberts v. United States Jaycees*, 468 U.S. 609, 631–33 (1984). She would grant full First Amendment protection to the internal workings of so-called expressive (i.e. noncommercial) associations. *Id*. at 633–35. She would grant limited First Amendment protection to the internal workings of nonexpressive (i.e., commercial) asso-

ciations. *Id.* at 634–35. Other justices, in the majority opinion, applying a sliding scale, ad hoc approach, would grant full First Amendment coverage to associational activity where appropriate to protect the expressive element of an association. *Id.* at 622. All justices agreed that the right of association is not absolute and is subject to compelling state interests (e.g., prevention of gender discrimination).

170. *Virginia State Board of Pharmacy* at 765.

171. *Principles of Corporate Governance: Analysis and Recommendations*, § 2.01 (Tent. Draft No. 2, 1981).

172. Wolfson, *supra* note 131 at 147–58.

173. 95 Ill. App.2d 173, 175; 237 N.E.2d 776, 777 (1968).

174. *Lowe, v. SEC*, 472 U.S. 181 (1985).

175. *Id.* at 185.

176. *Id.*

177. *Id.* at 185–86 (footnotes omitted).

178. *Id.* at 203–11.

179. *Id.* at 208.

180. *Id.* at 204.

181. *Id.* at 235–36 (White, J., concurring).

182. *Id.* at 228.

183. *Id.* at 232 (emphasis added and footnote omitted).

184. *Id.* at 234.

185. *Id.*

186. *Id.*

187. The concurring opinion states: "One does not have to read the Court's opinion very closely to realize that its interpretation of the Act is in fact based on a thinly disguised conviction that the Act is unconstitutional as applied to prohibit publication of newsletters by unregistered advisers." *Id.* at 226 (White, J., concurring).

188. *Id.* at 210, n. 58 (citation omitted).

189. *See, e.g.,* R. Posner and K. Scott, *Economics of Corporation Law and Securities Regulation* 155–94 (1980);

190. *See* Nowak, Rotunda, and Young, *supra* note 1 at 870.

191. 472 U.S. 181, 232 (1985) (White, J., concurring).

192. See T. Sowell, *supra* note 139 at 200.

193. *See* Note, *The Efficient Capital Market Hypothesis, Economic Theory and the Regulation of the Securities Industry*, 29 Stanford L. Rev. 1031 (1977).

194. *See* Matthews and Levine, *First Amendment Problems Complicate SEC Enforcement*, N.Y.L.J. 33, 44 (DEC. 10, 1984).

195. *United States v. Winans*, 612 F.Supp. 827 (S.D.N.Y. 1985), *aff'd in part, rev'd in part, sub. nom. United States v. Carpenter*, 791 F.2d 1024 (2d Cir. 1986), *aff'd* 484 U.S. 19 (1987).

196. *Id.*

197. 484 U.S. at 24.

198. *Id.* The justices split 4–4 on the Rule 10b–5 misappropriation count. Hence the convictions on this theory were sustained. The justices unanimously upheld the wire and mail fraud convictions. For an analysis of misappropriation doctrine as a form of protection of property rights in information and, more particularly, as a form of trade secrets law, see Wolfson, *Trade Secrets and Secret Trading*, 25 San Diego L. Rev. 95 (1988). The doctrine governing insider trading can be summarized as follows.

Corporate insiders, such as officers, directors, and control shareholders, have an affirmative duty either to disclose material information about their corporation before trading or must refrain from trading. *See, e.g., Dirks v. SEC*, 463 U.S. 646 (1983): *Chiarella v. United States*, 445 U.S. 222 (1980). However, Winans was a "stranger" to the corporations about which he wrote. He, therefore, had no fiduciary duties to buyer or sellers of their stock. However, the courts have developed the "misappropriation" doctrine. *See, e.g., Newman v. United States*, 464 U.S. 863 (1983); *SEC v. Materia*, 745 F.2d 197 (2d Cir. 1984), *cert. denied*, 471 U.S. 1053 (1985). Anyone, such as Winans, who misappropriates information or wrongfully abuses a special relationship with an employer (here the *Wall Street Journal*) or another, in connection with the purchase or sale of stock, violates SEC Rule 10b–5. Since the *Wall Street Journal* had a policy forbidding scalping and Winans knew of it, he misappropriated his special relationship with the *Journal* when he traded. That is, he misappropriated the *Journal*'s confidential schedule of forthcoming publications in connection with his stock trading. It may be argued that Winans violated the journalist's special relationship of trust with his readership (not only his employer) in connection with his purchase, and for that reason also violated Rule 10b–5. The latter interpretation, however, would create a relatively radical judicial doctrine, since it would impose Rule 10b–5 responsibilities on all journalists over a wide scope of behavior. In the SEC civil case against him (and at an earlier point in connection with the criminal case), the government asserted the more radical theory that he had violated a fiduciary duty to this readership in not disclosing the scheme, and hence had committed an actionable fraud in connection with the purchase or sale of stock. *See* Matthews and Levine, *supra* note at 44.

199. Insider Trading and Securities Fraud Enforcement Act of 1988.

200. Federal District Court Judge Stewart, in his opinion finding Winans et al. guilty, had the following to say on the media's objections to the indictment:

On January 21, 1985, the Reporters' Committee for Freedom of the Press, the National Association of Broadcasters, the Newsletters Association, the New York Financial Writers Association, the Media Institute, the Newspaper Guild, the Radio-Television News Directors Association, the American Society of Magazine Editors, the National Newspaper Association, and the Associated Press Managing Editors filed a motion for leave to file a brief as amici curiae in support of defendants' Rule 29 motion to dismiss various counts of the indictment. They filed another motion for leave to file a supplemental memorandum on April 23, 1985. Because of the timing of the latter motion, we did not require the government to respond to the points raised. However, we hereby grant both motions.

The arguments made by the amici with respect to the proper construction of the securities laws are adequately addressed in the text. Amici make a more narrow argument that states in essence that the government's theory rests on ill-defined duties for reporters and editors; criminalization of breaches of those duties will interfere with the editorial process and will create a threat to the amici's First Amendment freedoms. We are not persuaded that the government's theory does create any new duties; as the government stated in their reply brief, "this prosecution under the 'misappropriation' theory creates no obligations, but merely enforces pre-existing obligations as it finds them." Nor does the theory impose any duties at all on publishers and editors as to what they must do if a reporter does disclose trading or tipping. Editors must make decisions about whether or not to run articles all the time, and this theory does not affect that choice at all. If Winans were to have disclosed to his editors prior to publication the fact that he was trading in the stock slated to be the subject of a *Heard* column the following day, the editors had several choices open to them, including running the column and taking disciplinary action against Winans for his misconduct, as well as seeking criminal penalties. *United States v. Winans*, 612 F.Supp. 827, 843, n. 10 (S.D.N.Y. 1985).

201. See Manne, *Insider Trading and Property Rights in New Information*, in *Economic Liberties and the Judiciary* 317 (J. Dunn and H. Manne eds. 1987); Wolfson, *Comment: Civil Liberties and Regulation of Insider Trading* in *Economic Liberties* 339.
202. See *supra*, notes 194 and accompanying text.
203. *Basic Inc. v. Levinson*, 108 S. Ct. 978 (1988).
204. *See* Schneider, 3 *Insights* 3 (February 1989).
205. L. Tribe, *American Constitutional Law* 1054 (2d ed. 1988).
206. *Id.* at 1055.
207. *Id.* at 1056.
208. *Id.* at 1057.
209. *Id.* at 1057.
210. *Id.* at 1057, n. 10.
211. *Id.* at 1060–1061.
212. *Id.* at 1048.
213. *Id.* at 1042.
214. *Id.* at 1057, n. 10. Tribe has written: "One difficulty with this approach is that it permits nonjudicial determinations of what is commercial. As §12–18 made apparent, the dividing line between the 'economical' and the 'political' is hazy at best." *Id.*
215. Loss, *supra* note 37 at 129–130 (footnote omitted).
216. Tribe at 1054.

Bibliography

Abrams, A., *Chilling Effect on Corporate Speech*, New York Times, July. 6, 1986, 3, at 2.

Auerbach, J. *Unequal Justice* (1975).

Baker, *Commercial Speech: A Problem in the Theory of Freedom*, 62 Iowa L. Rev. 1 (1976).

Benston, *Government Constraints on Political, Artistic and Commercial Speech*, 20 Conn. L. Rev. 303 (1988).

Benston, *The Cost and Benefits of Government—Required Disclosure: SEC and FTC Requirements, An Appraisal*. In *Corporations at the Crossroads: Governance and Reform* (D. Demott ed. 1980).

Benston, *Required Periodic Disclosure Under the Securities Acts and the Proposed Federal Securities Code*, 33 Univ. Miami L. Rev. 1471 (1979).

Bentham, J., *Manual of Political Economy*, 1 J. Bentham's *Economic Writings* (1953).

Black, *Bidder Overpayment in Takeovers*, 41 Stan. L. Rev. 597 (1989).

Blasi, *The "Checking Value" in First Amendment Theory*, 1977 Am. B. Found. Research J. 521.

Blasi, *The Pathological Perspective and the First Amendment*, 85 Colum. L. Rev. 449 (1985).

Bork, *Neutral Principles and Some First Amendment Problems*, 47 Ind. L. J. 1 (1971).

Budd, M. and N. Wolfson, *Securities Regulation, Cases and Materials* (1984).

Butler and Ribstein, *The Contract Clause and the Corporation*, 55 Brooklyn L. Rev. 767 (1989).

Canavan, F., *Freedom of Expression, Purpose as Limit* (1984).

Cass, *Commercial Speech, Constitutionalism, Collective Choice*, 56 U. Cinn. L. Rev. 1317 (1988).

Chafee, Z. *The Blessings of Liberty* (1957).

Coase, R. H., *The Market for Goods and the Market for Ideas*, 64 Am. Econ. Rev. Papers & Proceedings 384 (1974).

Coase, R. H., *Advertising and Free Speech*, in *Advertising and Free Speech* (A. Hyman and M. Johnson eds. 1977).

Coffee, *The Uncertain Case for Takeover Reform: An Essay on Stockholders, Stakeholders and Bustups*, 1988 Wis. L. Rev. 435.

Coffee, *Regulating the Market for Corporate Control: A Critical Assessment of the Tender Offer's Role in Corporate Governance*, 84 Colum. L. Rev. 1145 (1984).

De Bondt and Thaler, *Anomalies: a Mean-Reverting Walk Down Wall Street*, 3 J. Econ. Perspective 189 (Winter 1989).

De Tocqueville, A., 1 *Democracy in America* (P. Bradley ed. 1945).

Director, *The Parity of the Economic Market Place*, 7 J. Law & Econ 1 (1964).

Easterbrook, *Manager's Discretion and Investors' Welfare: Theories and Evidence*, 9 Del. J. Corp. L. 540 (1984).

Easterbrook and Fischel, *The Proper Role of a Target's Management in Responding to a Tender Offer*, 94 Harv. L. Rev. 1161 (1981).

Emerson, T., *The System of Freedom of Expression* (1970).

Emerson, T., *Toward a General Theory of the First Amendment*, (1966).

Emerson, T., *First Amendment Doctrine and the Burger Court*, 68 Calif. L. Rev. 422 (1980).

Farber, *Commercial Speech and First Amendment Theory*, 74 Nw. U.L. Rev. 372 (1979).

Freeman, S., *The Fairness Doctrine: The Electronic Media and Free Speech* (Anti-Defamation League of B'nai-Brith, Civil Rights Division Policy Background Report, Sept., 1987).

Friedman, M. *Capitalism and Freedom* (1962).

Friedman, M., and Friedman, R., *Free to Choose* (1979).

Fromm, E., *The Sane Society* (1955).

Gilson, R., *The Law and Finance of Corporate Acquisitions* (1986).

Greenwalt, *Free Speech Justifications*, 89 Columbia L. Rev. 119 (1989).

Hamilton, R., *Cases and Materials on Corporations* (2d ed. 1981).

Hamilton, R. *Corporations, Cases and Materials* (3d ed. 1986).

Hayek, F. A., *Law, Legislation and Liberty* (1979).

Hazen, T., The *Law of Securities Regulation* (1985).

Himmelfarb, G., *On Liberty and Liberalism: The Case of John Stuart Mill* (1974).

Jackson and Jeffries, *Commercial Speech: Economic Due Process and the First Amendment*, 65 Va. L. Rev. 1 (1979).

Jensen, *Takeovers: Their Causes and Consequences*, 2 J. Econ. Perspectives 21 (1988).

Knight, F., *The Planful Act, in Freedom and Reform* (1947).

Kripke, H. *The SEC and Corporate Disclosure: Regulation in Search of a Purpose* (1979).

Levy, L., *Emergence of a Free Press* (1985).

Levy, L., *Legacy of Suppression* (1960).

Liebler, *A Proposal to Rescind the Shareholder Proposal Rule*, 18 Ga. L. Rev. 425 (1984).

Loss, L., *Fundamentals of Securities Regulation* (1983).

Manne, *Mergers and the Market for Corporate Control*, 73 J. Pol. Econ. 110 (1965).

Manne, *Insider Trading and Property Rights in New Information*, in *Economic Liberties and the Judiciary* (J. Dunn and H. Manne eds. 1987).

Marcuse, H., *One Dimensional Man* (1964).

Matthews and Levine, *First Amendment Problems Complicate SEC Enforcement*, N.Y.L.J. 33 (Dec. 10, 1984).

McChesney, F., *A Positive Regulatory Theory of the First Amendment*, 20 Conn. L. Rev. 355 (1988).

McChesney, *Commercial Speech in the Professions: The Supreme Court's Unanswered Questions and Questionable Answers*, 134 U. Pa. L. Rev. 45 (1985).

Meiklejohn, A., *Free Speech and Its Relation to Self-Government* (1948).

Meiklejohn, A., *The First Amendment Is an Absolute*, 1961 Sup. Ct. Rev. 245 (1961).

Meiklejohn, A. *Political Freedom* (1965).

Mill, J., 1 *Dissertations and Discussions* (1959).

Mill, J. S., *On Liberty* (Currin v. Shields ed. 1956) (1st ed. London 1859).

Mill, *On Liberty*, in *Utilitarianism, Liberty and Representative Government* (1951).

Milton, J., *Areopagitica, A Speech for the Liberty of Unlicensed Printing* (1959) (Everyman ed. 1927).

Monaghan, *Some Comments on Professor Neuborne's 65 Paper*, 55 Brooklyn L. Rev. 65 (1989).

Murray, C., *Losing Ground* (1984).

Neuborne, *The First Amendment and Government Regulation of Capital Markets*, 55 Brooklyn L. Rev. 5 (1988).

Note, *The Efficient Capital Market Hypothesis, Economic Theory and the Regulation of the Securities Industry*, 29 Stanford L. Rev. 1031 (1977).

Nowak, J., Rotunda, R., and Young, J., *Constitutional Law* (3d ed. 1986).

Painter, W., *Business Planning, Problems and Materials* (2d ed. 1984).

Peltzman, S., *Regulation of Pharmaceutical Innovation: The 1962 Amendments* (1974).

Pigou, A., *The Economics of Welfare* (4th ed. 1962).

Pinto, *The Nature of the Capital Markets Allows a Greater Role for the Government*, 55 Brooklyn L. Rev. 77 (1989).

Posner, R., *Free Speech in an Economic Perspective*, 20 Suffolk U.L. Rev. 1 (Spring 1986).

Posner, R., *Regulation of Advertising by the FTC* (1973).

Posner, R. and Scott, K., *Economics of Corporation Law and Securities Regulation* (1980).

Redish, *The First Amendment in the Marketplace: Commercial Speech and the Values of Free Expression*, 39 Geo. Wash. L. Rev. 429 (1971).

Redish, M., *Freedom of Expression: a Critical Analysis* (1984).

Reich, C., *The Greening of America* (1970).

Reynoldson, *The Case Against Lawyer Advertising*, 75 ABA Journal 60 (Jan. 1989).

Ribstein, *Takeover Defenses and the Corporate Contract*, 78 Georgetown L. Rev. 71 (1989).

Ryan, *Rule 14a–8, Institutional Shareholder Proposals, and Corporate Democracy*, 23 Ga. L. Rev. 97 (1988).

Schauer, F., *Free Speech: A Philosophical Enquiry* (1982).

Schauer, *Commercial Speech and the Architecture of the First Amendment*, 56 U.Cin L. Rev. 1181 (1988).

Schneider, Manko and Kant, *Going Public: Practice, Procedure, and Consequences* 27 Vill. L. Rev. 1 (1981).

Schneider, *Nits, Grits and Soft Information in SEC Filings*, 121 U. Pa. L. Rev. (1972).

Schneider and Shurgel, *"Now That You Are Publicly Owned . . . ,"* 36 Business Lawyer 1631 (1981).

Schoeman, *The First Amendment and Restrictions on Advertising of Securities Under the Securities Act of 1933*, 41 Bus. Law. 377 (1986).

Schucker, *Reagan's Tax Plan Is Unfair*, New York Times, June 12, 1985, at 27 col. 1.

Shiffrin, *The First Amendment and Economic Regulation: Away from a General Theory of the First Amendment*, 78 NW U.L Rev. 1212 (1983).

Siegan, B., *Economic Liberties and the Constitution* (1980).

Sommer, Jr., *Book Review*, 93 Harv. L. Rev. 1595 (1980).

Sowell, T., *Knowledge and Decisions* (1980).

Stigler, G., *The Economics of Information*, 69 J. Pol. Econ. 213 (1961).

Stigler, G., *The Theory of Economic Regulation*, Bell J. of Econ. and Management Science 2 (1971).

Stigler, G., *The Citizen and the State: Essays on Regulation* (1975).

Tribe, L., *American Constitutional Law* (2d ed.1988).

Winter, *A First Amendment Over-view*, 55 Brooklyn L. Rev. 71 (1989).

Wolfson, *Trade Secrets and Secret Trading*, 25 San Diego L. Rev. 95 (1988).

Wolfson, N., *The Modern Corporation, Free Markets vs. Regulation* (1984).

Wolfson, *Comment: Civil Liberties and Regulation of Insider Trading* in *Economic Liberties and the* Judiciary. (J. Dunne and H. Manne eds. 1987).

Index

About the Author

NICHOLAS WOLFSON is Professor of Law at the University of Connecticut Law School. He was previously Branch Chief, Special Counsel and Assistant Director at the SEC in Washington, D.C. Professor Wolfson is the author of several books and numerous professional articles, and is a frequent speaker on securities regulation.